JUDAS!

From Forest Hills To The Free Trade Hall
A Historical View Of The Big Boo

Clinton Heylin

First published by Route in 2016
PO Box 167, Pontefract, WF8 4WW
info@route-online.com
www.route-online.com

ISBN : 978-1901927-68-9

FIRST EDITION

Clinton Heylin asserts his moral
right to be identified as the author of this book

© Clinton Heylin

Photograph on photo section page 8 by Russell Pennell
© Victor Wright

Photographs on photo section pages 10-15 by Björn Larsson
© John Bauldie/Margaret Garner

Cover design:
GOLDEN

Printed in EU by Pulsio SARL

To Mitch Blank and Ian Woodward,
who do not heckle.

INTRO:
I Started Out On Burgundy,   7
But Soon Hit The Harder Stuff ...

THE 'I' OF THE STORM: 11
1. My Hands Are On Fire   15
2. The First Band Of The Hand   43
3. Seems Like A West Coast Freeze-Out   71
4. A Night With Bob Dylan   89
5. Doing The Tennessee Waltz   115

REAPING THE WHIRLWIND: 147
6. The Courage Of One's Convictions   151
7. Boy From The North Country   189
8. The Unforgiven   207
9. English Civil War   229
10. At The Still Point Of The Turning World   259

OUTRO:
I Do Believe I've Had Enough   288

Chapter Notes and Sources   293
Acknowledgements   302

INTRO:
I STARTED OUT ON BURGUNDY,
BUT SOON HIT THE HARDER STUFF...

We never did capture that sound on stage—the Blonde On Blonde *sound; we never did capture the* Highway 61 *sound on stage. What we did on stage was something different that we never recorded.*

—BOB DYLAN TO PETE OPPEL, NOVEMBER 1978

Although it was 1998 before Dylan sanctioned an official release of a 1966 show—thirty-two years after the possibility was first discussed in the halls of Columbia—it certainly wouldn't be true to say that the Live '66 sound was never recorded.

Actually, Dylan went out of his way to ensure the music he and The Hawks made between September 1965 and May 1966 *was* recorded, once he had his preferred rhythm section and was able to transcend all audio antecedents.

Following Dylan's explicit instructions, Columbia even ushered into the world a particularly electrifying example with almost indecent haste, before the letter columns of the English music papers had spewed their last concerning events still fresh in the collective conscious.

June 13 1966: barely a fortnight after Dylan left England's shores and a week before the release of his seventh album, Dylan's label released their third and last seven-inch preview for rock's most grandiloquent recalibration, *Blonde On Blonde*: 'I Want You' b/w 'Just Like Tom Thumb's Blues'.

After 'Rainy Day Women #12 & 35', Dylan's biggest hit to date, label execs had high hopes for 'I Want You', one of his catchiest constructs. For the label—indeed, all American labels—any single B-side was largely irrelevant. Hence, perhaps, the misleading report in *Billboard* suggesting the B-side was taken from his latest album.[1]

In fact, Dylan had arranged it so that the flipside to his latest chart-raid captured 'that sound on stage' in all its spine-tingling essence. *This* 'Just Like Tom Thumb's Blues' was from a show in Liverpool less than a month earlier. *It used to go like that, but now it goes like THIS!!!*

It was Dylan himself who selected this singular performance. Columbia hadn't even taped the Liverpool show—although the label did go to the trouble of taping the Sheffield show two nights later, and one in Manchester, the night after Sheffield.

Both were equally stormy affairs. Indeed, in the fullness of time, Manchester would supersede Liverpool in the general pecking order for Bobby's own battle of Britain. But the 'nightly ritual' of listening to the mono tapes made by Dylan's chosen soundman, Richard Alderson, for a movie he was shooting, had convinced the singer that 'Just Like Tom Thumb's Blues' should be the first vinyl bulletin from the precipice.

The song itself had been in the live set since Dylan unveiled his first post-Hibbing electric band at the Forest Hills Stadium, Queens, on August 28 1965. Repeatedly doused in wild mercury until it shone in the dark, by May 1966 it was a howl from the hinterlands, a kaddish to chaos itself, a paean to the kinda negativity that might yet pull him through.

Flipping between these two bookends for Dylan's electric era—'Tom Thumb's August 2 1965 studio incarnation and its May 14 1966 live reincarnation—is to intuitively chart his self-conscious descent into Rimbaud's 'unknowable region'.

To chronicle the ebb and flow of his mid-sixties maelstrom of drug-fuelled inspiration less instinctively—a *cante fable* of Bob aboard his *bateau ivre*—demands something else: a book's worth of explication, if not a library's. But no amount of explication can recreate the moment, fifty years ago, when avid Dylan fans flipped that single—described in a July 1966 *Record Mirror* review as 'probably the worst thing by Bob on record'—and found the sound of the apocalypse captured not in amber but on vinyl.

What in heaven *was* this sound!? It sure as hell wasn't the sound of

[1] In an era when The Beatles and Stones were releasing non-album gems like 'I'm Down', 'Rain', 'Play With Fire' and 'The Spider And The Fly' as UK flipsides, US labels preferred album tracks of no fixed abode, like the US B-side of 'Satisfaction', 'The Under Assistant West Coast Promotion Man'. A test pressing in the Mitch Blank Archives proves that the original intention was to put the album version of 'Tombstone Blues' on the B-side of 'I Want You'.

Highway 61. Rather, here was the sound of Dylan and The Hawks at the end of their world-tour tether, torn and frayed yet blazingly in tune, on English Cup Final Saturday, blasting away the boos (and there were a fair few that night) with an aural onslaught the like of which no nascent rock fan—no matter how hip—could have prepped for.

This was something new, and so startling it took Greil Marcus until December 1969 to contextualise it in the light of rock's then-trajectory, after Dylan's disappearance from view and The Band's (né The Hawks) emergence as contenders in their own right:

> The sound they produced was stately, extravagant, and visionary—there is nothing with which to compare it in all of Dylan's recordings. At the bottom of that sound was a rough, jerking marriage of blues and honky tonk, but over that were grafted the sorts of echoes that come from the music box of a circus merry-go-round: the fire and ice of Garth Hudson's organ and the young, brash clinches of Robbie Robertson's guitar. And it was loud, louder than anyone played in those days, but so musical and so melodic that the band could dance free and their audiences easily went with them.
>
> There was an urgency to those performances ... It's certainly there on [the Liverpool] 'Just Like Tom Thumb's Blues' ... Dylan's voice is tired, raspy, but even at the end of an endless tour he wouldn't quit. The music and the phrasing are nothing like the version on *Highway 61 Revisited*, and the real stars are Hudson and Robertson, Garth soloing weirdly in between the lines, Robbie punching notes in and out of Bob's shouts and screams until there is no separation between the singer and the musicians.

For the thousands first exposed to the Sound and the Fury on that '66 single, there had been not the slightest hint that this was Dylan's endgame on any of the four singles Columbia released in the aftermath of his *Highway 61 Revisited* breakthrough: 'Positively 4th Street', 'Can You Please Crawl Out Your Window?', 'One Of Us Must Know' and 'Rainy Day Women'.

When it came to the albums he made in these mercurial months, each was recorded with tried and trusted studio musicians—and Columbia released no less than four albums' worth of new material in the eighteen months separating *Bringing It All Back Home* from *Blonde On Blonde*. On these long-players, The Hawks (Robbie Robertson excepted) were nowhere to be seen—or heard—save on 'One Of Us Must Know', when their patented 'merry-go-round' sound vied with the fairground attractions provided by session stalwarts Al Kooper and Paul Griffin. It was as if Dylan was saving *his* band for the Main Event.

Even the non-album 'Can You Please Crawl Out Your Window?'—the one authentic studio representation of Dylan and The Hawks released in the moment—was little more than an afterthought at a session spent working on Dylan's latest, and greatest, exploration of human frailty, 'Freeze Out' (aka 'Visions Of Johanna').

In the end, none of these singles provided the building blocks to the bridges he burned nightly in May 1966, to the beat of Mickey Jones's pugilistic drums. Even those who had caught Dylan and The Hawks in flight Stateside—as they shuttled to and fro in their Lodestar, traversing the North American subcontinent in ever-decreasing circles for six months—found the ferocity of the performances from Liverpool and later, on bootleg, Manchester, wholly alien.

Gone is the vocal restraint and the reined-in playing on the few tapes that were made (mostly surreptitiously) at the American shows—Boston, Hartford, Berkeley, San Francisco, San Jose, Hempstead, Pittsburgh and White Plains—cast anew in brazen bronze strong enough to withstand whatever was hurled their way when the levees broke in Australia and Europe.

As Dylan told *Rolling Stone* writer Kurt Loder in 1987, 'What came out on record as The Band—it was like night and day. Robbie started playing that real pinched, squeezed guitar sound—he had never played like that before in his life! … [Back then,] every night was like goin' for broke, like the end of the world.'

Something happened *nightly* on that six-week-long 'world' tour that served to transform Dylan and The Hawks, making them sound ready to collectively fracture the very form itself. What happened, even those caught up in it did not fully understand. Nor were they greatly inclined to repeat the experiment. The toll was simply too great.

Thankfully, the tapes were now rolling: a cavalcade of ferric ferocity ringing out from Sydney to Sheffield, Melbourne to Manchester. To hear that seismic shift unfold before once-unknowing eyes all one really needs is to revisit a '66 show—take your pick—with the varifocals of hindsight and a good guidebook. The price of admission? Thirty pieces of silver.

PART ONE

THE 'I' OF THE STORM

Fanatic screaming erupted when Bob Dylan appeared on stage Sunday night. His black leather sports jacket, red shirt, tapered black slacks and electric guitar startled some in the audience and dismayed many. Sight of the Butterfield Band backing him up deepened their dismay. By his third—and most 'radically' rock and roll—song there was loud jeering and cat-calls from some parts of the audience. Then a regular battle between boos and cheers. Bob was obviously quite perturbed, the first time I have seen him so in front of an audience. (It must be said that he had rehearsed with the band for only an hour the night before and the poorly-balanced sound system made what could have been a great sound messy.) Bob dismissed the band, exchanged his electronic guitar for his more familiar acoustic one. When a cry arose for him to sing 'Mr Tambourine Man' he responded almost apologetically, 'Okay, if you want me to.' And he did, and then once again he had the old time thunderous near-unanimous applause. All in all, it was a dramatic confrontation.

—CARYL MIRKEN, 'NEWPORT: THE SHORT HOT SUMMER'
BROADSIDE #61, AUGUST 15 1965

Bob Dylan comes on stage, electric guitar in hand and accompanied by the entire Paul Butterfield R&B Band. He does three numbers including 'Maggie's Farm' and 'Like A Rolling Stone' (they all sounded more or less the same). Audience response at the end of the first is fairly good; after the second, only fair. Dylan walks off stage at the end of his third number, looking rather disgusted. Peter Yarrow tries to convince the audience that he had only allotted time for three songs; somebody else said it was because he was sick or because he couldn't get together with Butterfield's band, but the real reason was rather obvious: he left the stage because he was being booed by a large segment of the audience. It seems that there are some people who don't like electrified, amplified, reverberated, echo-chambered, rock'n'rolled Bob Dylan.

—ED FREEMAN, 'NOTES FROM A VARIANT STANZA COLLECTOR'
BOSTON BROADSIDE, AUGUST 18 1965

The set ended with his newest single release: 'Like A Rolling Stone'.
Clapping was void. Boos and hecklers' cries rang clear throughout the field.
Some, like myself, were stunned. It was awful—in the fullest sense of the
word: full of awe. Bobby left the stage abruptly. Peter Yarrow returned.
He could offer no words. The situation was incomprehensible. He asked if
people wished to hear more. Ironically, they did. But they wanted Dylan.
The old Dylan. Not a protégé of The Rolling Stones ... Bob sang 'It's All
Over Now Baby Blue'. The crowd changed colours. A standing ovation!
The cries of 'We want more', and relentless applause filled the air. Someone
yelled 'Mr Tambourine Man'. Dylan said, 'All right people, I'll sing that
for ya.' Applause again. ... At the end of the song, a standing ovation
commenced. Dylan bowed politely, smiling, saying, 'Thank you!' Perhaps
he was thanking them for letting him know how they felt about his folk/
rock endeavours.

—MICHAEL J. CARABETTA, 'IN DEFENCE OF DYLAN'
BOSTON BROADSIDE, AUGUST 18 1965

1. MY HANDS ARE ON FIRE
[July 26–September 4 1965]

MELODY MAKER, August 7, 1965—Page 7

THANK GOODNESS WE WON'T
GET THIS SIX-MINUTE BOB
DYLAN SINGLE IN BRITAIN

BOB DAWBARN LISTENS TO THE NEW SIX-MINUTE LONG BOB DYLAN SINGLE, AND COMES TO THE CONCLUSION THAT IT'S JUST AS WELL IT'S NOT SCHEDULED FOR BRITISH RELEASE.

BOB DYLAN's latest American chart entry is the world's longest single — a six-minute epic entitled "Like A Rolling Stone".

In Britain, CBS have no plans to release any Dylan single in the immediate future. And when a single is released, it is by no means certain to be "Like A Rolling Stone".

For once I'm on the side of a record company. Frankly I can't see "Like A Rolling Stone" pleasing either faction of Dylan's British fans — the folk collectors or the pop pickers.

To start with, Dylan is saddled with a quite horrific backing dominated by syrupy strings, amplified guitar and organ. Mick Jagger fans will also be distressed to learn that the song title refers to a rolling stone and not a Rolling Stone.

The lyric has its moments of typical Dylan imagery, but the monotonous melody line and Dylan's expressionless intoning just cannot hold the interest for what seems like the six longest minutes since the invention of time.

There are times when Dylan sounds faintly like Eric Burdon and, in fact, the song would be a much more suitable vehicle for the Animals than for the composer himself.

My copy of the disc bears the legend "Prod. by Tom Wilson." Somebody should have prodded Mr Wilson until he agreed to lock the backing group in the cellar until the session was over.

The paucity of "Like A Rolling Stone" is emphasised by the flip side which also runs for nearly six minutes. This is "Gates Of Eden", familiar to those who attended Dylan's British concerts and a track from his "Bringing It All Back" album.

This is just Dylan with guitar and harmonica. And without the extraneous backing noises one can concentrate on what the man is saying — and some of the writing is magnificent. What other popular writer would sing "The lamp post stands with folded arms"?

The problem posed by "Like A Rolling Stone" is the problem of Dylan himself at this stage in his career. His talents have become so diffuse—folk singer, writer with a social conscience, composer of hit songs, poet, satirist, pop star.

ELECTRONIC

The trouble comes when he starts mixing the roles. "Like A Rolling Stone" will offend the folk purists with its strings and electric guitars. It is unlikely to appeal to pop fans

It will offend the folkies
and it won't appeal to pop fans

because of its length, monotony and uncommercial lyric.

Those Dylan lyrics are another problem. He seems to be getting more and more obscure—there is an almost surrealist feel about some of his recent stuff when compared with the directness of songs like "Masters Of War", "Blowin' In The Wind" and "Don't Think Twice, It's All Right".

One imagines that this is all quite deliberate on the part of Dylan. He no doubt enjoys confounding the critics and upsetting the folk fans, who first bought his records, by going over to the electronic enemy.

That is his privilege. But it is also the record buyer's privilege to reject sub-standard Dylan. And that is what "Like A Rolling Stone" is!

The first time I played electric before a large group of people was at the Newport Folk Festival, but I had a hit record out, so I don't know how people expected me to do anything different.

—DYLAN TO SCOTT COHEN, *SPIN*, DECEMBER 1985

I couldn't go on being the lone folkie out there, you know, strumming 'Blowin' In The Wind' for three hours every night. I hear my songs as part of the music, the musical background ... I always hear other instruments, how they should sound.

—DYLAN TO RON ROSENBAUM, *PLAYBOY*, MARCH 1978

In the last weekend of July 1965, the vast American AM radio audience welcomed a new pop star, Bob Dylan. The name, vaguely familiar no doubt somehow, was all over the airwaves as his latest single enjoyed heavy rotation from California to Rhode Island.

That Sunday, he was certainly on the radio station to which the *Village Voice* music journalist Arthur Kretchmer was tuned 'on the way back from Newport ... when it ended the DJ came on in a high-pitched frenzy, "That was Bobby, BOBBY DYLAN!" He spewed some more and played the next number by the "Exhausts" or something.'

It was official: Dylan was no longer the sole property of folkies and, as Kretchmer (and Dylan) now knew, they weren't amused.

The day after the Newport Folk Festival's stormy conclusion—while Kretchmer and writers from mimeographed folk 'zines *Broadside* and *Boston Broadside* hastily filed in-the-moment reports—several frontline troops in the looming folk-rock war beat a hasty retreat to the *Sing Out!* offices in New York to regroup and review the events of a tumultuous weekend.

The first back that Monday morning was production assistant Deanna Rappaport, who explained to enthusiastic summer intern Richard Reuss, 'Dylan got booed off the stage for his rock'n'roll stuff ... He then came back a little while later with a non-amplified guitar

and did "Hey Mr Tambourine Man" and got a big hand.' Her own
position on the folk festival's primary talking point was unequivocal:
'I went to Newport to hear folk music … If I wanted rock and roll I
could just turn on the radio.'[2]

But the offices of the long-established folk periodical were
soon destined to ring with a familiar voice of dissent. Its leading
curmudgeon returned later that morning, still visibly vibrating from
the experience. Paul Nelson—co-founder of the folk 'zine *Little Sandy
Review* when Dylan was just another whiny Minnesotan trying to
sound like an Okie—had publicly criticised Dylan before, attacking
the more preachy material on his second album, *Freewheelin'*. It led to
a very public dressing down from Dylan in the program of the 1963
Newport Folk Festival. This time he was fully on the programme
and keen to give Reuss his own epiphanous take on the whole folk-
fest farrago:

> Paul said the festival was much better than last year. … He kept talking
> about the Dylan fiasco which made a very great impression on him,
> and he kept saying how dramatic it was and how it overshadowed
> everything else … Dylan was absolutely the greatest, Paul said, far
> better than Chuck Berry … [because] Dylan has the lyrics to go
> with the beat and the music. But he got a stone cold reaction. People
> yelled 'You stink' and 'Throw away the electric guitar' as his old
> fans turned on him. He left after three numbers with tears running
> down his face … Dylan came back with his regular guitar and did
> 'Baby Blue', also 'Tambourine Man' … Paul felt 'Baby Blue' was so
> appropriate as an encore [after] his sorry reception by the crowd:
> 'You could tell he was hurt.'

Nelson was already marshalling his arguments for the next *Sing
Out!* editorial. He had, after all, been brought in as the bi-monthly's
new editor the previous summer to shake the magazine up. It was a
remit given him by the magazine's owner/overseer Moe Asch, and
one he pursued with a vengeance.

So when Barbara Dane, the live-in girlfriend of *Sing Out!*'s
managing editor Irwin Silber (and an old acquaintance of Dylan's),

[2] Richard Reuss's unpublished diary from the summer of 1965, now lodged as part of
the Southern Folklife collection, provides the most reliable contemporary account of the
controversy from inside the corridors of the folk revival.

came into the office on Tuesday, she and Nelson quickly got into a heated debate about their respective weekend experiences. While Reuss jotted down notes, Dane suggested Dylan—or rather his manager Grossman—had severely miscalculated, and would be forced to rethink:

> Paul defended Dylan's rock and roll stuff. Barbara first made a few technical points: the amplifiers were still lousy (evidently a problem throughout much of the festival) … [and then] said, You know damn well there was a little bit of Al Grossman there saying, 'Okay Bobby boy, better do that stuff you've been fooling around with for the last two or three years since they all seem to want it,' completely misjudging the Newport audience because of the sales of Dylan's rock and roll album in the 'pop' market … Dylan had to realize that his audience expected a certain thing from him which in many cases filled a need in his audience. If he wished to switch his style so drastically, he had to realize that much of his audience … would seek to find their fulfilment in someone else, if not him … She felt that actually it was a very good experience for a young artist like Dylan to go through.

For all their previous familiarity, Dane evidently didn't know the former folksinger's mind. Yet she was not the only female on the highly incestuous folk scene who had known Bobby biblically and was initially convinced Dylan had miscalculated. Joan Baez, still as big a star in the contemporary folk constellation as her former paramour, informed *Broadside* after the conclusion of Dylan's set, 'Tonight Bob was in a mess. He's really very good. People just don't understand his writing,' thus managing to condescend to both sides of the argument with equal aplomb.

More openly aghast in the immediate aftermath was copywriter Carol Adler, who told the same broadsheet, 'This is the most hostile audience I've ever seen. I don't understand it.'

Dylan knew how she felt. As he sat backstage, dazed and bemused, festival organiser Theodore Bikel threw a few more verbal arrows his way. He hadn't appreciated Dylan hijacking 'his' festival with a rock band, and was still fulminating when delivering his withering verdict, 'You don't whistle in church—you don't play rock and roll at a folk festival.'

Unfortunately for Bikel and his fellow Newport committee members Pete Seeger and Alan Lomax, the other singer-songwriters who came to Newport to soak up the experience and provide the only possible future for this particular folk revival were firmly on Dylan's side.

Donovan, who arrived at the festival with Joan Baez, was one of those who (unlike Bobby's ex) loved the Dylan set. On his return to a Britain still unsure how to respond to the new six-minute Dylan single, he breathlessly informed *NME*, 'He was doing this great thing with electric guitars. It lasted a while and was fantastic, man. Electric guitars and folk, do they mix? Sure, if you want them to. Why not? Dylan uses electric guitars because he likes it that way. He doesn't care what people think.'

The original 'New Dylan', a non-performing but still-attendant Phil Ochs, also leapt to Dylan's defence even as assorted apostates from the once-Prince of Protest proffered Ochs the tainted crown. He even penned a letter to the *Village Voice*, the one non-folk periodical to give Dylan's Newport confrontation several column-inches:

> Some people saw fit to boo Dylan after each song [but] I think they were getting a needed dose of musical shock treatment. Dylan as usual was doing the unexpected, but was quite responsibly doing what any real artist should, that is performing the music he personally felt closest to and putting his own judgement before that of his audience. To cater to the audience's taste is not to respect them, and if an audience doesn't understand that, they don't deserve respect. The people that thought they were booing Dylan were in reality booing themselves in a most vulgar display of unthinking mob censorship. Meanwhile, life went on all around them.

These, then, were the protagonists caught up in the *initial* hullabaloo around Dylan's Newport set. For now, it seemed destined to remain an East Coast storm in a teacup. The week after, even *Sing Out!*'s publisher wasn't entirely sure whether the furore would die down by the time its next issue was due off the press in late September. (As such, Silber asked Nelson 'to come in to the office and talk about … how they were going to play the Newport festival next issue, play it up or down'.)

Dylan, for one, wanted to know the state of play. He seems to have sent Minnesotan friend Tony Glover to the *Sing Out!* offices the Friday after Newport to find out if something was happening—demonstrating how he *did* 'care what people think'.

Ostensibly there to find out how his book on blues harmonica was coming along, Glover took the opportunity to converse with both Nelson, an old friend from Minneapolis, and Silber, with whom he 'mildly argued'.[3] Glover had already caught a glimpse of Dylan's artistic response to the weekend's events, having attended the first session for Dylan's second (semi-)electric long-player the previous afternoon (Thursday, July 29).

Highway 61 Revisited would be wrapped up in just four inspirational sessions either side of the last weekend in July, which seems especially remarkable considering the views of Dylan's chosen guitarist, a key arbiter in his new sound:

Michael Bloomfield: The songs were written, and they had chord sheets. But there was no concept. No one knew what they wanted to play, no one knew what the music was supposed to sound like, other than Bob, who had the chords and the words and the melody. But as far as saying we're gonna make folk-rock records, nobody had any idea what to do—none … the producer was a non-producer. I don't know who he was … He didn't know what was happening, man! … We did twenty alternate takes of every song, and it got ridiculous because they were long songs … It was never, like, here's one of the tunes, we're gonna learn it, work out the arrangement, that just wasn't done. The thing just sort of fell together in this haphazard, half-assed way. … It was just like a jam session, it really was. But it was astutely mixed and I believe it was mixed by Dylan. He knew he had a sound in his mind. … He wanted [me] to play [more] like McGuinn. It was even discussed. He said, 'I don't want any of that B.B. King shit, man.'

That initial session, just four days after the Newport meltdown, began with Dylan working on two songs debuted at the folk-fest:

---

[3] Tony Glover's book on blues harmonica was due to be published by Oak Publications, the publishing arm of Moe Asch's Folkways Records.

'Tombstone Blues', played not in the brief electric set but during an acoustic afternoon workshop; and 'Phantom Engineer' (as he called it off-mic at Newport), a.k.a. 'It Takes A Lot To Laugh', the least successful of the three songs performed that Sunday with components of the Paul Butterfield Blues Band, now tried first fast, à la Newport, then slow and soulful.

He had a whole lot more he wanted to say, spending most of the late afternoon session (2:30–5:30) working on a song that, on one level at least, seemed to be taking the whole Newport thing personal: 'You got a lotta nerve to say you are my friend / When I was down, you just stood there grinning.' For now it was called 'Black Dally Rue', but he wasn't positive what title it would assume.

For those who thought the songs on *Another Side* were 'inner-probing' and 'self-conscious', there would be another shock in store. The final song of the day, recorded in a single remarkable take with just electric guitar and bass, was eleven minutes long. 'Desolation Row' was his most ambitious work to date and suggested that he was already several states of mind away from those who had booed his idea of electric blues.

Without reading a single review of Newport, Dylan had placed a barbed wire fence between himself and his former Fourth Street friends. These included *New York Times* folk critic Robert Shelton, who back in September 1961 had announced the emergence of 'a distinctive stylist' in the esteemed journal but now gave his Newport performance a lukewarm review in *Cavalier*.

It took Shelton a few more weeks to notice the wind of change was blowing away from him and to change direction. When he interviewed Dylan by phone for a pre–Forest Hills feature the following month, he quoted one of those 'truth attacks' Dylan directed at those without imagination verbatim, unaware he may have been numbered among them:

Bob Dylan: I know in my own mind what I'm doing. If anyone has imagination, he'll know what I'm doing. If they can't understand my songs they're missing something. If they can't understand green clocks, wet chairs, purple lamps or hostile statues, they're missing something, too.

After Forest Hills, Shelton realised Dylan's electrical experiment was no whim and signed on for the duration, dissociating himself from Silber and his worldview. It was an association that in Dylan's mind dated back to when the two deans of folk criticism found the songs on *Another Side Of Bob Dylan* obtuse, and Dylan's *previous* Newport appearance in 1964 a disappointment.

That final song recorded at the first *Highway 61 Revisited* session was a direct challenge to the mindset of anyone who had found 'My Back Pages' impenetrable. It featured not only 'green clocks, wet chairs, purple lamps [and] hostile statues' but characters straight out of some Hammer Horror movie Fellini secretly directed. Dylan had been pouring over the lyrics to 'Desolation Row' for days beforehand, but at the July 29 session he delivered it word-perfect, accompanied by a jangly, off-key electric guitar and a contrabass.

★ ★ ★

Asked twenty-two years later about whether being 'more or less drummed out of the purist folk movement ... was a painful experience', Dylan insisted he had always known his artistic intentions:

Bob Dylan: It didn't bother me that people didn't understand what I was doing, because ... I knew, when I was doing that stuff, that [it] hadn't been done before ... I knew what The Beatles were doing, and that seemed to be real pop stuff. The Stones were doing blues things—just hard city blues. But I knew that [what] I was doing ... hadn't *ever* been done before. [1987]

Even with hindsight, Dylan's own take on Newport rarely wavered. He challenged the scale of dissent that greeted him in a 1978 interview: 'They thought I didn't know what I was doing and that I'd slipped over the edge, but the truth is ... what the newspapers say happened didn't actually happen that way. There wasn't a whole lot of resistance in the crowd.'

What resistance rose up was bound to be futile:

Bob Dylan: I was aware that people were fighting in the audience, but I couldn't understand it. I was a little embarrassed by the fuss, because it was for the wrong reasons. I mean, you can do some really disgusting things in life and people will let you get away with it. Then you do something that you don't think is anything more than natural and people react in that type of riotous way. [1985]

Truth be told, the death of the folk messiah that night has been greatly exaggerated. The fabled shot of a tear running down Dylan's cheek is merely a bead of sweat. Whatever the *real* audience reaction, as far as he was concerned, 'You just try and dust yourself off and get on with it.'

And get on with it he did. He already knew he was far enough ahead to lob some verbal depth charges in the direction of the *Sing Out!* offices, if not on his next album, then with his next two singles. He had been working hard at the new lyrics, scribbling lines until he had a song, typing a fair draft and then correcting by hand, adding, subtracting lines until he had taken 'a rhythm thing on paper, all about my steady hatred directed at some point that was honest' and made it something poetical and truthful.[4]

He would use a weekend in Woodstock to put the finishing touches to at least four of the songs. 'Highway 61 Revisited' and 'Queen Jane Approximately' were two songs he planned to record the following Monday (August 2) but which had yet to arrive at a finished form. Returning to Woodstock after the Friday session, he knew that this was where he had completed his previous album and sensed it might be where he could wrap this one up, too.

On 'Highway 61 Revisited', he was assuredly setting the world to rights, character by caricature. Napoleon in Rags gave it up for 'Bony McFony' and 'Josephine', both of whom make an appearance in the original 'Highway 61 Revisited' typescript; the former has 'a thousand friends' yet only 'talks to himself' while the latter is another of those who 'makes the top of your head explode'.

'Queen Jane' may actually have been a song he started and finished in Woodstock. The trigger for the song can seemingly be found at the bottom of a typed copy of 'Highway 61'—with the single line, 'Won't you come see me, Lord Jim?' But then he gets out the legal notepaper, typewriter and a pen, and goes to work. The part-typed, part-handwritten draft of 'Queen Jane' reproduced in the *Mixing Up*

---

[4] Dylan gave this memorable quote—his attempt to describe what first inspired 'Like A Rolling Stone'—to a CBC journalist in February 1966.

The Medicine hardback book (included in the deluxe edition of *Cutting Edge*) may be the earliest such draft of a *Highway 61* song to survive; perhaps because that draft was left at the Grossmans', the widow subsequently trying to unsuccessfully sell it as her own property in auction, before it reverted to its legal owner.[5]

The lines at the top of the typed page make it abundantly clear what the approach of the song will be: 'youre scared more of yourself then [sic] you are of your ... creations'. By this stage, Lord Jim is no more. It is Queen Anne, not Queen Jane, who 'need[s] someone that you dont have to speak to'. But by the lower half of the page, she is Queen Jane, three of whose verses appear in rough disguise. She is still a long way from home, even as he warns her about those who 'tell you that they understand your pain'. The discarded double-sided sheet will need further work, both on the page and in the studio.

Another major song he worked on at his upstate typewriter, and perhaps on the bus he took back into the city on the Sunday, concerned someone who 'try[s] hard to fit in' only to find he is a square peg in a round hole. The typed prototype for 'Ballad Of A Thin Man' made it clear that Mr Jones was someone who, armed with his own press pass, used the pencil in his hand (which in the original draft was a 'hatchit') to dissect others' lives while staying resolutely in the closet himself:

> *you fought so hard / your whole life to get blessed*
> *by those who make you undress*
> *it must be terrifying to have so many people to impress.*
> *you ask obnoxious questions*
> *& you expect all the answers in just one word ...*

This song, recorded in just one complete take (and two breakdowns) the following Monday, would close the side 'Like A Rolling Stone' opened before becoming a most apposite precursor to the same cathartic comeuppance in concert.

'Thin Man' would also become the song he would be asked about most—after 'Rolling Stone'—as the more astute journalists realised

---

[5] At this stage Dylan may have been discarding most working papers, keeping only the fair copies.

Dylan had got them in his sights. Nora Ephron, the first fourth-estater to interview him after *Highway 61 Revisited*'s release, asked him outright, 'Who is Mr Jones?' Dylan replied, 'He's a real person. You know him, but not by that name.' Three months later, the same question reared its head again in a San Francisco TV studio, but Dylan still refused to give the man a singular identity: 'I'm not going to tell you his first name. I'd get sued.'

And yet, for all his insistence that Jones wasn't his name and that he 'wears suspenders', a cub *Time* reporter called Jeffrey Jones would publish a December 1975 article claiming to have inadvertently inspired him to write 'Ballad Of A Thin Man' by interviewing him at Newport. The then-college kid never considered the possibility that when Dylan mockingly called out over dinner, 'Gettin' it all down, Mr Jones? ... You going to write a story for *Time*, Mr Jones?' he might have already started to sketch 'Thin Man', inspired by an encounter with another *Time* reporter he had for a Savoy breakfast two months earlier.

Dylan himself, when asked in 1985 about this particular Mr Jones, expressed absolute amazement that anyone would want to own up to such an association. He further observed, 'There were a lot of Mister Joneses at that time. There obviously must have been ... for me to write that particular song. It wasn't just one person. It was like, "Oh, man, here's the thousandth Mister Jones."'

His response was a hundred and one nights on the road declaiming, 'Something is happening but you don't know what it is, do you ... Mr ... Jones!!' If his feelings weren't adequately expressed by the song itself—nightly rammed down critics' throats—it also provided a *raison d'être* for a ten-minute sequence in the still-unreleased 1966 tour documentary *Eat The Document*, editor Howard Alk intercutting every kind of Mr Jones (and even the odd Miss Jones) with live snatches of the song straight from Dylan's Inferno.

As of July 31 1965, Dylan was still obliged to play ball with the ballbusters, even with an album to complete, a band to rehearse, and a new way of performing to unveil. While he was thus distracted, the storm of controversy built up its own head of steam. In the twenty-four days separating the completion of *Highway 61 Revisited* from the Forest Hills unveiling of a full-on Electric Dylan, the legend of Newport began to overtake the facts.

★ ★ ★

That legend's first spark was provided by Arthur Kretchmer's August 5 *Village Voice* review. The weekly bible for East Village others hit the stands the very day Dylan put the finishing touches to a now-acoustic 'Desolation Row'. Beneath the banner headline 'It's All Right, Ma, I'm Only Playin' R & R', Kretchmer predicted how the myth's potency would continue to grow in inverse proportion to Dylan's retreat into an interior mindscape:

> Musically, the festival was obtuse and disappointing. Of five official concerts only one (Sunday afternoon) was satisfying ... mostly because of the brilliance of Mimi and Dick Farina ... [Yet] young girls ran through the Viking Hotel screaming, 'BOBBY! Donovan! Dylan! Look, mister, do you know who that is in the pool?' ... [as] the festival committee tried to force-feed a May Day atmosphere complete with militant Socialist restrictiveness to a generation that doesn't trust anybody who wants to run a machine. ... Sunday night Bob Dylan was booed for linking rhythm and blues to the paranoid nightmares of his vision. ... The irony of the folklorists and their parochial ire at Dylan's musical transgressions is that he is ... this generation's most awesome talent. And in 80 years you will read scholarly papers about his themes (terror, release).

Kretchmer hardly set out to absolve Dylan of his own burden of responsibility, calling him 'a man afraid and obsessed. He surrounds himself with people but will never be well-enough protected ... [because] for Dylan, this mass success has become another fear; another out-of-control situation.'

The *Voice*'s voice may even have witnessed Dylan mete out judgement on Jeffrey Jones, or some other poor sap, because he accused him of beginning to act 'like a mogul [who] surrounds himself with flunkies who feed him lines and laugh when he repeats them. At dinner he rotates the chicks at the place of honour next to himself.'

Nor was Kretchmer the only reporter that weekend who witnessed Dylan's increasing detachment from his fans, his new moddish attire already setting himself apart from those who still looked like sharecroppers. As Joe Boyd, the production manager at the festival, later wrote, 'When Mr Dylan arrived in '65 in a puff-sleeved dueling shirt, with a stoned-looking entourage, and sang "Mr Tambourine Man" at a Friday workshop [sic], the dream of the left died. You could [already] feel the tension between the generations.'

The man of the soil depicted on the cover of his third album had been returned in a box to Bowling Green. Even the ultra-staid *Boston Globe* called Dylan 'the aloof leather-jacketed idol of the topical song set'. Meanwhile, *Boston Broadside*'s Michael Carabetta, closer to the fray than the *Globe* scribe, suggested the new look played its part in the collective shock felt when the Fender guitar-toting Dylan took the stage at Newport:

> Gone was the well-worn suede jacket, dungarees and boots, the flat-top acoustic guitar. Those items of the past were replaced; replaced by a black continental suit, pointed black boots with Chelsea heels, and a solid body electric guitar. Was this he? The throng was bewildered somewhat.

Six weeks later, Nora Ephron jokingly asked the man himself about this 'sell-out jacket'. Dylan cracked a grin and wondered aloud, 'What kind of a jacket is a sell-out jacket? ... I've had black leather jackets since I was five years old.' But he of all hipsters knew that symbolism was not confined to the words he used, and he doubtless chuckled himself to sleep at night thinking about the epithets used by some reviewers that were reduced to commenting, unflatteringly, on his new image. For an old-school folkie like Jim Rooney, the new look was certainly symptomatic of a worried man:

> Bob is no longer a neo-Woody Guthrie, with whom they could identify. He has thrown away his dungarees and shaggy jacket. ... He travels by plane. He wears high-heel shoes and high-style clothes from Europe. The mountains and valleys he knows are those of the mind—a mind extremely aware of the violence of the inner and outer world. 'The people' so loved by Pete Seeger are 'the mob' so hated by Dylan.

Unwittingly, Rooney added his voice to the static already swirling around the event, having written his thoughts down in a letter (and sealed it with his hand) for the benefit of the Board of Directors at Newport—or so he thought. But that letter ended up on Paul Nelson's desk, and, with scant regard for Rooney, or the legal niceties, the editor decided to incorporate Rooney's privately expressed view into his consciously incendiary editorial on the great folk-rock showdown.

Nelson read the letter the day after he had told Silber, in front of Moe Asch, that 'he wanted to do an article for *Sing Out!* on Newport. Irwin … couldn't say no in front of Moe. He doesn't want Paul to do it, Paul says, because he might write something Irwin wouldn't agree with. [But] Moe has chewed out Irwin severely in the past for this kind of censoring … Irwin … is typing up an article [of his own] on Newport to be run in the next *Sing Out!*. [But] when Irwin gets to Dylan, he goes all over the place.'

Nelson also told Richard Reuss he liked the way Rooney's epistle 'stresses the generation gap of folksingers at Newport' and how 'the mood Pete [Seeger] had tried to create … was shattered by Dylan's intensely personal probings into the mind … unknown to the singers of Pete's generation.' But Rooney was not convinced Dylan knew what he was doing, whereas Nelson felt strongly he did. In fact, he had already discussed the shift in direction with Dylan at the festival; Dylan bluntly stated that he had 'used topical songs as a vehicle to get to the top and always considered them as a means to an end'.[6]

Nelson soon reeled off his riposte to Silber and his ilk, partly from his own notes, as well as using Rooney's letter, showing Reuss the article he had composed on August 17. Reuss found the argument 'devastating' but thought it 'will have to go in *Little Sandy Review* as Irwin will never approve it for *Sing Out!!*' Silber, though, did not have the final say. Asch did.

Before Nelson locked horns with Silber one last time, the latest issue of *Boston Broadside* was plonked across his desk. It only fuelled Nelson's determination to disavow those, like Ed Freeman, convinced that Dylan had misread the situation:

[6] This would become a familiar mantra. As late as 1969, Dylan told Ray Connolly, 'The reason I started off playing with just that acoustical sound was an economic one. Between about 1958 and 1963 it wasn't possible for a big rock band to make a living because they went out of fashion. But when The Beatles came along they opened it all up.'

The importance of the event ... lies not in what the crowd did or
didn't like, but in the fact that they actually had enough taste and
self-determination to have an opinion; that they could scream all
weekend for their hero and then boo him for doing something that
they thought was bad. ... It is heartening to know that the masses
has any taste at all and knows the difference between rock'n'roll and
folk music and prefers to hear the latter at a Folk Festival.

Compelled to take issue with another representative of folk's fourth
estate, Nelson openly disputed Freeman's assertion that 'Dylan was
not upset by the crowds, only by his inability to get together with the
band with whom he had had a short rehearsal period'. His view was
clear: 'Dylan *was* affected by the crowd's reaction and was [visibly]
upset.' Where he had the advantage over many eyewitnesses that
electric evening was his proximity—standing alongside Elektra's boss,
four feet from the stage:

Jac Holzman: That evening [at Newport] I was standing next to
Dave Gahr in the photographers' pit, below and in front of the stage.
Peter Yarrow introduced Dylan [as] the very special artist that he was
and from the moment he launched into 'Maggie's Farm', now fleshed
out with an incredible electric intensity, it was clarity and catharsis. ...
My friend Paul Nelson was standing alongside, and we just turned to
each other and shit-grinned. This was electricity married to content
... then suddenly we heard booing, like pockets of wartime flak. The
audience had split into two separate and opposing camps. It grew
into an awesome barrage of catcalls and hisses ... I couldn't believe
that those people weren't hearing the wonderful stuff I was hearing.
I looked directly into Dylan's face as he squinted in the darkness,
trying to figure out what was happening.

Both Holzman and Nelson were unaware of the war of words
going on behind them and only found out later about the kerfuffle at
the mixing desk. Holzman heard about it first, having 'got it directly
from George Wein (head of the Newport Folk Festival), who said
he was there when it happened. Pete Seeger did indeed want to cut
the wires of Dylan's electric guitar when Dylan came onstage. Wein
intervened and said to do that would cause a riot. Pete stalked off and

got in his car, rolled up all the windows, and sat there [with] tears rolling down his cheeks.'[7]

This contemporary account presents a very different version to the one Seeger later propagated (to myself and others): that he was upset by the sound mix, that was all. Seeger clung to that version for three decades. It would take a letter from Joe Boyd to the *New York Observer*, thirty-three and a third years later, to firmly shatter Seeger's unhistorical cotton-candy construct:

> I was in charge of liaison between backstage and the mixing console. We had an exciting sound check late Sunday afternoon. We knew then that the rumors were true, that Bob Dylan was going to confront the festival with rock'n'roll. When 'Maggie's Farm' hit, it was like an explosion. I was quickly summoned by an irate Alan Lomax, plus Pete Seeger and Theo Bikel, all members of the festival board. 'You have to get it turned down,' said Mr Lomax. He ordered me to climb the fence and demand the sound be turned down. I relayed the message. Middle fingers were extended from the hands of Albert Grossman, Peter Yarrow and the late Paul Rothschild, who was mixing the sound. I returned and relayed their message. Mr Seeger turned on his heel and stormed off into the parking lot. His wife Toshi burst into tears in George Wein's arms. Mr Lomax spat with fury. By this time, the three songs were almost over. There was no ax wielded.

At the time, Nelson went along with the legend of the 'ax wielded' because it suited his own polemical purpose, Seeger's (over)reaction providing a visually arresting metaphor for the generational conflict at the heart of their ideological spat. Other eyewitnesses were already painting the controversy in personal terms: less electric versus acoustic, rock versus folk, and more about Dylan versus Seeger, Grossman versus Lomax. A clash of personalities, not ideologies.

It helped the burgeoning legend that Seeger got his way, or appeared to. After all, didn't Dylan return with an acoustic guitar and give the crowd what it wanted? Again, it took Boyd to point out, this time in a 1986 interview with the *Telegraph*, that it was not so simple or straightforward:

[7] The quote comes verbatim from Richard Reuss's diary, drawing on a conversation he had with Paul Nelson.

Dylan had been scheduled for forty minutes—certainly half-an-hour. People had not come all that way to see twenty minutes of Bob Dylan [sic]. ... So Yarrow was poised to go up ... and suddenly they're finished. ... There was a huge roar from the crowd but ... you know, MORE and BOO sound very similar if you have a whole crowd going MORE and BOO. ... I think it was definitely evenly divided between approbation and condemnation from the crowd. Well, this roar went on for quite a long time and Yarrow then went on stage and, I think, rather embarrassingly, began to do his impression of a Las Vegas compere, 'C'mon, folks, let's hear it for Bob Dylan.' ... No Bob Dylan. Bob Dylan was hiding in a tent.

Much has been read into Dylan's return with a borrowed Martin guitar and his choice of 'encore'. But as Nelson explained to Reuss just a fortnight later, 'Dylan's band had only rehearsed three numbers, and if Dylan were to do more songs, he *had* to use a regular guitar. So although it looked as if Dylan were yielding to the crowd when he came back and played "Baby Blue", he really could do nothing else.'

Although endless accounts portray Dylan singing 'It's All Over Now Baby Blue' and leaving the stage, the song he was really ramming down the committee's throats was 'Mr Tambourine Man'. A confirmed classic, it had received its US debut at the previous Newport, when it was one of those songs Silber deemed 'inner-probing, self-conscious—maybe even a little maudlin or ... cruel'.

Now that the song sat at number one in the singles chart, courtesy of The Byrds—Dylan's full version having been finally captured on the acoustic side of *Bringing It All Back Home*—it was cheered to the rafters. Thus did Dylan make the subtlest of points: I was ahead of you then, and I'm ahead of you *now*.

From this time forward—when songs like 'It's All Over Now Baby Blue' and 'Tambourine Man' would serve as hors d'oeuvres, not the dessert—he would be prepared for anything. Of the three songs from his 'inner-probing, self-conscious' fourth album Dylan would retain throughout 1965, two would be given the treatment Silber feared most: rocked up.

★ ★ ★

Fully half of the vacant slots in his first full-blown electric set the following month would be given to songs Dylan only recorded in the aftermath of Newport, companion pieces to the six-minute hit single which first announced his new direction—home. *Highway 61 Revisited* was already rolling off the pressing plants when the daily papers announced Dylan was to play two open-air shows in New York and Los Angeles on consecutive summer's end weekends. 'Twas time to tell who's been left behind.

It was almost like these songs had been written more to bolster the electric live set than compile an album his label could sell in droves. Of the nine songs on his forthcoming long-player, Dylan played six at Forest Hills and the Hollywood Bowl and rehearsed another.[8] Only 'It Takes A Lot To Laugh' (which even in its up-tempo 'Phantom Engineer' guise had been the weak point in the Newport electric set) and 'Queen Jane Approximately' (which would have to wait twenty-two years for its live debut) were considered surplus to requirements.

This time Dylan would be as prepped as his new four-piece—drummer Levon Helm and guitarist Robbie Robertson from Toronto's Levon & The Hawks, organist Al Kooper and bassist Harvey Brooks from the *Highway 61* studio band—having booked two weeks at Carroll's rehearsal hall. If the latter two had already spent time with the likes of 'Tombstone Blues', 'Just Like Tom Thumb's Blues', 'From A Buick 6' and 'Ballad Of A Thin Man' in the studio, for the other attendees fully five-eighths of the electric set would be unreleased and, on first listen, unfathomable.

If Kooper and his friend Harvey Brooks had helped define the R&B roar of *Highway 61*—which was now the sound in Dylan's head—the inclusion of Robertson and Helm was essentially forced upon him by the haste with which he needed a backing band, and the reluctance of guitarist Mike Bloomfield (who had his own Butterfield Blues Band duties) and drummer Bobby Gregg to be live lab rats. He later made light of his providential choice:

Bob Dylan: Mary Martin kept pushing this group who were out in New Jersey—I think they were in Elizabeth, New Jersey, or Hartford,

---

[8] The title-track, scheduled as a possible encore at Forest Hills, was never actually played.

Connecticut, or some town close to New York. She was pushing them and she had two of the fellows come up to the office so we could meet. ... No more, no less. I just asked them if they could do it and they said they could. (Laughs) These two said they could. And that was how it started. Easy enough, you know. [1969]

It wasn't really so easy, or so serendipitous. Both Helm and Robertson had appeared on John Hammond Jr's *So Many Roads*, the first white electric blues album of its kind. Recorded the previous fall by Dylan's good friend, it provided enough of a calling card to lead Dylan to invite Robertson to a groundbreaking single session in June 1965. There he is in the corner of the room, behind the shades, at the playback for 'Like A Rolling Stone', while Eugene Smith snapped away for a *Life* feature that never appeared.

So when Dylan informed a journalist the following fall that he had known Robertson 'for a while', it was not one of his smokescreens. It was Hawks drummer Helm who didn't really know what he was taking on. Of course, when the two itinerant Canadian bar-band musicians accepted Dylan's out-of-the-blue offer, neither knew what long-term future the position might hold. But as Robertson had discovered only the other day, when you ain't got nothing, you got nothing to lose.

This time, Dylan decided to give fans a little advance warning. He proceeded to inform the fifteen thousand people with Forest Hills tickets to expect 'some electricity' this time, via a phone-call interview with the *New York Times*' Robert Shelton:

> I'll have some electricity and ... [maybe] four new songs. Time goes by very fast up there onstage. I think of what not to do rather than what to do ... I can't sing 'With God On My Side' for fifteen years. What I write is much more concise now than before. It's not deceiving.

Dylan remained focused on playing the material he had been writing, making precious few concessions to the expectations of an audience bound to be split between old and new fans. The first part of the electric set would comprise three unreleased songs and a radical rearrangement of 'It Ain't Me Babe', a song already given the folk-rock treatment by The Turtles (and a country-rock treatment by Johnny Cash).

He was going for broke, six years after he left Bobby Vee's band to become a folksinger and acoustic guitar picker. It took some adjusting, for him *and* them. As he admitted in 1968, 'It's more complicated playing an electric guitar because you're five or ten feet away from the sound and you strain for things that you don't have to when the sound is right next to your body.' Forest Hills Stadium was a long way from his rock'n'roll debut at the Hibbing High School Auditorium even if the reaction was shockingly similar.[9]

At least this time there was an actual sound check captured on camera by his official photographer, Daniel Kramer. In fact, the level of preparation was unlike any concert to date, as Kramer noted in a 1967 photo-study:

> In the past, Bob would bring his guitar, some harmonicas, and his small case of microphone equipment. On this day, things were approaching the conditions of a recording studio. There were many microphones to unpack, microphone stands to assemble, and dozens of coils of cable to unwind. The instruments had to be set up and arranged on stage. Microphones had to be placed and then balanced for sound. There were problems caused by the rustling sound made by the wind as it rushed by the mike heads. Voice levels had to be balanced so they could be heard over the sound of the instruments. It went on and on. Half a dozen people worked at it, and the musicians and Dylan were constantly needed for sound checks. It was an astonishing contrast to the preparation required for the first Dylan concert I attended almost a year earlier.

When the folk fans arrived at the stadium on an August evening with a distinctly autumnal feel, the sight of all those banks of speakers only heightened the chill factor. But perhaps they could allow their hero the benefit of the doubt. After all, as an attendant Robert Shelton reported, 'Mr Dylan [first] appeared alone with his guitar, harmonica, plaintive voice and seven of his folkish songs, among them … a major new work, "Desolation Road" [sic] … filled with the incongruities of black humour and macabre imagery'. 'Desolation Row's incongruous

[9] A young Bob Zimmerman was famously booed off the stage at his high school on his live 1957 debut with The Golden Chords.

imagery prompted audible laughs from the attentive audience, who remained in good humour throughout.[10]

The rest of the acoustic set, 'To Ramona' excepted, Dylan devoted to songs from his fifth album, *Bringing It All Back Home*, bringing warm applause from those who had come fearing the worst and polite applause from those who sensed he was just warming up. At the end of a heartfelt 'Tambourine Man', the crowd were informed there would be a short interval. While fans chatted about what they had heard so far, Dylan gave his first and last pep talk to musicians as Daniel Kramer sat and watched:

> He told them they should expect anything to happen … He told them that the audience might yell and boo, and that they should not be bothered by it. Their job, he said, was to make the best music they were capable of, and let whatever happened happen.

If Newport had been Dylan venturing into the unknown, the confrontation in Queens was one he fully expected and even to some extent orchestrated. He certainly can't have imagined getting a hopped-up Murray The K to introduce him would go down well with the older folk. And nor did it. As *Variety*'s Herm Schoenfeld reported, 'The temper of the Forest Hills audience could be gauged from the reaction to Murray Kaufman. … Kaufman's close association with the "Top 40" school of pops earned some vigorous boos from a large section of this folknik crowd, who neither needed nor wanted an explanation for Dylan's conversion to rock'n'roll.'

Shelton suggested Murray The K was left 'barely able to shout his blessings on Mr Dylan and his new mood before the audience howled and booed its disapproval'. Dylan's appearance onstage with 'an excellent rock'n'roll quartet', far from assuaging these fans, only served to further incense them. Launching into a raucous 'Tombstone Blues', Dylan's band and a raft of amps drowned out further expostulations from the stands. But it was a temporary cease-fire. The 'Mods', as *Village Voice*'s Jack Newfield dubbed the 'folknik crowd', were reloading:

---

[10] This ten-minute epic still proved so challenging to *Billboard*'s reporter that he convinced himself it was vocally 'reminiscent of the late Jimmie Rodgers'.

After the first rock song, the Mods booed Dylan. After the second someone called him a 'scumbag', [to which] he replied coolly, 'Aw, come on now.' After the third, the Mods chanted sardonically, 'We want Dylan.'

Like Nelson at Newport, Newfield felt there was something decidedly generational about the conflagration:

> The Mods booed their former culture hero savagely after each of his amplified rock melodies. They chanted … and shouted insults at him. Meanwhile, the Rockers, in frenzied kamikaze squadrons of six and eight, leaped out of the stands after each rock song and raced for the stage. … The factionalism within the teenage sub-culture seemed as fierce as that between Social Democrats and Stalinists.

Things were getting heated. The chants of 'We want Dylan' seemed to be orchestrated, or so thought Dylan's future manager, as of now just another thirteen-year-old fan of the 'new' Dylan. *Newsday*'s Joseph Gelmis had never seen anything like it:

> 'Traitor,' some shouted as Dylan and his quartet finished a song. 'Where's Ringo?' a young voice in the stands taunted. Then, from the seats where 15,000 faithful had defied temperatures in the low 50s and winds that boomed like doomsday through the microphone, a chant started: 'Where's Dylan? We want Dylan. We want Dylan.' Dylan's only reply to the catcalls and gibes was a sad shake of the head and a plaintive, 'Ah, ah, come on.'

This was all great copy—and this time the mainstream media was on hand to see the drama unfold before their largely unknowing eyes: *Billboard*, *Variety*, the *New York Times* and *Newsday* had all sent emissaries. If Newport was a boondock escapade—important only to campfire folkies and trust-fund Commie kids—this was the Forest Hills Music Festival. Frank Sinatra, Barbra Streisand and Peter, Paul & Mary had all preceded Dylan's appearance that month, and sold out. So had Dylan, both literally and metaphorically.

Halfway through the electric set, things began to change. Many of the dissenters began to pay more attention, probably because of a conscious concession on Dylan's part to play two recognisable songs in a row: 'It Ain't Me Babe', 'with a muted rock beat', followed by 'Maggie's Farm'. According to *Billboard*, 'Thereafter, each song brought mixed boos and applause; finally the boos died away.'

Meanwhile, the ritual of wave after 'wave of Rockers sprint[ing] for the stage … was repeated by co-ed guerrilla bands after each succeeding song'. Finally, after the Mods' wrath had largely subsided, Jack Newfield witnessed them 'join the Rockers in wildly applauding Dylan's new[est] song of the evening, which he sang while playing the piano standing up'.

The song in question, 'Ballad Of A Thin Man', would prove a popular choice at every show for the next nine months.[11] Leading quickly into 'Like A Rolling Stone', it couldn't help but bring down the house. Yet a pencilled-in two-song encore never happened. Instead, 'Dylan and his musicians slipped away … to the candy-striped tent behind the stage without a goodbye or a wave.'

Back at the *Sing Out!* office, the debate raged all the next (work) day, with Richard Reuss convinced that 'the audience split down the middle pretty much, although more were against him than for him'—a view at variance with most other eyewitnesses. For Nelson, 'the audience changed on Dylan simply because he used an electric guitar the second half'—true—'and was immature in their change'.

Shelton called the audience 'immature', while accusing them of showing their feelings rudely in his *New York Times* review. Dylan, though, wanted an honest response, as he demonstrated back at Grossman's apartment after the concert when he launched into another 'truth attack' on some unfortunate girl, witnessed by, among others, Daniel Kramer:

> Bob, relaxing in his stocking feet, asked a young lady who had been at the concert for her opinion of what she had seen and heard. She replied that she had no feelings. Finally, under some pressure, she admitted that she did not particularly like the new music. Asked if she had booed, she replied that she had not. Why not, was Dylan's question. Why hadn't she made her feelings known? She would not answer. If you don't like something, you should let your feelings be known—you should have booed, Dylan told her.

[11] In Al Kooper's *Backstage Passes*, he suggests that such was the furore at Forest Hills that Dylan was forced to play the piano intro to 'Ballad Of A Thin Man' over and over again until the crowd calmed down. The lo-fi audience tape firmly refutes Kooper's account.

Headlines in the following day's (and weekly) papers suggested a victory on points for the singer with his own penchant for boxing analogies:

> 'Dylan Conquers Unruly Audience'
> 'Show Sold Out, But Did Dylan?'
> 'Mods, Rockers, Fight Over New Thing Called "Dylan"'
> 'Bob Dylan Moves Too Fast For Fans'

The furore even made the English music papers, where *Record Mirror*'s Norman Jopling reported, 'Bob Dylan was greeted with boos and one yell of "traitor!" when he sang rock'n'roll songs during a concert at America's Forest Hills Music Festival.' This must have seemed quite incredible to the *Mirror* readers, coming less than three months after two triumphant all-acoustic affairs at the Royal Albert Hall. (Next time, it would not go so well, and it would behove The Beatles to berate the barrackers from their private box.)

★ ★ ★

Unfortunately, The Beatles could not be on hand, or hold Bob's hand, at Forest Hills. They were too busy fighting their own battles with their fanatical fans on the West Coast, at the very venue Dylan was scheduled to play a week later. *Their* problem was not an overly negative audience—quite the opposite. So loud were the hormonal screams of yet another audience of adulatory adolescents at the Hollywood Bowl that even if one had wanted to hear their brand of Merseybeat, one couldn't.

The leakage into the onstage microphones being used to record a live album proved so loud the band could not hear itself, and the album itself was scrapped. The contrast with Dylan's performance a week later would prove marked enough to draw comment from the *LA Times*' veteran entertainment reporter, Charles Champlin:

> The incidentals were the same as for The Beatles' concerts last Sunday and Monday—the Hollywood Bowl virtually sold out, the parking lots overflowing and Highland Avenue a tangle, the hip young crowd dressed in bell-bottoms, shifts and, for the boys, sports shirts of unparalleled finery. The monumental difference was

that his vast audience paid folk singer Bob Dylan the compliment of pin-drop silence while he was performing. His rewards thereafter were thunderous applause, a scattering of whistles, but no screams, which is interesting because there was obviously at least a partial overlap between his audience and The Beatles'.

If the contrast with The Beatles' Bowl gig was acute, so was the contrast with Forest Hills.[12] Even Champlin—who in his review suggested 'that Newport had the right idea—the added sound drowned the lyrics in several instances, [and] undercut Dylan's individuality, putting him in a bag ... which is already overcrowded'—admitted his own criticism was in no way indicative of the majority view.

This was a crowd who set far more store in the pop journalism of *KRLA Beat* than their patronising parents' paper of choice. And *KRLA Beat* gave Dylan at the Bowl a full page and the headline, 'We Had Known A Lion'. Its young female reporter, Shirley Poston, was unapologetic about joining in the cheers for the song most there had come to hear:

When the time came to honor the most-shouted request of the evening, Dylan searched momentarily for his C harmonica, couldn't find it, asked the audience for help and tuned up with a mouth harp that was helpfully hurled onto the stage by an unknown friend indeed. He should have flung it back. Gently, of course. And returned to the piano. [But] this was the moment the majority of his audience had been waiting for. Dylan, in the flesh and blood, singing the number one song that has made him the idol of millions instead of just thousands. It was probably the moment he'd been waiting for, too. He knew the song by heart. So did his audience. Unfortunately, the band did not ... but Dylan made the best of it. There hadn't been time for the group to learn the intricate arrangement, so the band just more or less played on.

The soundboard recording of the Bowl show—which emerged in the nineties (along with similar tapes of Simon & Garfunkel and Buffalo Springfield, from the same in-house source)—confirmed

[12] Actually, self-styled hipster and *LA Free Press* scribe Paul Jay Robbins thought 'the audience for this concert, as a whole, [was] not too receptive to the New Amplified Dylan'. But he was largely alone in this view.

Poston's view. This 'Rolling Stone' not only lacks those great intuitive Bloomfield fills but Kooper's swirling organ, a trademark of the 'new' sound, was rendered largely inaudible by the crude PA. The tape at least shows Dylan making a manly fist of the half dozen new songs, which he was still content to sing and not shout.

A delighted Dylan left the stage confident that the after-effects of the earlier East Coast storm had barely made it to the Hollywood Hills. But when it came to stupidity and incomprehension, the West Coast media had at least as many subscribers as the East Coast tabloids—as was proven the following afternoon, when Dylan gave his first bona fide American press conference in a bungalow at the Beverly Hills Hotel. It would prove to be the first of many declarations of independent thought Dylan would have to make over the next nine months when having a face-off with a sea of squares:

Q: Are you interested in getting through to your audience?
A: I don't have to prove anything to anyone. Those people who dig me know where I'm at—I don't have to come on to them. I'm not a ballroom singer.
Q: Do you feel you belong to the public now?
A: I don't have any responsibility to the people who are hung up on me. I'm only responsible for what I create. I didn't create them.
Q: What about those in the audience who aren't grooving with you?
A: I'm not interested in them.
Q: How do you feel about the power grabbers, those who can directly and indirectly influence what you do?
A: They can't hurt me. Sure, they can crush you and kill you. They can lay you on 42nd Street and Broadway and put the hoses on you and flush you in the sewers and put you on the subway and carry you out to Coney Island and bury you on the Ferris wheel. But I refuse to sit here and worry about dying.
Q: Do you think anything of consequence happens at these things?
A: Interviewers will write my scene and words from their own bags anyway, no matter what I say. I accept writers and photographers. I don't think it's necessary at all, but it happens anyway…

Anything he said to defend his new music or his right to artistic autonomy was destined to fall on stony ground. As he informed another *Los Angeles Times* reporter, in another lifetime, 'It was right to be vague [in those press conferences] because they were trying to dig a hole for you. If you took it seriously and gave serious answers, you'd just get hurt. You had to respond in a way that wouldn't hurt you.'

Dylan emerged from the Beverly Hills bungalow without a scratch, and with a newfound determination to play the press at its own game, spinning ever more absurd webs of wordplay around his victim/s while tarantelling to his own tune. By the time he gave his second LA press conference, three months later, Dylan's answers would perfectly mirror the edge his music had acquired in the interim.

The Hollywood Bowl proved to be the last live experiment with the Kooper/Brooks pickup band. After some prodding from Robbie and Levon, Dylan had asked the Toronto-based Hawks if they would fly with him into the eye of this electrical storm.

2. THE FIRST BAND OF THE HAND
[September 15–November 28 1965]

A 6-MINUTE
SINGLE?

WHY NOT!
when you have
6 minutes of
BOB DYLAN

singing his great
new song
"LIKE A
ROLLING
STONE"
ON COLUMBIA
RECORDS

What they would have seen in '66 or '65 ... was a much more demanding show [than 1974]. People didn't know what it was at that point. When people don't know what something is ... they start to get weird and defensive. Nothing is predictable and you're always out on the edge. Anything can happen.

—DYLAN TO CAMERON CROWE, 1985

Barely had Dylan begun his electric experiment than a rethink was required. Despite telling Paul Jay Robbins, on the night of the Bowl show, that he planned to keep working with these guys, neither Kooper nor Brooks was psyched by the prospect of more hostile crowds, especially as this folk-rock forum was heading south, to Texas, in just over a fortnight—a source of some concern. As Kooper later wrote, 'I began to give serious consideration to making my exit from this travelling circus. I mean, look at what they did to J.F.K. down there.'

Test-pressings of *Highway 61 Revisited* were thus dispatched to Toronto, where the rest of The Hawks were awaiting the return of their erstwhile leader, Levon. Their future frontman and general lifesaver would be along to check they had done their homework just as soon as he got a few promotional interviews for the new long-player out of the way. After all, how hard could it be for them to learn the same eight or nine songs their lead guitarist and drummer had already locked down?

Back in New York, editors already seemed to know that sending a female reporter (or two) to interview the folk-rock king was the best way to get a hearing—or at least to avoid one of his devastating 'truth attacks'. Even journalist Mary Merryfield emerged unscathed, though her questions suggested she thought she was meeting a folk troubadour, only to be confronted by a man for whom 'there are no answers. If a question can't be answered by a question then I know it really can't be answered.'[13]

---

[13] The Mary Merryfield interview was not published until November 21, in the *Chicago Tribune*, but there is little to indicate when the interview itself was done; it remains a possibility that the lady journalist dredged up a much earlier interview.

Frances Taylor, writing for the *Long Island Press*, also escaped a tongue-lashing. Instead, Dylan patiently explained that he was 'writing now for the people who share my feelings. The point is not understanding what I write but *feeling* it'—even though he suspected a gal who co-wrote songs with Pete Seeger would remain sceptical. The minute she began asking him about topical song, he put her straight: 'Have you heard my last two records, *Bringing It All Back Home* and *Highway 61*? It's all there. That's the real Dylan.'

The best mid-September interrogation came the day Dylan met Nora Ephron. Sent by the *New York Post*, Ephron was generally on the ball and genuinely amused by a Dylan who rejected every label applied to him or his music, from 'poet' to 'folk-rocker'. He admitted to her that he had been on the verge of quitting when he chanced upon this 'whole other thing', such was his disenchantment with the folk scene:

> Folk rock. I've never even said that word. It has a hard, gutter sound. Circussy atmosphere. It's nose-thumbing. Sound like you're looking down on what is … fantastic, great music. … What I'm doing now—it's a whole other thing. We're not playing rock music. It's not a hard sound. These people call it folk rock — if they want to call it that, something that simple. It's good for selling records. As far as it being what it is, I don't know what it is. I can't call it folk rock. It's a whole way of doing things … I've never written anything hard to understand, not in my head, anyway, and nothing as far out as some of the old songs. They were out of sight.
>
> Some people work in gas stations and they're poets. I don't call myself a poet because I don't like the word. I'm a trapeze artist … I was doing fine, singing and playing my guitar. It was a sure thing … I was getting very bored with that. I couldn't go out and play like that. I was thinking of quitting. … It was very automatic … [but] I like what I'm doing now. I would have done it before. It wasn't practical to do it before. … And I know that it's real. No matter what anybody says. They can boo till the end of time. I know that my music is real, more real than the boos.

When Ephron ventured to ask what the band brought to the live experience, she was told in no uncertain terms, 'They wouldn't be playing with me if they didn't play like I want them to.' In fact, he had no idea if they played like he wanted until he got to Toronto and checked out Mary Martin's ears.[14] He was essentially placing his faith, and career, in the hands of a young secretary at Grossman's office.

As he later told Jann Wenner, '[Martin] was a rather persevering soul, as she hurried around the office on her job … and knew all the bands and all the singers from Canada. She was from Canada. Anyway, I needed a group to play electric songs.' The *Rolling Stone* editor asked where it was that Dylan heard them play. He replied, 'Oh, I never did hear them play.' And, in a sense, that was true.

In September 1965, The Hawks were a bar-band with no real frontman who, after jettisoning Ronnie Hawkins to embark on a 'pop' career, had three singles to their name and were so far off the radar that tunnel-digging equipment would have been needed to locate their sales figures. The other three had returned to Toronto's Yonge Street at the end of August, no further on than when they backed Ronnie Hawkins on the same strip more than a year earlier.

Levon Helm later proclaimed, in his myopic 1993 memoir, 'The Hawks were *the* band to know about back then. It was an "underground" thing … we were like a state secret among hip musical people because nobody else was as tight as they were.'

But this was baloney bespattered in bullshit. The Hawks were on the road to nowhere, and Dylan was about to take perhaps the biggest gamble of his career to date. And he knew it. The one time he caught their act was at a largely instrumental set in a New Jersey nightclub—which is why the 'sound of '65' flew to Toronto mid-September to rehearse for two days with the entire five-piece, trusting to still-unerring musical instincts.

All he had to go on was the way Robbie Robertson used a Fender guitar to counterpoint his own singing without ever overplaying (as even Bloomfield did sometimes). When a friendly LA journalist asked Dylan, after the Bowl, why he didn't play lead himself, he got straight to the point: 'Robbie does things I can't do, which the songs need done.'

Hopefully, the rest of The Hawks could play with a similar unobtrusive velocity. The one thing they would need to do right away

---

[14] Ian Woodward, in a recent *Isis* article, dates the interview after Dylan's return from Toronto. I am unconvinced. The two weeks between LA and Toronto remain my preferred attribution.

was put their heads down and keep playing while everyone around was saying, 'Dump the band':

Bob Dylan: We were all in it together. We were putting our heads in the lion's mouth and … I had to admire them for sticking it out with me. Just for doing [that], in my book, [means] they were gallant knights. [2000]

When Dylan took the Lodestar to Toronto on September 15, to rehearse for upcoming shows in Texas and New York, he was flying by the seat of his pants. But even on such a hush-hush mission, other distractions crowded in. Such was the media interest in the New Dylan that, even when sneaking into Toronto for a secret rehearsal or two, he found a spare hour to talk with local journalist Robert Fulford, whose interview ran in the *Toronto Star*, affording Dylan the opportunity to remind his Canadian fans the arrow of truth could still pierce through the dust of rumour:

Bob Dylan: I don't care what people do. They're there. And if they come to do their thing, whatever it is—if they come to boo, or clap, or cheer—well, I don't really come in contact with the audience. There's the lights there and all. They couldn't have a reaction in the world that would scare me.

The week *Highway 61 Revisited* appeared in the shops, he informed Fulford, 'If you listen to [the] early records and the recent ones, you can see the band really makes no difference.' He failed to fool Fulford, his readers or himself. He needed musicians who could take his audience and his art to a whole other level; and had to hope The Hawks could attain said plane without further ado.

★ ★ ★

A week after his Toronto jaunt, Dylan met up again with the now-retained Hawks in the Wild West: Austin, Texas, to be exact. Dylan was again travelling in style: his own twelve-seat jet, purchased on his behalf by Ashes & Sand, the management company Grossman had set up on his (and his own) behalf. This Lodestar could comfortably carry him, the band, Grossman, assorted hangers-on and sidekicks from coast to coast. It would carry the load for the next six months as Dylan and The Hawks flitted from east to west, north to south, in bursts of activity that were not so much one tour as a sustained campaign for hearts and minds.

The most trusted companion on these weekly jaunts was Bobby Neuwirth, a folksinger Dylan had met at the Indian Neck Folk Festival in May 1961, whose sense of humour and street savvy made him a perfect foil for Dylan's razor wit. Neuwirth's road duties included sifting the young and the hip from the dead-from-the-neck-up. On the Texan trip, his first test came at the Villa Capri hotel, when a student journalist turned up and began asking some guy with 'long hair, tight pants, elf boots, dark glasses, purple shirt' if he knew where one might find Neuwirth.

The young colt was asking Dylan himself. Once Neuwirth vouched for the reporter (and the pair stopped laughing), he was given a rare day pass into the inner portal. Such would be the pattern throughout the world tour; at a time when the hip and the square were as night and day, one look was all it took:

'You mean, Bobby Neuwirth the FOLKSINGER?' laughed Dylan, and out ran Bobby N, who was serving as a sort of aide-de-camp, and was running around frantically trying to locate, among other things, a set of drums for the band's drummer. You cannot even rent a set of drums in Austin, it seems, not to mention the fact that it being after ten o'clock, you cannot even buy whiskey. I apologised. Bobby threw around some introductions and headed back for the telephone. Dylan was engaged in a conversation about folk-singing with someone wearing a red beard on the other couch, the red beard doing most of the talking ...

After a few minutes I thought of a place to borrow a set of drums and get a bottle of booze, and I headed back for the car. By this time Bobby N was sitting beside the swimming pool with two girls with Day-Glo blonde hair.

Go-go girls they were, fresh from Dallas for the opening of another discotheque in Austin, and they had come to the Villa Capri hunting for Bob Dylan, and they had found Bobby N in HIS tight pants, elf boots, dark glasses, long hair and so forth. ... Bobby was teasing them. Bob Dylan the FOLKSINGER? In AUSTIN? No, I didn't know THAT! I'm just a pore cowboy on mah way through Austin on a trail drive!

In their desperation they turned on me: 'You're with Bob Dylan, aren't you? ... Are you sure this gentleman isn't Bob Dylan?' They turned on Bobby again. 'ARE YOU BOB DYLAN?' ...

A local beatnik showed up with three-dollar-a-litre bottles of Mexican rum, room service managed to come up with some ice and some tumblers. ... Bobby came grinning in the door with the go-go girls. They were stricken. Bob Dylan actually was there. One of them tiptoes across the room and—Lord help me, this is the truth—asked Bob Dylan if she could just touch him; this was alright, so she reached out and touched him with the tip of her finger, on the knee, I believe it was. She and her friend then fell into reverent silence.

I felt it was my duty ... to ask Bob Dylan a few questions so that I might have something to write about. ... But Dylan wasn't offering any philosophy that night—at least not in my direction. ... We ended up talking about rock and roll music, which was getting back to my level. Another go-go girl came in and sat beside Dylan on the couch, saying her name was Maggie. She was the chief go-go girl. [By now] the bourbon was gone ...

By the time the Mexican rum did come, Dylan was all questioned out, having just spent the afternoon at another pre-concert press conference. Predictably enough, it was frequented by impertinent pressmen and feisty female fans. One of the latter, Judith Adams, attended on behalf of the local KUT-FM station. She forwarded *San Francisco Chronicle* music critic Ralph J. Gleason her own eyewitness account of another surreal exercise in non-communication:

Dylan was quiet, gentle and immensely patient. The guy from the Austin paper missed the whole point. According to him, we were all sitting around, waiting for the Word from Dylan. It wasn't that way at all. Dylan, with his slightness and quietness, took us all aback. Any questions asked of him was tantamount to an attack on him. And Dylan is not the kind of guy one asks questions of easily. You feel that if you know his songs, you know him, and what the hell kind of questions can you ask him? Someone asked him if he was a Christian. And someone else inquired if he were trying to change the world with his songs. He finally asked her if she knew what he was saying in his songs and she admitted she didn't, really. And yet he [remained] marvellously patient.

Again Dylan's verbal riffing sailed over the hacks' heads. Asked to define himself, he said he saw himself as 'a trapeze artist'. The person who asked him if he was a Christian received a perfect parry: 'Well, first of all, God is a woman. We all know that. Well, you take it from there.' And still they wanted to know if he really believed he could change the world.

That was the plan: concert hall by concert hall, audience by audience. In Austin, Dylan finally got to play his rocked-up rearrangement of 'Baby Let Me Follow You Down', a song rehearsed for Forest Hills having already received electroshock treatment at the hands of Bert Berns and The Animals. Judith Adams was bowled over:

> After the intermission the stage was lit up with a fabulous magenta—the exact embodiment of the Purple Grotto that Al Collins used to talk about. After the first song it just went from fabulous to sublime until 'Baby Let Me Follow You Down' which tore the place up. He started out just kind of hitting his guitar and then suddenly the whole thing came together and it was 'Baby Lemme' and everybody screamed. It was a torrent of sound to go with his words, an absolute avalanche. My God, you couldn't sit still.

If the KUTe reporter 'couldn't sit still', the rest of the audience was more restrained. As the student reporter from *Texas Ranger* noted, 'They applauded politely at the end of each of Dylan's numbers, and in the middle of some of them, at the appropriate places, of course, but there was no yelling, whistling nor, needless to say, dancing in the aisles. … This Austin audience sat like a bunch of toads … and when the concert was over … filed quietly out without so much as a riot.'

Yet Dylan was perfectly delighted by the reception he received—the most positive to date. With a welcome absence of booing, he allowed himself to have a ball. As the *Ranger* reported, the once-static-with-stage-fright singer could barely contain himself. 'Dylan [would] roar back and shout, jump across the stage, sometimes walking right up to the soloist in the middle of their solos and grinning in their faces, waving around the Fender Jazzmaster electric guitar.'

The Hawks were just the kind of musical throwbacks who could propel Dylan's new music forward. For the Canadian troupe it was a new experience. A club act for half a decade, they bluffed their way through that first concert, assuming the Municipal Auditorium audience might be the largest hall they would have to win over. But the following night, the eight thousand SMU Coliseum in Dallas was filled to capacity.

The last time Dylan stopped off at this gas station, it was less than three months after Kennedy's assassination, and when he asked for directions to Dealey Plaza, a local man replied, 'You mean where they shot that bastard Kennedy?' Thankfully, this time the police would provide altogether better protection when an impressionable young female fan thought she had seen Dylan bathed in his own messianic aura:

> The young people, who were predominant and to who[m] he addressed his message, apparently dug him throughout. One blonde girl, in the evening's only untutored incident, walked as mesmerized to the stage apron while Dylan was in mid-song and attempted to touch his feet. Even when two policemen escorted her away, she turned and stared raptly at her ideal, then slumped to the floor before being led out. Dylan, gifted with a sense of humor, smiled but never lost a note.

Dylan was doing his best not to succumb to the distractions teen-mania pop celebrity status now accorded him. At one point in the acoustic set, 'when some clamoured for their favourites, instead of the scheduled number', he asked for silence.

He was less concerned about the reaction after the intermission; with the contrast between his demeanour in the acoustic and electric halves again proving striking enough to draw comment from the *Dallas Times Herald*:

> He is not a showman, but then that is not one of his targets. In fact, in seeking out the role of anti-star Dylan simply strolls onstage without introduction, fanfare or special lighting. He acknowledged his audience slightly, absorbing himself in his music until the second half when he apparently got a kick from the big beat behind him.

He toyed with the combo members, pacing them and working with them, much in the jazz style.

For all the obvious enjoyment he drew from another electrifying performance there was no encore. At the end of 'Like A Rolling Stone' Dylan spun round on his Cuban heels and 'strode off-stage with the band' before having second thoughts and returning to the microphone to inform the throng, 'Audiences in Austin and in Dallas are the best.'

It was a most uncharacteristic expression of appreciation from a man of many words in his songs but few words onstage. And he meant it most sincerely. At a West Coast press conference in December, asked about the booing, he observed, 'They've done it just about all over, except in Texas ... they didn't boo us in Texas.' He expanded on the theme to Allen Ginsberg a few days later: 'We played in Texas and it was groovy down there, it really was. It's different down there.'

His conviction that Texas audiences 'got' him—in a way that others did not—never wavered. He informed a French reporter a full eight months afterward that 'the south of Texas [is] the world where ... I'm really understood'. By then, Dylan was hurting for just such a reaction, having just played the Free Trade Hall, where he was called every name under the sun—even the man who betrayed Christ.[15]

However, no amount of shows in West Texas would replicate the kind of media coverage a New York gig generated. So, barely five weeks after his victory on points at Forest Hills, Dylan returned to Carnegie Hall, the scene of his famous October 1963 acoustic showcase, with his third live band of the summer, determined to ram The Hawks down the folkniks' self-righteous throats.

★ ★ ★

While Dylan was taking his message to Texas, Carnegie Hall had staged a whole evening of music designed to pretend Newport had never happened. The 'Sing-In For Peace' concert on September 24—one last excuse for communal handholding before mass

[15] Eight *years* later, back on the road for the first time since those name-calling days, Dylan remained convinced he had a special relationship with the Lone Star state, telling a *Rolling Stone* reporter he was looking forward to playing Texas because 'they're more receptive to my kind of music, my kind of style'.

communication scrambled the message—was headlined by Joan Baez, the self-appointed leader of a committee dedicated to getting America out of Vietnam.

Meanwhile Dylan—misleadingly listed as a member of that committee in the concert ads—was opening both Texas shows with 'Tombstone Blues'. It said everything that needed saying about the conscription of American youth—'The king of the Philistines his soldiers to save/ Puts jawbones on their tombstones and flatters their graves ... then sends them out to the jungle.'

The latest issue of *Sing Out!*—for sale at the Sing-In For Peace—suggested it was embroiled in its own uncivil war between partisans of folk-rock and its naysayers. Paul Nelson, having formally tendered his resignation as editor of the folk 'zine, had secured from Moe Asch a promise that his final piece, on Newport, would run unexpurgated and Silber-free. Asch kept his word, and the most important article of Nelson's writing career—guaranteeing him tickets for Dylan concerts for *years*—ran as is. It concluded:

Like it or not, the audience had to choose. Whether, on the one hand, to take the word of a dignified and great humanitarian whose personal sincerity is beyond question but whose public career more and more seems to be sliding ... toward a *Reader's Digest*–Norman Rockwell version of how things are ... or whether to accept as truth the Donleavy-Westian-Brechtian world of Bob Dylan, where things aren't often pretty, where there isn't often hope, where man isn't always noble, but where, most importantly, there exists a reality that coincides with that of this planet ...

Make no mistake, the audience had to make a clear-cut choice and they made it: Pete Seeger. They chose to boo Dylan off the stage for something as superficially silly as an electric guitar or something as stagnatingly sickening as their idea of owning an artist ... They were afraid, as was Pete Seeger (who was profoundly disturbed by Dylan's performance), to make a leap, to admit, to consider, to think. ... It was a sad parting of the ways for many, myself included. I choose Dylan. I choose art. I will stand behind Dylan and his 'new' songs, and I'll bet my critical reputation (such as it may be) that I'm right.

For the surly Silber, Nelson's piece was merely the opening salvo. There would be no more open letters addressed to Dylan in *his* folk 'zine. Instead, every mention of Dylan, whether in its editorial or letters page—and, for the next three issues, Dylan's act of apostasy dominated the *Sing Out!* letters page—read like the wounded wail of a bereft ex-lover. Silber's own 'review' of Newport in the same issue was one such piece entirely shot in black and white:

> The Festival's most controversial scene was played out on the dramatically lit giant stage halfway through the final night's concert when Bob Dylan emerged from his cult-imposed aura of mystery to demonstrate the new 'folk rock'. … To many, it seemed that it was not very good 'rock', while other disappointed legions did not think it was very good Dylan.

The next issue of *Sing Out!*, due in late November, would jettison any sense of equivocation, or balance, as Silber grabbed the helm and headed for the isle of irrelevance. And rather than trusting anyone else on his ever-rotating staff to review Dylan's Carnegie Hall 'comeback', he dispatched himself, delivering an overview full of righteous indignation for his aptly-named 'Fan The Flames' column:

> The evening itself was a compendium of recent Dylan LPs, half of the program done 'straight', with unamplified guitar [sic], the second half to the accompaniment of a painfully neurotic electrified supporting cast.
>   Apparently this was the statement that Dylan will be making at similar concerts throughout the country in the coming months. As evidenced through his recent recordings, this statement is basically a philosophy of alienation and paranoid fear. Having proclaimed himself an apostle of 'freedom' where answers are to be found only 'on your own', Dylan's music at Carnegie Hall essentialized the fundamental isolation of white, middle-class, teen-aged America— rejecting the false values of a corrupt society [yet] unable to find any new values anywhere. To some, this psychotic vision represented truth—and art. But to others, this writer included, it was a death wish set to music, the ultimate philosophy of fear.

For those readers seeking some light relief from Silber's heavy-handed tub-thumping, there was little solace on the letters page, which included a long letter from Jim Rooney expressing his 'distress' at Nelson's misuse of his own private critique of Newport, concluding, 'I would never be caught in the kind of stupidity that Nelson [has] got himself into.' The self-same page also carried the first of a number of Dylan obituaries published over the next nine months, usually by someone returning from a show.[16] This one, from Kathleen Ivans in Whitestone, New York, had been penned after the New York concert:

> Folk fans the world over are mourning the death of Bob Dylan, who died at Carnegie Hall on Oct. 1st, 1965. In a short but brilliant career, Mr Dylan amassed fans and fame with his electrifying performances. He leaves a legacy of only four albums [sic] which contain some of the finest folk music ever written. His last illness, which may be termed an acute case of avarice, severely affected Mr Dylan's sense of values, ultimately causing his untimely death.

Yet no matter how many column inches Silber gave his fellow Luddites, his was a pyrrhic victory. In the final end he would lose the war—and many former leaders into the bargain. The 'Mods' simply didn't have the numbers, and the tide of history was against them. Silber himself might have realised this when he wrote, between gritted teeth, 'Dylan had total acceptance at Carnegie Hall. Perhaps those who were enamoured of the "old" Dylan didn't bother to get down to the box-office in time to get their tickets.'

Whatever the reason, the reactionaries who had made such a racket at Forest Hills were very much in the minority at Carnegie Hall, making Dylan's latest performance something of a triumph. The *Village Voice*'s Jack Newfield led the way in a tickertape parade of press plaudits:

> They booed Bob Dylan at Newport in July, they insulted him at Forest Hills in August, but last Friday night at Carnegie Hall they

---

[16] The most subtle of these comes in *Blow-Up*, where a door to a club The Yardbirds are playing at has a flyer that reads 'Bob Dylan R.I.P. May 27th, 1966'.

screamed for more of his 'folk rock' poetry. 'I didn't think you would like it,' he said shyly before doing the first encore anyone could remember him doing. The concert was almost a Defend Bob Dylan Rally. ... The second half of the concert was devoted to Dylan's amplified band. At the beginning there were a few boos, perhaps a conditioned response from the previous concerts ... [but] on this third try, it became clear he had sold his new style to his fans. After each tune the cheers grew deeper and wilder. And Dylan, tense and frail, his diction better and his voice more magnetic than ever before, was clearly enjoying his vindication.

Most other reviewers followed Newfield's lead. *Billboard*'s Herb Wood voiced a soon-familiar suspicion that the marked contrast between the dynamism of the second half and Dylan's subdued manner during the acoustic set was wholly deliberate—an example of Dylan making a point not with words, but with sound:

Opening the program with solo performances of several of his lengthy folk-oriented songs ... after a short intermission Dylan began the commercial segment of the program, backed by two electric guitars, electric organ, piano and drums. His performance was electric in contrast to the slow, somewhat tedious opening. It was obviously designed to convince Dylan's more 'ethnic' fans that his switch to the teen sound was actually a good idea.

The well-respected *Herald Tribune* reviewer William Bender was more conflicted about what he heard, having become so enamoured with the first half he gushed about 'a vision that burns its way through the mechanical forms of the folk songs that shot him to fame ... He's a religious philosopher ... He's a poet ... He's a lover of the open road ... He's a surrealist painter.'

After the interval, though, the elder Bender found himself pinned to his seat by 'the sheer noise of the "folk rock"—Dylan's invention, combining elements of folk music and rock'n'roll ... The din that came from the electrified guitars, organ, drums and piano was unbelievable. The beat was great—no one with two feet could deny that—but the words were inaudible. And so was the message.'

Nonetheless, Bender recognised that the singer struck 'a chord of empathy' with his audience. Daniel Kramer, again on hand to snap a visual record, summarised the collective view: 'The mood was different. His audience was beginning to understand his new music, and they showed it in their response. The tide had turned.'

The Hawks—Helm and Robertson excepted—may have even started to wonder if their erstwhile leader had been pulling their legs. What booing?!

Three gigs, three rapturous receptions. And the following night was more of the same. Dylan and the guys headed out to New Jersey, where The Hawks had just played a month-long residency, as another adult reporter looked on wide-eyed at the rapt way this largely teenage audience listened to this electric poet they came in their thousands to see:

> Dylan sings to them about violence and rebellion. Rebellion against war and racial prejudice—against most kinds of prejudice. But he also sings about love and laughter and Tom Thumb. Actually it doesn't matter what he sings—he always has his audience. And it's growing bigger by the day. Like at the Newark Mosque [where] the response grew louder, more enthusiastic with each number. Everybody was listening intently, too—for Dylan casts a spell when he sings ... He seems to be singing directly to you.

One eyewitness, Peter Stone Brown, who had been at Forest Hills, recalled that, this time 'there was no booing'. Even when 'they started with "Tombstone Blues" ... probably the loudest thing I ever heard in my life', the crowd cheered. Photos of the performance (by Thom Cronin) show a relaxed Dylan, a grinning Robbie Robertson and the audience 'listening intently'.[17]

Once again, Dylan gave his adoring East Coast fans an encore: his latest single, 'Positively 4th Street'. Shooting up the Hot Hundred, Dylan's latest verbal barb was already leaving the diminishing number of Dust Bowl balladeers far behind.

---

[17] A judicious selection of these Newark shots appears in the *Mixing Up The Medicine* book, a companion to 2015's *Cutting Edge* deluxe edition.

★ ★ ★

And yet Newark would not merit inclusion in Dylan's shortlist of places they *didn't* boo him, in response to a question at a December 1965 press conference. He *did* cite Atlanta, where he performed the week after Newark, following on from shows in Baltimore and Knoxville (where the audience response has gone unrecorded).

At this stage he was still offering some explanation to reporters, in this instance Ann Carter of the *Atlanta Journal*, concerning the 'mathematics' his music contained, and the equations he had already rejected—'I don't play rock'n'roll. I do play with electricity. I like it. The only reason I didn't do it before is because I couldn't afford it.'

Asked to explicate the worldview driving his new songs, he was a tad more enigmatic. 'I can accept sword swallowers, hunchbacks, girls with one leg ... I accept everybody. I never hide Kleenex from anybody, and I always try to keep one eye on the ashtray.'

Carter nodded her head and hurried off to catch the show at the Municipal Auditorium, where she hoped to learn what he had really meant. She found everyone there quite determined to have a good time, Dylan included:

> A group of around 4,500 young people at City Auditorium Saturday night did 'take care' and applauded Dylan wildly for his performance. ...The second part of the program, judging from applause, was the most [sic] popular. Dylan, still dressed in British-cut grey suit, played an electric guitar. ... He concluded the performance with 'Rolling Stone' and took one curtain call, despite shouts of 'more'.

He had played his last encore of the world tour—boos or no boos. 'Positively 4th Street' was now slotted instead between 'Thin Man' and 'Rolling Stone'. The sudden end to proceedings allowed him to head for the airport before the house lights even came on, while the leased Lodestar allowed him to play the most poorly organised of schedules.

Spreading the folk-rock gospel from place to place, The Hawks found themselves playing Worcester, Massachusetts, one weekend, Providence, Rhode Island, the next, with a show in Burlington the following night. Two shows in Boston were scheduled for the last weekend in October—just not on consecutive nights. Instead, his booking agent slotted Hartford in between, making his northeast 'tour' seem like a work of random imprecision.

If touring by plane made such a schedule possible, even with one's own airborne transport, best-laid plans could go amiss. The Burlington show was an hour late starting. As one irate representative of the local *Free Press* complained, 'Hundreds of ticket-holders were forced to stand in the rain while the gymnasium remained locked. The official explanation was that Dylan's plane had been late due to [the] bad weather.' Which was perfectly true. Those in attendance were at least 'rewarded with a performance lasting nearly two hours'. Not for the first time, though, problems with the sound in the auditorium played havoc with a critic's appreciation:

> A muddy amplification system with too much volume prevented many of the audience from hearing the words to some of the songs. This was especially true during the second half of the concert when the screaming electric instruments tended to drown out Dylan's singing. Nevertheless, the powerful melodies, pounding rhythm and the lyrics came reaching out to all corners of the nearly full hall with the essential Dylan message. ... Most came away from the concert with their heads full of Dylan's expansive melodies, renewed in the faith of rebellion. They took him to heart because he calls a spade a bloody shovel, and he doesn't stop short of the big questions.

If Dylan and The Hawks were at the very cutting edge of mid-sixties rock performance, they had very little control of the venues or the sound systems. No regular concertgoer in 1965 would have been able to hear all the nuances Dylan heard on stage, because as the folk-rock emperor himself told Jeff Rosen in 2000, 'These stages were created for people who stood on stage and recited Shakespearean plays. They weren't made for this kind of music we were playing. The sound was pretty archaic, really.'

So when the lines of communication got scrambled, it was not always Dylan's fault, or even something of which he was consciously aware. Another critic, reviewing Dylan's 'homecoming' gig in Minneapolis the first week in November, was honest enough to admit:

Whatever [my] personal reaction was, the overall reaction was great. Those that remained [for the second half] sat through another fast-moving hour of loud jamming and hoarse shouting. Dylan yelled out his songs just barely above the rumble of the bass and the fantastic accompaniment of the rhythm guitar. The words were really unintelligible—yet many followed enjoyably, having memorized most of the words, especially the refrains: 'How does it feel?' or 'You've got a lot of nerve'. The feeling was exciting, and with the heavy drum beat, and the wail of the harmonica, you felt you were where the action was. Dylan, too, looked, as I said, a bit more active, as he bounced about, with his back to the audience at the beginning of each song, to get his band synchronized.

Sound problems aside, the first month of real touring had gone well, which is perhaps why Dylan gave a surprisingly straight radio interview in Detroit on the twenty-fourth, to WATM's Allen Stone, before giving the Motor City an Oktoberfest preview of the volume most bands playing the Grande Ballroom in a year or two would perform at.

But if Dylan felt he had pushed back the lapping waters of discontent, he was wrong. The tide was still coming in and from a seaboard he had always considered a second home. Boston and Hartford were cities he thought he had long ago made his own. In the early days, the former had been a regular home away from home, which is perhaps why when he broke into 'Baby Let Me Follow You Down' at one of the Boston shows—a song he first heard in Eric Von Schmidt's Boston apartment in the summer of '61—he dedicated it to Betsy Siggins, the owner of the Club 47.[18]

Dylan suggested in San Francisco that Boston was another place that was boo-free. The passing review in *Broadside* also fails to refer to any catcalling, though it noted the contrast in Dylan's demeanour between first and second halves:

Dylan, when playing unaccompanied and unelectrified, was less animated than my record player. During the second half of his concerts, with drums, organs et al., he blew his mind. Obviously, he enjoys his new sound and the wide range of moods his instrumentalist[s] can produce.

[18] This, to me, is the only credible explanation for Dylan prefacing the song by suggesting it's for Betty/Betsy, as he appears to do on the often-misattributed Boston audience tape.

This was not how Hawks drummer Levon Helm remembered it. 'We were seriously booed during a two-night stand at the Back Bay Theater in Boston,' he later wrote. 'That's when it started to get to me. I'd been raised to believe that music was supposed to make people … want to party. And here was all this hostility coming back at us.'

It has to be said that one cannot hear any hostility on the four-song tape a sloppy drunk Dylan fan seems to have made of one of the Boston shows. But then any boos are equally inaudible on the tape of the Hartford show Ashes & Sand had sandwiched between the two Bostons. And yet, according to a review that ran in the *NME*, Dylan met real hostility in Hartford that night—though it was as nothing to the hostility he encountered next time he played the same venue in May 1980:[19]

> Bob Dylan shocked his fans by appearing here with a five-piece band backing him for the second half of his concert. They rocked it up and as Bob walked to an organ [sic] to accompany himself in 'Ballad Of A Thin Man' he was mocked with cries of 'Go back to England' and 'Get rid of the band'. He took this in his stride, however, as he continued … 'Like A Rolling Stone'. He left after that number, not saying more than two words during the whole show.

Neither tape, in fairness, provides much of an aural window into the sonic world of Dylan and the Levon-led Hawks. All four circulating songs from 'Boston' are incomplete, and are not exactly enhanced by a running commentary from taper and friend. The Hartford taper not only attempted to squeeze a ninety-minute show onto one side of a C90 cassette, but preferred to prioritise the acoustic half. What these recordings—the only audio documents of this lineup—do suggest is that the band were still finding their way into the songs. Thankfully, Dylan had quickly learnt how to project himself vocally over a band who played fucking loud.

He was now confident enough with this direction to head home. The week after Boston, he and The Hawks flew to Minneapolis. Dylan knew the audience would include his immediate family, long-

---

[19] He even seems to have recalled the occasion fifteen years earlier, telling the audience that night, 'I know I been through here before … I remember singing a song called "Desolation Row". You're clapping now, you weren't clapping then! … 'Desolation Row", "Maggie's Farm", "Subterranean Homesick Blues", all that stuff … wasn't accepted very well at the time.'

standing friends like Tony Glover, and a large number of Minneapolis folkies still wondering what happened to the young tyke who had left for New York five years earlier to *'shoot lightning through* the sky in the *entertainment world'*.

An article from a *St Paul Dispatch* writer who was as ill-disposed toward Dylan as he was ill-informed would later claim he 'refused contact with anyone, horsed around during his show and generally left a sour taste in his wake. ... [While] in Minneapolis, he said, "Why should I see these people? They had no time for me when I was nothing. Why should I see them now?"'

In fact, Dylan went out of his way to track down old friends, spending the night before his November 5 Auditorium show trawling the old haunts, as one local journalist was able to report:

[A friend] acted as Dylan's guide around Minneapolis for two hours Thursday night, after Dylan and three companions chanced to stop her and a friend in Dinkytown to ask of the whereabouts of Tony Glover. ... The six of them travelled around to the Scholar, a few bars, and finally McCosh's Bookstore as Dylan sought Glover and reminisced of his Minneapolis days. ... The main thing Dylan was interested in was the Minneapolis scene, and what was done around here for excitement. Dylan questioned the girls much more than they questioned him, for he, and his manager, kept refusing to answer any 'fan' questions. Dylan ... asked who was popular around here; both as a folk singer and popular rock and roll. He asked especially about himself, and the writeups he received—tearing an advertisement of his upcoming concert out of the paper to save.

His hair was very real and long ... His clothes that night were 'grubby' and he wore shades most of the evening until my dear friend commented on how brilliant the sunlight was—causing a grin and a discarding of the glasses. He seemed very quiet. ... Everywhere they went she had to go in first to see if the path was clear, then the group followed. They ended up sitting in McCosh's Bookstore and remained there for about an hour. ... Then it was over, Dylan dropped her and her friend off at home (so they could do homework) and then he proceeded to drive around town [till] early Friday morning.

The above article suggests the two schoolgirls Dylan picked up not only recognised this 'false knight on the road' but were somewhat in awe of the 'grubby' folk-rock messiah. After he returned them unharmed, he finally tracked down Glover, who got his first opportunity to talk to his friend's new lead guitarist.

Having personally experienced Newport—and his friend's stunned reaction to it—Glover wanted to ask Robertson 'how he felt about the booing'.

'Doesn't really matter much,' Robertson laconically replied. 'We're just playing the best music we know how—that other stuff is *their* problem.'

Meanwhile, Minneapolis passed off largely without incident, with only a smattering of audible discontent for reporters to report:

> For a little over an hour, Dylan … gave the audience an exact replica of what they have heard, or would hear, in an hour's sitting in front of a record player. The process would seem very boring and unbearable, if it were not for the preconditioning of the 'fans'. … [But] when the lights went off for the second half of the concert, the 'New Dylan' appeared on stage. Now he was visibly a little tighter, and a little happier, as he bounced around the stage in his 'highheeled boots' giving last minute instructions to his 'big beat' electrified rock and roll band

★ ★ ★

Sound problems continued to dog Dylan and the band throughout November, so much so that Cleveland critic Glenn Pullen thought he heard, in the first half, 'the new musical leader of modern rebels turn[ing] his vocal guns on people whom he doesn't like. Old-fashioned parents and "square-headed teachers", war-mongering politicians and segregationists.'

Mr Pullen's ears, already made of cloth, did not need the further handicap of two hands over them throughout the second half, as he found 'what came out of the amplifiers was a tremendously big beat sound, exciting to the young generation but deafening to the few adults in the audience'.

If The Hawks were starting to enjoy themselves, there was the daunting prospect of two mid-November shows at Toronto's Massey Hall, allowing the individual Hawks to visit familiar haunts. Dylan was not so free with his time. He found he had agreed to his second

Canadian interview of the year, with Margaret Steen of the *Toronto Star Weekly*.

Ms Steen, presumably just his type, found a Dylan willing to turn on the charm, although he never forgot he was on the record. He concluded their convivial conversation by reminding her, 'If I met you in a bar somewhere, or even at a party, I could tell you more. We could talk better. But you're a reporter, you're here for your interview—and where will it all get either of us? Nothing will happen.'

Actually, something more than mere word games did happen. Dylan even elucidated the difference between his old songs and his new songs, providing his only coherent definition of 'the mathematics of song', a term he used repeatedly in his mid-sixties interviews:

Bob Dylan: Before, every song had to have a specific point behind it, a person, a thing. I would squeeze a shapeless concept into this artificial shape. ... Now? ... Well, for one thing, the music, the rhyming and rhythm, what I call the mathematics of a song, are more second-nature to me. I used to have to go after a song, seek it out. But now, instead of going to it I stay where I am and let everything disappear and the song rushes to me. Not just the music, the words, too ... I was still keeping the things that are really really real out of my songs, for fear they'd be misunderstood. Now, I don't care if they are.

He also went to some pains to delineate the difference between his current music and rock'n'roll, all the while steering clear of the dreaded term, folk-rock.

Bob Dylan: It's easy for people to classify it as rock and roll, to put it down. Rock and roll is a straight 12-bar blues progression. My new songs aren't. I used to play rock and roll a long time ago, before I even started playing old-fashioned folk ... when I was a kid.

Despite being set to play two sold-out shows at the Massey Hall, he admitted he no longer knew what his fans thought, and cared not a jot how his former fans expressed themselves:

Bob Dylan: Four years ago I used to sing in Village coffee houses, 50 people and they were packed, fire inspectors all over the place, you know? Then I knew my real fans. Now, these concerts, I don't know them, I don't know why they're there. I don't know what they think about when they go away … [but] if they like it or don't like it, that's their business. You can't tell people what to do at a concert. Anyway, paying out $4 for a ticket to come and boo—is anyone groovy gonna do that?

Groovy or not, The Hawks' hometown or not, the Toronto two-nighter ended up being something of a throwback to Forest Hills and Boston; and this time local journalists knew the name of the band responsible for tarnishing their hero and trashing his music. The *Star* did not send Steen, but rather Tony Ferry, who was *not* a rock'n'roll fan—or much of a music critic. Unlike Dylan, he cared greatly about the feelings of those who felt betrayed by the new Bob:

> There were many harsh verdicts. Someone said in the middle of a song, 'Stop turning your back to us.' As he plugged in an electric guitar, they cried, 'Let's hear the words, forget the electronics.' A folksong fan walked out crying, 'Dylan, you're doing it for money!' and at the back of the hall came the ultimate insult … 'You're another Elvis.' … Here was Bob Dylan who once was a purist, a folk-poet of America in direct line to Woody Guthrie, now electronically hooked up to a third-rate Yonge St. rock & roll band which he has now contracted. That great voice, a wonderfully clean poet's voice, is buried under the same Big Sound that draws all the Screamies to a Beatle orgy of pubescent kids at Maple Leaf Gardens. The aforementioned third-rate Yonge St. rock & roll band, called Levon and the Hawks, does most of the electronic fronting for Dylan, who seems now to be faking his own guitar playing. The Big Sound drowns out all his message, but elicits hysterical squeals from a small segment of young girls who dart to the front of the stage like they dig his sound but are totally deaf to his lyrics.

The *Globe and Mail*, snubbed by Dylan on all three Toronto trips to date, joined the public execution with unalloyed glee, its carping critic adopting the same tone as the paper's gratuitous headline, 'A

Changed Bob Dylan Booed In Toronto'. The paper's Bruce Lawson manned his post valiantly, even as he baulked at a Dylan 'reinforced by The Hawks and almost every electronic gadget ever invented to boost noise to the unbearable level':

> 'I'm going back to New York City, I do believe I've had enough,' wailed Bob Dylan at Massey Hall last night. 'Booo!' shouted somebody in the packed audiences. 'Ssss!' went someone else. 'Elvis!' spat out a third. There was some weak applause in Dylan's support. Most of the audience appeared to be sitting on their hands. … A few people walked out of the concert hall soon after the second (rock) part of the performance began.

If Dylan carried on regardless, Levon Helm was once again feeling the strain. The drummer had never expected 'a mixture of cheers and boos' and took the Toronto reviews to heart. Margaret Steen's revealing interview and a rave review of the two shows in the popular Canadian weekly magazine, *MacLean's*, would not appear till Toronto windows were filled with frost. But Peter Gzowski—the co-author of Canada's unofficial national anthem, 'Four Strong Winds', a song Dylan himself would cover in the near future—challenged the churlish consensus of Toronto's dailies:

> The second half, as they say, was something else: the New Music. … Everything [was] boosted electronically. A microphone rested on the piano's most resonant plane. The guitars were plugged into a battery of chrome-plated, suitcase-sized amplifiers, whose red control lights blinked on and off in the half-light of the stage. 'Visually,' a member of the audience remarked later, 'it was like some kind of super-pop art. It reminded me very much of a John Cage concert, all wild and surrealistic.' At Dylan's signal, Levon and the Hawks exploded into sound like a squadron of jet planes, a leaping, rising, crushing wave of sound that pulsed the air and rocked the floor. In the balcony, I could feel the bass notes through the soles of my shoes. … Yet for all the throbbing emotion of the music, the audience remained physically quite still. No one stood. No one shouted. … Instead, there was rapt attention. As Dylan, in his curious, Guthrie-esque accent, wailed the poetry of the lyrics into the microphone, the young fans mouthed the words along with

him [while] the grown-ups, some looking simply puzzled, strained
to hear through the din.

★ ★ ★

By the time that glowing review ran, Helm had relinquished his drum
rise, having decided to tender his resignation the day after another
two-nighter in Chicago, where, according to Helm, there was yet
'more booing'. It seems the trick was to only play a single show in
each city. Where Dylan's popularity justified a double-header—as it
did in Boston, Toronto and Chicago—the temptation to pay 'out $4
for a ticket to come and boo' was proving too great to ignore.

The cities in question had been mainstays of Dylan's touring
schedule even in the days when his road crew consisted of someone
to carry his guitar case—hence, perhaps, why disaffection seemed so
rife in these regions. Again when Dylan blew into the Windy City
a two-nighter inspired animosity from the audience, as the *Chicago
Tribune* reviewer made clear:

> Throughout the second half ... Dylan was booed by the folk purists
> who wanted him to unplug his guitar, send his cohorts off the stage,
> and start singing the way he did before intermission. This was more
> than balanced, tho, by rock and roll enthusiasts in the audience who
> were now hearing what they had paid their money for.

Dylan's response to any name-calling from folk reactionaries was
to turn it up some more, a strategy he retained to the bitter end. He
was first accused of doing exactly this at the final November show
in DC. His accuser was *Washington Evening Star* reporter Lawrence
Sears: 'The second half used an ensemble of three electric guitars,
piano, drums and electric organ. They produced a Niagara of sound.
All began at top volume, and later increased the decibels.'

A reviewer of the Columbus, Ohio gig, at the midpoint between
Chicago and Toronto, had already ruefully recalled, 'The sound of
all those instruments amplified many times over through the huge
speakers at "Vets" was almost deafening, but the audience seemed
to like it.'

Dylan had now found another way to make the contrast between
the acoustic and electric halves more pronounced: 'After nearly every

song in the first half of the programme he paused to retune his guitar. "My electric guitar never goes out of tune," he told the audience.' At the volume at which The Hawks played, and with Dylan's scratchy rhythm-guitar rendered all-but-inaudible in the mix, there was no way of telling.

In Chicago, the sound was again so bad that *Tribune* reviewer Bruce Plowman heard songs that 'protested against the social order and its inequalities, cried out against war, and warned that a new order is coming'. Dylan had stopped writing those kinda songs before the fourth album and stopped performing them after All Hallow's Eve 1964. Studs Terkel, who had given Dylan a forum on his popular radio show on his first visit to Chicago, in April 1963, had arrived hoping against hope to see the protest singer he met then. For him, the experience was almost too painful to bear:

> Second half. Metamorphosis out of Kafka. Boy no longer alone. Four colleagues plugged into wall sockets. Organ glows fluorescently, all orange and green. A good night for Commonwealth Edison … 'cause we have electricity and all. Content is overwhelmed.

Someone like Terkel, a dyed-in-the-wool musical reactionary who had stopped listening a year earlier, still seemed to think his belated complaints would register with the rock'n'roll recidivist. If Dylan had ever been the type to apologise for letting anyone down—lover, friend or foe—the inclusion of 'It Ain't Me Babe' in the electric set was directed at all who took his musical choices personally. He had already informed Joseph Haas of the *Daily News*, on the afternoon before the first Chicago show:

Bob Dylan: It would be silly of me to say I'm sorry, because I haven't really done anything … I have a hunch the people who feel I betrayed them picked up on me a few years ago and weren't really back there with me at the beginning. Because I still see the people who were with me from the beginning once in a while, and they *know* what I'm doing. … I don't even understand [the booing]. I mean, what are they going to shatter, my ego? And it doesn't even exist, they can't hurt me with a boo … I don't feel alienated, or disconnected, or afraid. ... [Sure,] some day I might find myself alone in a subway car, stranded when the lights go out, with forty people, and I'll have to get to know them. Then I'll just do what has to be [done].

Haas also found himself on the receiving end of the nth recalibration of the now-familiar anti-folk-rock mantra from Dylan's wild mercury mouth: 'It's not folk-rock, it's just instruments. ... I call it the mathematical sound. ... It's not just pretty words to a tune or putting tunes to words, there's nothing that's exploited. ... [Now] I can hear the sound of what I want to say.'

Dylan was determined to follow that sound, no matter how often it resulted in communication breakdown. Hence his latest song, which was about trying to make a connection—and failing; or, to apply Bruce Plowman's description of the (probable) live debut of 'Long Distance Operator', 'It's an enigmatic discourse directed at the operator, urging her to put his call through to his baby.'

This raucous R&B number was the first new song Dylan had introduced into the set since The Hawks joined up—and almost the first thing Levon Helm would record with his old band when re-joining them at the end of 1967. Its inclusion suggested Dylan had got over the disappointment of trying—and failing—to teach Helm and co. a handful of new songs at a recording session in early October. It might even have convinced him they were ready to record his most difficult song to date—and perhaps his greatest—a ten-minute magnum opus called 'Freeze Out' all about dislocation and disaffection in the End Times.

It was time to crack the nightingale's code, with or without Levon, who quit after Washington, a show which, to Helm's mind, again involved 'a lot of booing and a couple of fights'. He felt he was getting out just in time.

Robbie didn't think so, and told him as much: 'Lee, we're gonna *find* this music. We're gonna find a way to make it work so that we can get something out of it.' The Canadian-born guitarist would prove as good as his word.

3. SEEMS LIKE A
WEST COAST FREEZE-OUT
[December 3–19 1965]

America's Largest Teen NEWSpaper

KYA BEAT
Edition

MFP

LOVE THIS

Volume 1, Number 26   SAN FRANCISCO, CALIFORNIA   15 Cents   January 22, 1966

The Man, The Myth, The Music: The Man They Call DYLAN

In the old days ... I did New York, San Francisco and Austin. The rest were
hard in coming.

—BOB DYLAN TO BEN FONG-TORRES, JANUARY 12 1974

In early September, Dylan had flown to LA with his new electric
band, the Forest Hills boos ringing in his ears, some less-than-ringing
endorsements straining his eyes. Three months later, to the day, he
returned to the West Coast with a different combo (guitarist excepted)
and some equally contentious reading matter to catch up on.

By now, he was all but inured to the criticism that continued to
rain down on him—especially from the direction of the *Sing Out!*
offices—but was no less anxious to be kept abreast. For this flight there
was a new issue of *Sing Out!* to mull over; conclusive proof his new
music had got under Irwin Silber's skin and Nelson had been right to
jump ship. The January 1966 issue seemed like one sustained assault
on 'The Big Beat of Folk-Rock-Protest' and its avatar from Duluth.[20]

Not only did Silber allow himself an opportunity to compare and
contrast the Sing-In For Peace with Dylan's Carnegie jamboree, but
Jim Rooney got to 'correct' Nelson's presumptuous Newport review.
Bookending a bumper issue were lengthy pieces by Josh Dunson—the
title of which, 'Folk Rock: Thunder Without Rain', said it all—and
fellow Village songsmith Tom Paxton. Paxton's piece was provocatively
called 'Folk Rot'. It missed the mark by a league but barely three. Paxton
had taken the whole thing personal; he didn't care about the facts:

> One thing should be clear right away: it isn't folk, and if Bob
> Dylan hadn't led, fed and bred it no one would ever have dreamed
> of confusing it with folk music. ... Not only is he the All-hip

---

[20] Silber then had the gall to voice his disappointment when Dylan's publisher duly denied
Sing Out! permission to incorporate the lyrics (and music) for 'Like A Rolling Stone' into this
sustained, issue-long assault on his new sensibility. The January 1966 edition was published
the last week of November 1965.

(keep those threatening cards and letters coming in, folks) but the thundering herd in his wake has so ravaged and savaged his song bag that recordings of his songs by beat groups now number in the hundreds. The question of why he took this road is academic. It could have been on the advice of his manager. It could have been at the urging of his parasites, or at the behest of John Lennon ... who introduced him to the screamies of England. In the end, though, it was his choice. ... Bob Dylan plugged in and rocked.

Starting from an even more skewered base point, Dunson attempted to wrap his argument in a wafer-thin thesis that cast 'race music' and folk-rock as twin siblings of old style folk-blues, but with only the former retaining that old familiar feeling. The explanation was simple: folk artists whose labels supported them had surrendered their integrity and sold out to 'The Man':

> The contrast between folk rock and what might be considered protest 'race music' is great indeed. ... The music that Barry McGuire, Bob Dylan and Jody Miller use is dull noise that more often than not gets in the way of the words. There is none of the tension, the vitality, the excellence that is part of the better 'soul' records. There is just no guts to it ...
>
> There is something slimy and powerful about the Top Forty industry that contaminates and controls most things that come into contact with it. There are full-page ads for Dylan ... in *Billboard* and *Cashbox*. ... [He] is the central figure in folk rock, [and] has given the pop world a number of literate songs on love. But musically, he has utilized one rock and roll cliché after another. His side men can keep a beat, but there is no soul. When the words come through, they don't mean very much.

In this context, a reprint of Frances Taylor's September interview acquired an aura of negativity summarised by its final sentence: 'His most devoted followers still hope Dylan will some day sing to them of reality, as he once did in clear, sharp tones and lyrics they can remember.' The likes of Taylor may have been on Dylan's mind when he gave vent to his feelings about small-time journalists in San Francisco, when asked if he 'found that the text of the interviews ... which have been published are accurate to the original conversations?'

Bob Dylan: That's another reason I don't really give press interviews. … They just take it all out of context, or just take what they want to use; and they even ask you a question and you answer it, and then it comes out in print that they just substitute another question for your answer. … It's not really truthful, you know … so I just don't do it. … [But] then they write bad things.

★ ★ ★

A fortnight of concerts up and down the West Coast—San Francisco included—were an integral part of a year's-end mini media-blitz that would include two press conferences, both filmed. Each was set up by Columbia's West Coast promotion man, Billy James, the first person to provide *real* label support for the callow Midwestern folksinger some wag once cruelly dubbed 'Hammond's Folly'.

Now based out west, James had helped orchestrate The Byrds' ascent. When he arranged for their happy-clappy brand of folk-rock to be endorsed by Dylan during a visit to LA in spring 1965, it was also an opportunity for Dylan and James to rekindle their former friendship, which had been soured by Andrea Svedberg's October 1963 *Newsweek* hatchet job, for which Dylan had initially blamed James (who'd set it up).

This time around, San Francisco would be the main base of operations, with Los Angeles and San Diego the afterthought. There may also have been a change of hotel in LA. Dylan hinted to Allen Ginsberg backstage at the Masonic Auditorium that his penchant for all-night hotel sessions might have caused a problem: 'I can go for a long time if I dig what's happening, but we had a lot of bullshit at the hotel. They didn't want me staying there.'

In San Francisco, where they flew first, Dylan could call on another influential figure, Ralph J. Gleason, a friend of Lenny Bruce and a renowned jazz critic/sleeve-note writer. The music critic at the *Chronicle*, Gleason had been a late convert to Dylan, finally seeing the light at a February 1964 Berkeley Community Theatre gig he was obliged to review. Ever since that day they had got along famously, with Gleason even earmarked to write the sleeve notes for an *In Concert* album assigned a fall 1964/winter 1965 release.

Dylan was looking forward to renewing his acquaintance with the man who had been with Lenny Bruce the October 1961 night he was busted at the Jazz Workshop. In fact, San Francisco's law enforcement agency had made rather a habit of brandishing obscenity charges, the most notorious (and futile) being one filed against City Lights Books for publishing Allen Ginsberg's *Howl and Other Poems* back in 1956. It all made for a most unlikely West Coast headquarters for the counterculture.

Yet City Lights had gone from strength to strength in the decade since *Howl*. At one point in 1964, owner Lawrence Ferlinghetti, an important poet in his own right, had even entered into correspondence with Dylan about publishing a book of poetry, before Grossman headed him off at the pass, signing his client with the mainstream Macmillan, much to Dylan's growing chagrin.

As a form of contrition—as well as a way to beef up his own beat credentials—Dylan agreed to visit the City Lights store when he first hit town, to join the hallowed company of Ferlinghetti, mutual friend Allen Ginsberg and Michael McClure. The others did not seem quite sure what their role might be. After a brief photo shoot outside the store to memorialise the occasion, they all retired to a local watering hole, where photographer Larry Keenan saw various beats jump through hoops to impress the folk-rock king.

Larry Keenan: After[ward], everybody was sitting around the table at Vesuvio's—there were about twelve people everybody was ordering hard liquor. [The waiter] gets around to Dylan and he orders tea. And everybody changed their order to tea. … These guys were all heavyweights in their own right and they [changed their orders because] *he* ordered tea.

City Lights was merely the first of a number of commitments seemingly designed to widen the divide that now separated Dylan from the residents of Squaresville. Gleason, having already run a couple of previews in the *Chronicle*, had arranged for Dylan to give his first televised press conference the afternoon of his first Berkeley concert for local public broadcast station KQED.

Dylan arrived accompanied by Allen Ginsberg, whom had been prepped with a question of his own, which may or may not have been the one Ginsberg asked: 'Can you ever envisage a time when you'll be hung as a thief?' The fifty-minute press conference would provide the perfect distillation of Dylan's mid-sixties press persona, eighteen months before *Dont Look Back* did the same for an international audience.

It all began, appropriately enough, with a young film student George Lucas, telling a startled Dylan he had been thinking an awful lot about the symbolism behind the *Highway 61 Revisited* cover photo (shot by Daniel Kramer on the downtown stoop of a friend's apartment). Once Dylan deflected Lucas's earnest enquiry, the conference settled into a familiar pattern. Asked to define himself as a singer or a poet (apparently incompatible), Dylan said he considered himself 'more as a song and dance man, y'know'. Asked if he would 'stick with folk-rock', he snapped, 'I don't play folk-rock.' Requested to explain himself to someone 'well over thirty', he sent up the besuited pressman by labelling himself as 'well under thirty. And my role is to just stay here as long as I can.'

When one suspicious scribe asked if it was fun to put on an audience, Dylan sidestepped the implied critique: 'I don't know. I've never done it.' And when someone he made look like a chump took umbrage, he pulled a metaphorical rug away: 'You want me to jump up and say "Hallelujah" and crash the cameras and do something weird? Tell me, tell me. I'll go along with you. If I can't go along with you, I'll find somebody [who will].'

But he wasn't just playing Mr Send-Up. He also genuinely tried to communicate with the occasional interrogator and the TV cameras. When a question made sense, or suggested a serious enquiry, he opened up far enough to offer a glimpse of the man in him. He was even willing to admit the experience of seeing him live these days might be challenging:

Bob Dylan: We've played some concerts where sometimes they have those very bad halls. You know, [bad] microphone systems. So it's not that easy for somebody to come and just listen to a band as if they were listening to one person. ... It's a lot of electronic equipment now, a lot of different things which have to be taken care of, so we need a lot of people. We have three road managers and things like that. We don't make any big public presentations, though, like we never come into town in limousines or anything like that. We just go from place to place, and do the shows. That's all. ... We've had some bad nights, but ... most of the time, it does come across. Most of the time we do feel like playing. That's important to me. ... The aftermath and whatever happens before and after, is not really important to me; just the time on the stage.

Asked if he found time to write on the road, and what songs he might be working on, he talked for the first time about making a 'whole album consisting of one song', only to promptly make a joke of what was a perfectly serious ambition. 'I don't know who's going to buy it. That might be the time to leave.' Here was also something of a hint that his new songs might not be obvious chart material:

Bob Dylan: We just made a song the other day which came out ten minutes long, and I thought of releasing it as a single, but they would have [had to] cut it up. It wouldn't have worked that way, so we're not going to turn it out as a single. It's called 'Freeze Out'. You'll hear it on the next album.

In fact, his whole approach to composition was starting to change as the pressures to record and tour and record grew and a new methodology seemed to be slowly taking shape:

Bob Dylan: I might write all night and get one song out of a lot of different things I write ... so the songs I don't publish, I usually do forget.
Interviewer: Have you ever taken these scraps, as you call them, and made them into copied songs?
Bob Dylan: No. I've forgotten the scraps. I have to start over all the time. I can't really keep notes or anything like that. ... Robbie, the lead guitar player, sometimes we play the guitars together ... something might come up ... I'll be just sitting around playing, so I can write up some words.

This was the first time Robertson's role as sounding board and personal amanuensis had been mentioned (leaving one to despair at how many of those unrecorded scraps were lost to the night). It seems Dylan had decided to verbalise the process by which he took 'twenty pages of vomit' and distilled it down to 'Like A Rolling Stone', which had already broken the three-minute rule for singles by running to six minutes and still peaked at #2. But that song had a classic pop hook, courtesy of 'La Bamba', and his latest song did not. Though he was still aiming to give form to the formless, he was no longer trying to preach to the converted.

Bob Dylan: These songs aren't complicated to me at all. I know what they are all about. There's nothing hard to figure out for me. I wouldn't write anything I can't really see ... I just went through the other thing of writing [obvious] songs, and I couldn't write like it anymore. ... I would start out [and] I would know what I wanted to say before I wrote the song. ... But now, I just write a song, I know that it's just going to be alright, and I don't really know exactly what it's all about, but I do know the minutes and the layers of what it's all about.

Predictably, the press that afternoon were more concerned with controversy than composition technique, asking a number of times about the Big Boo. By now, it was as water off a drake's back. Not only did Dylan seem greatly amused by the fuss, he had his patter down. 'You can't tell where the booings going to come up. Can't tell at all. It comes up in the weirdest, strangest places ... [but] I figure there's a little "boo" in all of us ... they've done it in a lot of places. They must be pretty rich to be able to go some place and boo.'

He had more pressing concerns, having flown west with the Levon-less Hawks—probably on December 2 1965—and a stand-in drummer, the rock-solid Bobby Gregg. Helm had left everyone in the lurch by leaving the day after Washington without notice or explanation. Thankfully, Gregg was no folk-rock ingénue. He had played on both the recent albums. And yet Dylan told Ginsberg backstage in San Francisco that it would be the 'same show—we can't take a chance with the new drummer'.[21]

Of far greater concern than Gregg's ability to keep a beat was how he might react should Dylan receive a stormy reception at the Berkeley Community Theatre. It was, after all, another two-night residency, and recent ones had not always gone to plan.

[21] Ginsberg decided to test his new portable reel-to-reel by recording his conversation with Dylan backstage, prior to the concert. It was Dylan who suggested he tape the actual performance.

Dylan need not have worried—on either front. According to
Larry Keenan, everybody else hushed down those who tried to boo
before they could clear their throats; while Bobby Gregg's pugnacious
presence kept the dynamics of a band who loudly but efficiently
backed Dylan to the hilt, the *Berkeley Barb* reviewer even noticing
how Dylan had 'a gas of a drummer, who plays like a huge teddy bear'.

Gleason's focus, in his own *Chronicle* review, was solidly on the
frontman. He was keen to insist, 'They didn't boo Bob Dylan in
Berkeley when he brought out his electric guitar and his rock'n'roll
band. Instead they cheered and shouted "bravo! bravo" when he
finished his hit, "Positively 4th Street". On both the Friday and
Saturday night shows, a curious rapport existed with the audience.'

The *Chronicle* critic's contemporary account was confirmed in the
nineties by the emergence of a tape of the electric set, purportedly
made by Allen Ginsberg, sitting front row centre with his fellow beats
and a few Hell's Angels who had just arrived from the coast. By the
end of the evening, the spirit of 'Howl' had prevailed, with Gleason
on hand to spread the gospel:

> Both nights the second half wiped everybody out. Dylan's rock'n'roll
> band, which caused such hooing and horror-show reaction at the
> Newport Folk Festival and elsewhere, went over in Berkeley like the
> discovery of gold. It made a great sight. Here was one of America's
> greatest singers (who is also America's greatest poet) standing there
> like an I. Magnin mannequin clutching an electric guitar, backed by
> racks of amplifiers, loudspeakers, flanked by an electric organ, a piano,
> another guitarist, an electric bassist and a drummer [while] overhead,
> making a surrealistic stage set, [were] four paintings by Bobby
> Neuwirth. In each painting, from the space man to the rock'n'roll
> players, the figures were an abstraction of Dylan's own image, or so
> it seemed to me after two glasses of milk and a Hershey bar.

★ ★ ★

Significantly, the Berkeley tape—the earliest complete electric Dylan/
Hawks set extant—communicates The Hawks' commitment to
keeping it tight and on the beat. Instrumental explorations are rare
and brief, abruptly curtailed by the resumption of Dylan's nasal whine.
Even without the benefit of being there, it is clear to any attentive

listener that the Bay Area audience are with him all the way. Even the quirky stop-start rearrangement of 'It Ain't Me Babe', rather less successful than its Rolling Thunder faux-reggae incarnation, gets a big hand. The highlight of the electric set, though, is a 'Just Like Tom Thumb's Blues' that builds and builds into a mighty torrent of sound.

Dylan continues to enjoy himself, though he says nothing between songs, not even when launching into 'Long Distance Operator', the title of which defeated Gleason both nights. Greil Marcus, a student of words looking to polish his critical lens, later opined, 'If you weren't there, it will be difficult to convey the visual power of their performances. There were Bob and Robbie Robertson, like twins on the stage, charging each other for the solos, their fingers only inches apart.'

Ginsberg seemingly missed taping the acoustic set that night, which featured a live debut of 'Visions Of Johanna'. But he made up for it the following week, capturing the second San Francisco show in its entirety, including a solo 'Visions Of Johanna' which Dylan introduced a tad misleadingly, 'This song has not been recorded. It's called "Something Like A Freeze Out".'

It receives a long harmonica intro before Dylan continues to tweak the lyric—playing '*games* when you're trying to be so quiet' and '*boasts* of his misery'. The line about Mona Lisa not finding her knees draws an appreciative laugh from the crowd, suggesting they are paying attention throughout. 'Desolation Row' also draws whoops of applause during the harp break.

The San Jose show the following night—also taped by the Beat bard—adhered to the Berkeley template, again without a word of protest from the auditorium. The likes of 'Ballad Of A Thin Man', 'Positively 4th Street' and 'Like A Rolling Stone' are all warmly applauded as soon as they become recognisable, and even the unknown 'Long Distance Operator' (with a new line about 'waiting for it to collide') goes down well.

Also preserved, thanks to our sense-of-history man, was a pre-show conversation with Dylan, informal and friendly, in which the singer admits he had 'spent a lot of time with Marlon Brando' in LA, talking to him for three hours. He also discussed with Phil Spector the idea of Spector producing Ginsberg—'He's very interested in that.' But the most telling remark comes when Ginsberg asks about his current music. 'I don't know what the fuck it is I do. I didn't set out to do this, I can tell you that, but … the songs aren't bullshit songs.'

Seeking an honest explanation from Dylan of *why* he was doing this usually set him off—even if it was a friend asking. Hence a remark he made in LA to Barry McGuire, then at the height of 'Eve Of Destruction's fifteen minutes of fame: 'People ask me how come I'm using a rock'n'roll band—ain't that weird? Other than the fact that I dig it—if I told people why, it would be all over!'

McGuire was struck by the reverence with which his friend's music was now greeted. 'The concert was really like going to church. There were thousands of kids there, and they just sat and listened!!'

The *San Diego Tribune* reviewer came away equally impressed from a gig the week after Berkeley:

> Dylan's voice creeps through your ear and insults your brain with its many discordant notes but you don't mind. His harmonica shrieks through the hall but you lean forward and listen for more. Dylan appeared on the stage with just his guitar and harmonica during the first half of the concert but had a piano, an organ, a guitar, bass and drums to back him up after the intermission. He switched from folk to folk rock music but his lyrics and images stayed powerful and provocative.

Problems with the sound seem to have temporarily abated, even as Dylan continued to crank it up. Marlon Brando, who attended one of the LA shows at the singer's invitation, later said The Hawks were one of the loudest things he'd ever heard in his life.

But when Dylan ventured into the hills and dales surrounding LA and San Francisco, some stick-in-the-muds were waiting to chirp their chorus of displeasure. In Pasadena, one stunned gig-goer noticed:

> Once the music started the weirdest thing started to happen, people started getting up and leaving. They didn't dig the ELECTRICITY. What a bunch of chumps, because Dylan and his group were ROCKING. There were these two guys sitting in front of me, one was tall and skinny and he looked like a jealous bird, the other guy wore glasses, and they jumped up in disgust and ran for the door.

And yet every West Coast show was a sell-out. Indeed, additional shows in Pasadena, Santa Monica and San Francisco were added to cater for demand. As the tour stretched into the third week of December, Dylan even agreed to a second LA press conference in order to publicise additional shows without subjecting himself to direct interrogation.

By the time he got to the TV studio, though, he had a bad feeling, and a poison headache. This crew cut lot were secret suspender-wearers to a man, nonplussed as to why Dylan was even there. At one point he was actually asked, 'What is your reason for your visit to Los Angeles?' Dylan began to spin one of his surreal yarns, 'I'm here looking for some donkeys. I'm making a movie about Jesus …' when he remembered he was here to sell tickets and not complain: 'Besides, I'm playing a few times here and there. I'm really here on business.'

Dylan wasn't the only one taken aback by the sheer ill-will of the straight men dispatched to interrogate the interloper. He did have allies, mostly in female form. Printed 'pop' media, in fortnightly and monthly guises, had recently sprung up in the Hollywood Hills, with both *KRLA Beat* and *TeenSet* equal opportunity employers. Their female journalists seemed particularly keen to counteract the mainstream media view (two years after The Beatles burst upon the scene) that all this great music was disposable junk. The reporter from *TeenSet* was appalled at the treatment dished out to Dylan, and wrote so:

> The conference was attended by reporters, photographers and television newscasters who spent forty minutes asking questions and another hour trying to figure out the answers. The first question was, 'How many protest singers are there?' … Dylan denied throughout the entire press conference that he was a protest singer and that he was trying to cause controversy by the songs he writes and records.
>
> 'I'm just an entertainer. I'm not on trial and I don't have to explain my feelings,' he said at one point in the conference. He described his friends as 'horrible people, midgets and thieves'. He told the gathering that he wasn't happy about his accomplishments and that he was really sort of disappointed because his life's ambition was to drive a bus.

Dylan, to his credit, kept his cool throughout, even when asked at the very start how many protest singers there really were. An incredulous Dylan suggested, 'It's either a hundred and thirty-six or a hundred and forty-two.' The general laughter did not dissuade further impertinent enquiries from the LA frat house:

Q: What would you call your music?
A: I like to think of it more in terms of vision music. It's mathematical music. I use words like most people use numbers.
Q: Can you elaborate a little more on that, you're losing me again?
A: Oh I'd hate to do that! ...
Q: Why are you putting us, and the rest of the world, on so?
A: I'm just trying to answer your questions as good as you can ask them.
Q: I am sure you must have been asked a thousand times—what are you trying to say in your music? I don't understand ONE of the songs.
A: Well, you shouldn't feel offended or anything. I am not trying to say anything to you. If you don't get it, you don't have to really think about it, 'cause it's not addressed to you.

The out-of-depth pressmen did their very best to get Dylan to rise to the bait, but the more insulting the question, the more mockingly mordant the slurred rebuttal. In the end they had to resort to four letter words like 'love', 'pain' and 'drug' (as in 'drurrrg song'):

Q: Do you really feel the things that you write?
A: What is there to feel? Name me some things.
Q: We are talking about standard emotions—pain, remorse, love.
A: I have none of those feeling ...
Q: I think 'Puff The Magic Dragon' and 'Mr Tambourine Man' were considered by some to be endorsements of marijuana smoking.
A: Well, I didn't write 'Puff The Magic Dragon'. [As for] 'Mr Tambourine Man', there's no marijuana in that song; at least I've never heard of it before.
Q: Bob, why is there such a widespread use of drugs among singers today? [*Laughter.*]
A: I don't know.
Q: Do you take drugs yourself?
A: I don't even know what a drug is. I have never even seen a drug. I would not know what one looked like if I saw one ...

He kept a straight face throughout, while the small sorority of sister-reporters looked on in wry amusement. One calling herself 'Eden' wrote a lengthy feature about the press conference in the widely syndicated *KRLA Beat*. It would be the most balanced eyewitness account of one of the more farcical press conferences of the era. Eden was initially inclined to spring to Dylan's rescue but soon realised he was wholly impervious to their slings and arrows:

It became somehow like a giant Alice-in-Wonderland zoo, grotesque, with all of the animals peering out from behind their fiberglass bars at all the odd-looking people on the outside.

Reporters and journalists and TV cameras all had come to see a freak in a sideshow, all had come to be entertained. ... Instead, they found a man—*Dylan*. Some people were nosey, and asked questions which were out of place: How much money do you make, Bob?

'I don't know how much money I make and I don't ever want to find out. When I want some money, I just go and ask for it, and then I use it. When I want some more I go and ask for some more.'

Some round-looking people tried to squeeze their questions into little square pegholes and hoped that Dylan would follow after. They tried to pin him down: How exactly do you write your songs and poems?

'I just sit down and all of a sudden it's there. I just sit down and write and the next thing I know, it's there.' ...

Some questions were quite foolish, like those who tried to ask them: How do your parents feel about your success? 'Well, I hope they can handle it!' Sometimes words were spoken, and their speaker was Bob Dylan ...

'I'm just an entertainer, that's all. I'm addressed to everyone.'

'I sing mostly love songs—I like to sing and play.'

'I'm gonna write a symphony with words—I don't now if it's gonna be vague or not. There will be one song in one key, and another song in another key. Everything will be happening all at once.'

Sometimes people threw their verbal harpoons at him, only to find him throwing them right back—with deadly aim! 'I bet you couldn't name one thing I participate in—go ahead, I *dare* you!' And there was no one there to accept the challenge.

People asking foolish and irrelevant questions found that they received their answers in direct accordance. Why did you come to California, Bob?

'I came to find some donkeys for a film I'm making!' Are you gonna play yourself in the film? 'No, I'm gonna play my *mother*, and we're gonna call it "Mother Revisited"!' …

It was like an operating room with a hundred amateur physicians all trying to dissect one human form. But they couldn't make the crucial incision, and the anaesthetic worked on *them*, instead.

And then the man named Dylan rose and slowly left the room. The TV cameras turned off their blinding klieg lights, and the radio men turned off their prying microphones. Slowly all the reporters and the journalists disappeared through the one-way door, returning to their one-way lives. And then the room was quiet—there was no one left inside.

★ ★ ★

At the end of proceedings, Eden went in search of Billy James, 'Manager of Talent Acquisition and Development for Columbia Records', hoping he might explicate what had just happened, having known the artist since Dylan signed to Columbia. But he couldn't quite believe what he'd just seen, either:

Billy James: I think he will make attempts to like people even when it's obvious to him that they dislike him. His evaluation of silly questions and a questioner's evaluation of a silly question may be different. [But] I think it's ludicrous for one human being to ask another human being—'Don't you have any feelings?' Nevertheless, someone did ask that question. So the question deserved a silly answer, and he said 'No!'

As an exercise in communication, LA had been another mismatch. If articles in *NME*, *TeenSet* and *KRLA Beat*, all written by women journalists, were firmly on his side, in Pleasant Valley the conference went largely unreported, perhaps because its emissaries left none the wiser. They should perhaps have interviewed Dylan's publicist instead:

Billy James: I don't think he directs his work toward anyone—I think he works. People respond to this work or they don't. Any 'act' is communication, so of course—what he does, communicates. If everything could be explained in words, art wouldn't exist in the first place, and it's grossly unfair to expect an artist to explain his work in other words. ... They accepted him when they could identify with him easily. When they could buy a corduroy cap and a harmonica holder just like this. When he sang songs of social protest ... when he was communicating on a level that was understood quite readily by a certain segment of his audience—then he was accepted. When he moved on—he picked up people and lost people—every step of the way. It hasn't moved smoothly ... [but] he has become the most significant creator in the field of literature and popular music in the United States. His influence is quite, quite far-reaching—musically and verbally.

As a summary of Dylan's then-position in pop culture, this could hardly be bettered. It had been a year of extraordinary achievement— the West providing the best reception to date—but he needed a break to preserve his sanity. In a few days' time he could look forward to a six-week rest even as the stream of product flowed forth. Columbia already had his next single—'Can You Please Crawl Out Your Window?'—in the can, with every right to think it would match or surpass the Top 10 success of 'Positively 4th Street'.

Dylan was anxious to board his Lodestar after three weeks on the West Coast, though not so anxious that he couldn't spend a few days at the Castle in the company of Warhol superstar Edie Sedgwick and a besotted Bobby Neuwirth. He was heading home to his new bride, Sara, and the prospect of their first baby in January, leaving California to The Byrds, The Beach Boys, The Beau Brummels and his old friend, Barry McGuire.

McGuire had enjoyed several evenings in Dylan's company during his time in LA, and was sad to see him go. Sad *and* afraid. He had become the second friend to voice his concern in print that Dylan might be taking on more than any man could bear, confiding to Eden, 'He's so fragile—so frail—he looks like they could really hurt him. He's so very delicate, that I just sort of want to be his bodyguard to make sure that no one hurts him.'

The same concern had been voiced in print by another former folksinger wondering whether to follow the sound of folk-rock. The ever-conflicted Phil Ochs had given a long, rambling interview in *Broadside* in which he not only let rip at the whole folk-rock phenomenon but also warned Dylan he might not have much time left before he had to 'quit singing':

Phil Ochs: Dylan has this whole aggressive thing—this whole attacking, putting down. This is part of his style, like in his new single, 'I wish you were standing in my shoes so you could see what a drag it is to see you ...' And also in 'Like A Rolling Stone' ... no sympathy, but a hatred, a real aggression coming out. And all this done on the stage, and done great. It's not done in any sophomoric way at all. And it has a very disturbing effect on people ... Dylan is LSD on the stage. Dylan is LSD set to music. ... [He] has managed to convene a very dangerous neurotic audience together in one place, who are all hipped on him on different levels. They aren't all listening to him in the same way. That's the danger of it. ... Some of them are there looking for the lost symbol of the message singer. And none of them have any right to him. That's the thing that none of them really understand. Dylan is an individual singing. And these people want to own him. And that's what a lot of Dylan's songs are about—You can't own me. [But they're] sitting there and saying we want the old Dylan or we want the new Dylan. That's bullshit, that's nonsense. It's a very sick thing going on there. And it's because of this neurotic audience that Dylan has got. And that is why Dylan ... will have to quit singing.

Given Dylan's insistence on reading (and reflecting on) everything written about him at this juncture—as well as his long-standing relationship with Sis Cunningham and Gordon Friesen, co-founders of *Broadside* (with Pete Seeger)—it seems highly unlikely he did not read Ochs's concerns.

Yet the topic does not seem to have come up when next they met at the end of December. Dylan had barely touched down in New York before he was back to his swinging ways, descending on old Village haunts like the Limelight to hold court, his retained jesters ever ready to put down anyone foolish enough to play this game of thrones.

Running into Ochs at a regular Village watering hole, a speeding Dylan insisted on playing him a test pressing of his latest single. 'Can You Please Crawl Out Your Window?' was one more example of 'the whole ... putting down' thing, rush-released in three weeks to head off a version by The Vacels, who had gotten their hands on a rare mispress of 'Positively 4th Street' featuring an alternate 'Can You Please Crawl Out Your Window?' and copied it note for note. Dylan and The Hawks remade the song as the inevitable whiplash from another car-crash relationship of Miss Lonely.

When Ochs told him he didn't think it would be a hit, some uncharacteristic 'real aggression' came out. Dylan ordered Ochs from his car and left him at the curb. It was another symbolic parting of the ways. Ochs would soon be proven right on both counts: 'Can You Please Crawl Out Your Window?' would stall at #58, applying an unexpected check on Dylan's commercial ambitions, forcing a rethink as to his relationship with The Hawks.

Ochs was even more prescient in his evaluation of the 'very sick thing going on' between his former mentor and 'this neurotic audience'. At the end of his *Broadside* ruminations, Ochs began wondering aloud about 'what's going to happen. I [really] don't know if Dylan can get on the stage a year from now. I don't think so.' Dylan was not sure he'd even be around.

4. A NIGHT WITH BOB DYLAN

[October 1965–January 1966]

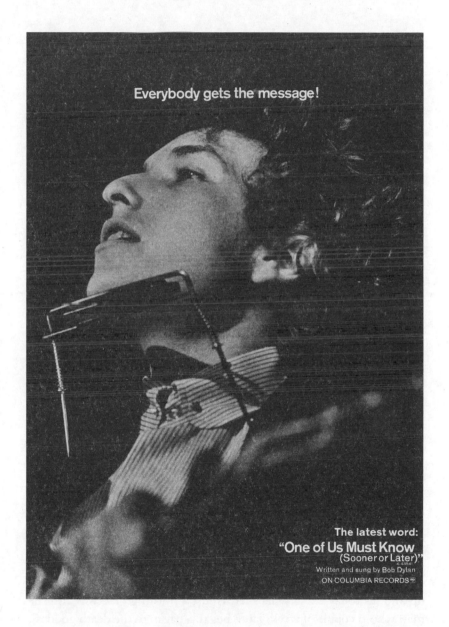

I try not to make any plans ... I have a concert schedule I keep, but other people get me there. I don't have to do anything. ... Getting married, having a bunch of kids, I have no hopes for it. If it happens, it happens.
—BOB DYLAN TO JOSEPH HAAS, CHICAGO, NOVEMBER 26 1965

It would be February 1966 before the story of Dylan's secret marriage to Sara Lowndes the previous November made it into the papers. (He could blame the ever-informed Nora Ephron, who blew his cover in the *New York Post*.) So, when Dylan said, four days *after* he tied the knot with a woman seven months pregnant with his child, 'Getting married, having a bunch of kids, I have no hopes for it,' it was taken at face value.

Whether he was quite ready for fatherhood was another question. His lifestyle suggested not. Even back in New York, the nights could be long and the public glare unrelenting. The other time the subject came up that fall—in a long, discursive interview with Nat Hentoff intended for men's magazine *Playboy*—Dylan painted a surprisingly bleak scenario, one which did not involve a long-term future, suggesting he felt he might not return from Rimbaud's 'unknowable region':

Bob Dylan: [Any] kid [of mine] wouldn't open his eyes anyway until [he was] five or six years old. I wouldn't imagine I'd even be around by that time ... I mean, I'm not counting on being around. ... If somebody told me right now, 'You're gonna have to die in an hour,' there would really be nothing that I'd have to clean up, y'know, no unfinished business ... I could very easily accept it.

He seemed to be living with the same existential despair as the characters scattered across the last two albums, feeling that, 'in terms of really hard reality, tomorrow never comes. Like, you always wake up and it's today ... so what's left is just a nothing.' He was also the man who, a couple of weeks later, began a paean to the death goddess,

Johanna. In fact, a certain fatalism—and the presence of one or more witchy women with a kiss like death—imbue a number of songs he began sketching out for *Highway 61 Revisited*'s successor. The question was, did he have anything left to offer his inner muse? Hentoff got to play father confessor to these inner doubts:

Bob Dylan: I don't know what else I can do. I'll continue making the records. They're not gonna be any better from now on. ... Whereas, when I made my last record, before this, I still knew what I wanted to do on my next record. I don't know what I'm gonna do on my next record, but I know it's gonna be the same kind of thing, just a little different. ... This last record, it's just too good.

If references to shows in Cincinnati and Buffalo are to the actual gigs, then the original Hentoff interview dates from mid-November. But the mention of Atlanta might suggest the week after Newark, in early October, a day or two after the first studio session with The Hawks on October 5 proved something of a bust.[22]

Even the 2015 release of the entire October 5 session on an eighteen-CD mid-sixties studio smorgasbord fails to elucidate the purpose of this session. One can only assume Dylan's goal was to have a single A-side in the can as a potential follow-up to 'Positively 4th Street'. If so, he arrived at the session unsure which among the half-formed ideas he had brought suited the format best. Which may well be why he set about recording single-verse versions of four separate songs: 'Medicine Sunday', 'Jet Pilot', 'I Wanna Be Your Partner' and 'Can You Please Crawl Out Your Window?'—only one of which he went on to complete.

It seems this was his intention all along. Before attempting the evening's first song, 'Medicine Sunday' (twice), Dylan told producer Johnston, 'We're just gonna do one verse, Bob!' Yet an earlier rough draft of the lyrics (put up for auction by Christie's New York in 2013) contains at least one more verse:

> *the jack o diamonds was talking to the queen of hearts*
> *saying i know you want my loving, but you want it free of charge*

---

[22] Not that photos of Dylan, Rick Danko and co. in a booth at Ondine's taken the same evening suggest those assembled were in the pit of despair.

He had also penned a couple of attempts to compose a catchier burden, of which 'I know you want it from me / Honey, but I just can't pay' offers a different slant to the one he ended up using (twice): 'You know you want my lovin'/ Mama, but you're so hard.' The working drafts strongly suggest he intended 'Medicine Sunday' should run to three verses. But a one-verse version is all he ever tried.

He also prefaced a rehearsal take of 'I Wanna Be Your Partner' that evening by asking, 'Are you ready to take this? OK, one verse.' Even the one song that was ready to go, 'Can You Please Crawl Out Your Window?', was abandoned after two one-verse takes. Maybe he had simply forgotten the rest of these songs along with the guitar case he had left in the Lodestar with a series of draft lyrics.

Eventually, a choice needed to be made. And it was a slightly odd one. The second session that day, which ran from 11:30pm to 2:30am, would be spent working up 'I Wanna Be Your Lover' with the midnight crew. A song that put *Highway 61 Revisited* and *Rubber Soul* in a blender on a three-minute spin cycle, it had a welcome levity and wit but still seemed more of an album track than a Top 10 single.

Whether it would have been a hit, we'll never know, but the last three takes of the evening were all complete—and all have something to recommend them. The one listed as take 5 comes closest to the live sound, with Robertson threatening to take off at song's end. Take 6 reins Robertson in while having the greater pop sensibility. This would be the take marked as 'master', later popping up on a compilation reel bootlegged as *The LA Band Session* in the early seventies. But it was the punchier take 7 that was ushered into the world first, on 1985's *Biograph*.

A session scheduled for the following evening was cancelled, suggesting Dylan had either got what he had been looking for or despaired of finding it now. Whatever his reasoning, 'I Wanna Be Your Lover' would never be a single. When he finally gave Columbia a follow-up to 'Positively 4th Street', it was a remake of 'Can You Please Crawl Out Your Window?', another lyrical rehash of the *Highway 61* vibe.

Perhaps it was the lyrics to 'I Wanna Be Your Lover' that continued to bother him, having at least partly evolved from another song. Because the most interesting of the lyrics he worked on before touching down in New York was one he never even recorded. Initially called 'Inside The Darkness Of Your Room', Dylan added a bracketed subtitle ('Uranium Sunday') on a second fragmentary draft, by which time it was shedding lines to 'I Wanna Be Your Lover'.

What 'Inside The Darkness Of Your Room' and/or 'Uranium Sunday' was never in danger of becoming was 'Absolutely Sweet Marie'. Yet this is precisely how it was described in the 2013 Christie's catalogue: 'Comprising draft lyrics for the song Absolutely Sweet Marie ... [though] only a few words hint at the final version.'

'Inside The Darkness Of Your Room' bears about as much resemblance to 'Absolutely Sweet Marie' as 'Song To Woody'. The three-word phrase it shares, 'six white horses', is a traditional commonplace Dylan didn't think twice about using again. It had been a familiar component of 'She'll Be Coming 'Round The Mountain' for a century or more.

For all of 'Sweet Marie's sensuous charms, 'Inside The Darkness Of Your Room' is actually the more interesting lyric; partly because, chronologically, it is the starting point for *Blonde On Blonde*. Here, for the very first time, are the first cousins to those characters who will inhabit *Blonde On Blonde* (and, with a lil' existential twist, the Big Pink demos).

Here is pretty Mary, another death goddess ready to kill 'the first boy ... to put love into words for her'; a drunken Maid Marian, possibly on the game; and the four horsemen of the apocalypse, quietly determined 'to get him before he flips'. Nor is 'the darkness' suffusing the song confined to the inside of her room. Rather, it soon becomes all-pervasive and all consuming:

> *Oh my God, all the clocks are exploding ...*
> *i wanna be inside [the] fire of your breath/*
> *yes, I guess i'd like to burn to death ...*
> *& there's nothing left but me & you lady*

A case of 'Stuck Inside of Mobile' meeting 'Temporary Like Achilles' at the dark end of the street. Yet Dylan never reclaimed the song—which ultimately donated the line 'she's 5 ft. 9 & carries a wrench' to 'Jet Pilot' and its refrain to 'I Wanna Be Your Lover'—

from the jet pilot in question, Victor Quinto, who died in 1977, leaving the lyrics in his loft for his daughter to discover.[23]

The idea of (writing about) being in thrall to a death goddess in her lofty room was one Dylan saved for another rainy day. When the notion was resurrected, substantial work would be required before it could reclaim the night.

Meanwhile, he would have to be content with watching 'Positively 4th Street' ascend the charts. After all, as he informed Nat Hentoff, 'The only outlet I know of is records, [though] I don't know who buys the records. It's the same with the magazine. I have no idea really who buys the magazine except that I know it's a very funny-looking group of people.'

Such a 'funny-looking group of people' was Dylan's intended audience for a couple of hours' stream-of-consciousness conversation with the man who had written the sleeve notes to his breakthrough album, *Freewheelin'*, back in May 1963. Nat Hentoff, who had given Dylan his first *Playboy* mention in June 1963, singling him out as the Great White Hope for folkniks in a feature on the folk revival, was the chosen conduit between Dylan and *Playboy*'s randy readers. Meanwhile, Dylan was insisting he had nothing left to say:

Bob Dylan: I'm not trying to say anything any more. Once upon a time I tried to say 'Well, I'm here, listen to me.' ... I don't have to say that any more ... [Now] the songs would be there if anybody listened to them or not. They're not manufactured songs ... I know what they are, but I can't tell somebody what they are ...

I don't think in terms of the people that listen to me. ... I certainly wouldn't run over them on the street or anything. ... If somebody needed a mouthful of water, I'd probably give [it] them ... but I guess there are a lot of people that want to see me done away with ...

When I wrote those [old] songs ... they were written within a small circle of people ... that heard them. And when some of them were brought finally to the outside, somebody else who heard 'em just weren't equipped really to take it and know it the same way. ... But I also ... took the time out to write [other] things. The other stuff I was doing didn't resemble those songs at all. They resembled more

---

[23] The full story was told in an episode of the *History Detective* TV series, with record dealer Jeff Gold transmuted into a 'Dylan expert'.

what I'm writing today. … [Now] every time I write a song, it's like writing a novel. Just takes me a lot less time, and I can get it down … I can re-read it in my head … I don't have to hold anything back now. Before, I used to have to hold things back. … If I just came out and sang 'Desolation Row' five years ago, I probably would've been murdered.

★ ★ ★

A feature interview for *Playboy* was both an acknowledgment of Dylan's growing importance and an admission he was something of a curiosity to many folk. For anyone who thought he might be the poster boy of the new intelligentsia, he made it plain he had a mile-wide anti-intellectual streak running through him. This former university student—albeit for barely a year—placed very little store in the benefits of college:

Bob Dylan: I don't have to have any degree. I don't have to take any tests. I don't have to sort any kind of philosophies out in my mind. I don't have to memorize anything. I don't have to look like the next person. I just don't have these problems … so I don't have to rebel against this … I would like to go to one [of these colleges], just to relax once in a while … just to sit on the banks of some river, most of them are on rivers, you know. Just do that. But I can't imagine going to any classes, or reading any books that they would give me. … Just going to school reading and writing and taking tests and learning why things happen, it just [seems] ridiculous in the face of things that are going to happen whether you know why they happen or not. … Who cares who the first President of the United States was and who cares where Africa is?

Nat Hentoff, a jazz critic of comparable stature to Ralph J. Gleason and another friend of Lenny Bruce, was an ideal confessor. He had written the first important profile of the young folksinger, for *The New Yorker*, in June 1964; here, at the cusp of a great change, he elicited results which were fulsome and wide-ranging.

Not surprisingly, Dylan was keen to distance himself from anyone and everyone who had ever thought he was a protest singer, insisting (quite correctly) that protest songs had very little to do with real folk music:

Bob Dylan: You can just about pinpoint the people that don't like [what I do]. You can walk down the street and you see and know who wouldn't like it. ... The way they light a cigarette—you can tell. ... [But] if somebody's really got something to say, and they really can help somebody out ... obviously they're gonna be done away with. ... I'm not asking anyone, 'Which side are you on?' And which side can you be on? I mean, is there really only two sides to anything? ... I respect folk music ... but it's not a thing to play with ... [or] have folk song groups and have folk gatherings and 'let's all sing a bunch of folk songs'. It's not that kind of thing at all. ... People just lost the point. ... These people in the South ... they talk about roses growing out of peoples' brains and lovers who are geese, and swans who turn into angels ... that's what I would think of [as a folk song]. I certainly wouldn't think of any twenty-two year old kid going to a labour rally and singing some union songs.

Now on another side of the great folk/rock divide, Hentoff wanted to know, 'How does it feel?' The singer offered a surprisingly straightforward answer:

Bob Dylan: I'm working now a lot, because I dig it now ... I was gonna quit. When I was playing all by myself ... I was very mixed-up on how long I was gonna really do it, play by myself. ... I would never want to do it again. ... I've written a lot of songs ... but to get up on stage and sing 'em night after night, gets a little hard. Because you're not really there in your right mind half the time. ... I used to play these concerts. I used to say [to myself], 'Well, would I come to see me tonight?' And ... to be very truthful [I'd think,] 'No, I wouldn't come.' But now ... I've gotta say, I would ... I know what we're doing is different. I don't know what exactly it is that we're doing... I know that it's different, though. It's not folk-rock ... but I'd listen to it. I actually dig it.

When Dylan relaxed, he sometimes rambled, and Hentoff let him do so. One such ramble suggested the desire for revenge in some of his recent songs was a true reflection of the poet-self: 'I don't really worry too much about people who say they've been hurt by me, because ninety-nine times out of a hundred, it's not me that hurts them.'

OKTOBER '66
75 CENT-12 FRANK
No.130-11e JAARG.
VERSCHIJNT MAANDELIJKS

BOB DYLAN

MEER DAN
1,5 MILJOEN
LEZERS

Despite all of the hurtful press directed his way in the last year—or perhaps because of it—Dylan welcomed the opportunity to open up to one of the few figures who had been a cheerleader through the simple years. And open up he did. On the book he owed Macmillan, which he now had serious doubts about: 'I've a book coming out but it's very average to me, you know. I can't really be excited about it. I've worked on it hard at certain times. But now it's all done [and] it means very little.' About leaving home when he was young: 'I'm not the only one that left there and traveled around. ... Everybody left there. I don't know really of anybody that stayed there. ... Everybody my age I know left. ... From my very first time of consciousness, I knew I wanted to get out of there.' He even addressed the contentious subject of drugs: 'To know pot, or to know any drug, is fine, and it's not gonna fuck you up ... [but] the people that really actually think that they got their answers through pot, probably never even smoked pot.'

Hentoff had skilfully secured what he later described as 'an almost unusually straight interview ... a quite sober, almost historical, biographical account [with] a lot of opinion ... [typically] sardonically funny. But just a straight interview.' He dispatched the edited transcript to *Playboy* in Chicago, and waited for the cheque.

Meanwhile Dylan, still battling the armies of incomprehension, continued to feed old allies from the fourth estate the odd juicy bone of contention. The most hilarious of these was a piece depicting 'A Night With Bob Dylan'. It ran in the *New York Herald Tribune*'s Sunday magazine the second week of December—alongside a 'think piece' by William Bender called 'Bob Dylan: Man & Music'—but without a by-line, or any real indication whose 'night with Bob Dylan' it was. Whoever had come along for the ride, it was evidently a helluva night:

Bob Dylan picked himself up from the revolving turntable, staggered into an armchair, waved his hands above his head and sat down to watch the tube. On it, Soupy Sales was grinning from a mask of cream pie.

It wasn't Dylan's pad; he had borrowed it from someone or other. On the floor, a mink rug played tablecloth for several cups and saucers, ashes and the ashtrays that the ashes had been intended for. On a couch opposite Dylan's armchair sat Robbie Robertson, whom Dylan refers to as 'the only mathematical guitar genius I've ever run into who does not offend my intestinal nervousness with his rearguard sound'. Robertson, who plays lead guitar in Dylan's band, was strumming an autoharp ...

The doorbell rang. It was Brian Jones of The Rolling Stones with a limousine waiting outside. Dylan wiped Soupy Sales' face off the TV tube, Robbie Robertson wiped the autoharp off his lap and everybody split. Dylan was the last to leave. He took the Temptations' record off the turntable, hid it under his double-breasted corduroy jacket and winked at a light bulb. His tea, unsipped, was left to cool in its cup.

In the limousine, Charlie, the chauffeur, asked if the group was going downtown. 'I'm getting off at the next block,' said Dylan. 'These other people're going downtown ... .' 'Thank you, sir,' said Charlie. 'No, we're not going downtown,' said Milly, a friend of Brian [Jones]'s. 'Shut up!' said Dylan, 'shut up and quit making that racket or else you'll be thrown to the fire inspectors ... and they're very hungry.' 'What?' yelled Milly. The car stopped at the corner and Milly, one way or another, was thrown out. ... 'Watch the fire inspectors!' yelled Brian.

Clearly a composite of several such occasions, the piece—subsequently attributed by some sources to Al Aronowitz and Dylan—seems to accurately reflect Dylan's nightlife in the months he was 'staying up for days in the Chelsea Hotel' (where he and his bride-to-be had taken an apartment down the hall from Robertson). The fact that his fiancée, Sara, has been airbrushed out of the article should come as no great surprise. However, she was certainly at her beau's side the night Dylan, Jerry Schatzberg and Brian Jones had dinner (probably on November 8). New York photographer Don Paulsen caught her unmistakeable profile as he was snapping Dylan and Jones.

The following night, Jones and Dylan were together again, Neuwirth and Robertson in tow. The night of the big New York City blackout, they spent most of the evening jamming in Jones's hotel room at the City Squire Hotel. Two evenings earlier, Jones and the rest of the Stones met up with Dylan at the Phone Booth after midnight, fleet foot from two scream-along shows in Newark across the bay.

Jones enjoyed hanging out with Dylan *and* Robertson. When the latter invited him to the Cafe Wha? to see some new hot guitarist, Jimmy James, he was delighted to tag along. What he saw so blew him away that he returned to London still raving about the guy. When ex-Animal Chas Chandler heard about James, he hotfooted it back to New York, signed him up and rechristened him Jimi Hendrix.

Where the Stones (and The Beatles) were concerned, Al Aronowitz was a familiar New York chaperon. So he was probably there in person on one or more of these November nights. If so, he may have witnessed Dylan and Jones attempt to write a song together during a Wilson Pickett session they gatecrashed. Any such effort, though, came to naught. Brian Jones was never a songwriter, no matter how essential to the early Stones' sound he was. As for Dylan, he was still working from scraps left at the side of *Highway 61*.

All that changed within days of tying the knot with the saintly Sara at a private Long Island ceremony on November 22. Still in love with song-titles that bore no (overt) relation to the lyrics, Dylan wrote 'Freeze Out'; and, with it, answered a rhetorical question he had raised with Nat Hentoff. After castigating 'all the intellectual [authors of] books [that] just appeal to a small group of people ... who are just going to talk among themselves about it', he wondered aloud, 'What would happen if all of a sudden *Ulysses* came on the radio one day?'

'Freeze Out' raised that very possibility. If the stick-in-the-muds presiding over the folk world were kith and kin to the fossils running the museums, he had moved to another world, where people were plugged in to a pop culture that had never been more vibrant:

Bob Dylan: The *Sing Out!* world just overlaps into that kind of world ... of putting books on the shelf. Once you read a book, you just put it on a shelf and there it is. If you wanna buy a painting, you've gotta go out and pay a lot of money for a painting. If you wanna see paintings, you've gotta pay to go in the museum. ... [Instead of] straining to go see all these Broadway plays and museums ... [what if] the same thing is on the radio?

★ ★ ★

'Visions Of Johanna' addressed this very question in song, pointing the finger at the cultural codifiers with 'Inside the museums, Infinity goes

up on trial', a line in the fourth verse which came relatively easily, as
did the first three. It was the fifth and final verse which gave Dylan
a deal of grief, subjected to a number of rewrites leading up to an
all-important session at Studio A on November 30. At one point he:

> *Mourns the death of infinity's codes*
> *Who've taken everything back which was owed*
> *Used by (the) nightingale(s) of the road*
> *Still left on the fish truck that loads*
> *My conscience explodes.*

By the time of the session, 'the death of infinity' has been dispensed
with; it is the nightingale's code he chooses to examine existentially,
even if 'Everything's gone which was owed'. But these lines would
continue to bother him. A further rewrite would be necessary before
its near-perfect realisation at a session in Tennessee on Valentine's Day
1966. That struggle with a vital song probably reflects his own inner
struggle to overcome intimations of mortality below the surface of
this most unlikely wedding song.

Having worked tirelessly and meticulously on the lyrics, Dylan
arrived at the late-November session prepared to do the same in the
studio even if it took all night. But the gods of serendipity were not
on his side. Trusting to chance and utilising a band unfamiliar with
the very idea of a song that broke all the rules of popular song was not
the way to go. The session, which started promisingly, soon began to
veer off the rails, driven as it was by a tavern band with little studio
experience and only one way of playing: all cylinders firing. Lines
as evocative as 'But Louise she's alright she's just near / She's delicate
and seems like the mirror' were treated like a drive-by shooting by
The Hawks.

In fact, that evening's first full version of 'Freeze Out' rather
continues where the band had left off two nights earlier, in Washington.
But Dylan isn't looking for a rollicking roar from a well-oiled R&B
machine, even with Bobby Gregg holding down the beat. After the
second of three vamped-up 'rehearsal takes', all put down on tape,
Dylan sings the band the first verse at the tempo he wants them to
play at and tells them, 'I don't want to get it too fast.' When they
give him their idea of medium tempo, he says, 'That's way too fast.'

A third take breaks down before Dylan again takes them to task, 'That's not the sound, that's not it! The only one to play hard is Robbie.' It is Dylan issuing all the instructions. Johnston is evidently there to run tape and check levels. By take eight—the version on the *No Direction Home* CD—they have a complete take but the meaning of the words has been left in the fish truck. It is slowly dawning on Dylan that maybe these guys only know how to play Moondog Matinees and Midnight Rambles.[24]

Such an epic song had need of something more understated, more measured. Yet the tutoring Dylan perseveres as over the next three hours an arrangement is sculpted, take by take, breakdown by breakdown, until it has less of the honky-tonk, more of the country station.

The fourteenth and final attempt—marked on the studio sheet, I know not why, 'funny ad-libs'—would be the one transferred to the 'LA Band' 'comp' reel, his audio shortlist for an album he had informed Hentoff was 'gonna be the same kind of thing [as *Highway 61*], just a little different'; an album he would ultimately replace with something a lot more mercurial.

'Visions' would survive the transition, but The Hawks would not. Dylan, in his heart of hearts, knew he had failed to realise this inspired night-time vision. Which may be why, when the song made its live debut three days later, it was in the acoustic set, where it would remain till the end of the world tour.

Another 'Long Distance Operator' he did not need. He did, however, need to keep piling up the singles. And whatever concerns he had about The Hawks' ability to pick up a difficult new song in the studio, 'Can You Please Crawl Out Your Window?' was something they'd already rehearsed, though perhaps not recently.

Dylan is forced to call out after a second breakdown, 'Does everybody know the song because the right chords aren't coming across?' But again he persevered until, providentially—at the end of a long night—they re-cut 'Can You Please ...' in just three complete takes (and half a dozen breakdowns), duly rediscovering their potency

[24] Columbia, in this period, assigned take numbers to both incomplete takes (or 'breakdowns') and false starts. However, when the indexing was done for the 2015 *Cutting Edge* set, multiple false starts and breakdowns were sometimes indexed as a single track, rather muddying the water as to what is a take and what is not. My take numbers adhere to the ones given in the Sony tape database, unless otherwise noted.

as a band. The release of the first Dylan and The Hawks single—*if* it was a hit—would reinforce his movement away from the folk-rock sound every reviewer continued to attribute to him:

Bob Dylan: A lot of my songs, they were becoming hits for other people. There was The Byrds, [who] had a big hit. Some group called The Turtles had some hit. Sonny & Cher had a hit with a song of mine. People were sort of writing a jingly-jangly kind of song ... which seemed to have something to do with me. ... You know, 'I Got You, Babe', is some kind of take-off of me, something I wrote ... [but] I didn't really like that sound ... folk-rock, whatever that was. I didn't feel that had anything to do with me. It got me thinking about the *Billboard* charts and the songs which become popular, which I hadn't thought of that before.

And yet Dylan refused to transfer such a glorious roar of retribution to the live shows. This near neighbour of '4th Street' was never even taken for a test-run onstage. It was as if Dylan was stung by its failure to chart higher than #58 and he had no MBE to return. Or perhaps it was a sensibility already adequately expressed in the live set. Either way, it was high time he re-employed his standing band to do what it did best: lobbing a large rock through the window of folk.

★ ★ ★

While Dylan was taking his new music to every corner of the English-speaking world, at *Sing Out!* they continued to barricade themselves inside folk's four enclosed walls, convinced that 25,000 subscribers spoke with a voice louder than thunder and that Dylan and his folk-rock friends would be swept away in the coming storm.

Interest in Dylan's act of apostasy was such that a reprint of Paxton's intemperate *Sing Out!* article 'Folk Rot' and an edit of Frances Taylor's interview became grist for a new jazz-pop monthly, *Sound & Fury*. These reprints signified something; *S&F* trying to strike the kind of balance Silber forsook by asking Henrietta Yurchenco to come to Dylan's defence. As Folk Music Editor of *American Record Guide* and the voice of WNYC's *Adventures In Folk Music* since 1939, Yurchenco had clout in the close-knit folk community. She also recognised *Highway 61* as two steps forward:

From the start Dylan's poetry was characterized not only by the acuteness and individuality of his vision but by his gift for words and imagery. His poetic tools have been sharpened, particularly in his recent album. ... Virtuosity for its own sake, which sometimes needlessly halted the poetic flow, is now not so pronounced ... his construction is more disciplined, less erratic.

Yurchenco's compelling portrait of the man she had known since 1961 gave her considered conclusion—that 'in this time of dreary conformity and intellectual cowardice in a world gone mad, Dylan's words and music are fresh and alive'—as much power as anything written during the Great Folk Scare of 1965.

Others who had known Dylan in the Village were also inclined to spring to his defence. Robert Shelton's riposte to Silber's blinkered belligerence may have been wholly expected, but it was welcome nonetheless. Shelton, having been straddling the folk/rock divide for some months, contributed a four-page Dylan feature to the July 1965 issue of *Cavalier*, a poor-man's *Playboy* with a residue of rock content.

Entitled 'The Charisma Kid', Shelton's piece was laced with occasional comments from Dylan himself, offered during a brief supper at the Lion's Head, wedged in before the Paul Butterfield Blues Band's April 1965 New York debut at the Village Gate. The most telling of these was, 'I'm in the show business now. I'm not in the folk-music business. That's where it's at.' Dylan's not-so-believable list of fellow club members included Roscoe Holcomb, Jean Ritchie, Little Orphan Annie and Dick Tracy. Pre-Newport, pre-'Rolling Stone', Shelton noted that Dylan had already become 'part of the Beatles backlash [for] using electrical background instruments and reworking the rhythm and blues tunes of Chuck Berry'.

As such, Silber and Paxton certainly cannot have been caught off guard to find themselves on the other side of the podium from Robert Shelton— and Murray The K—during a folk-rock symposium at the Village Vanguard in late December. What Silber did not see coming was Shelton's sideswipe when he suggested that 'folk-rock' songs represented a form of 'social protest that has no relation to anything that's real'. After Silber provided as evidence 'two full-page ads last week in *Billboard* providing the lyrics in full for two songs attacking

those who burn draft cards and march in peace parades', Shelton
pricked his righteous red balloon:

> Once again we have another example of folk purism carried to
> its ultimate phone-booth forum. Irwin, you put out an exciting
> publication called *Sing Out!*, which reaches approximately 20,000
> people. ... Would you rather have your 20,000 followers be
> completely educated to know the entire ... segregation-integration
> story from beginning to end or do you prefer reaching ten million
> people?

When Paxton joined the argument, reciting the full lyrics of a
Mann–Weil song, 'Home Of The Brave', a Top 30 hit for Jody Miller
that he considered 'garbage', things went from bad to worse for the
Sing Out! team. Shelton pointed out that the same team also wrote
the magnificent 'We've Gotta Get Out Of This Place', 'a beautifully
economical statement of a rather major social problem'.

At this juncture, moderator and closet Dylan fan Paul Krassner
finally mentioned the elephant in the room, asking Silber directly,
'Are you talking about rock folk, [or] particularly Bob Dylan?' Silber
responded, 'I'm talking about mass culture. But yes, I'm talking about
rock folk and Bob Dylan, too.' No matter how many times Silber and
Paxton went round the houses, it all came back to Dylan.

Dylan was playing to the masses the night of said symposium, but
he finally got to read a transcript of the evening in the March 1966
Cavalier, published in time for the resumption of touring, the first week
in February. Seven pages of *Cavalier*'s twenty-page 'folk-rock-protest'
special were devoted to the Vanguard showdown—almost as many
as were devoted to some particularly well-endowed topless women.

In fact, Dylan must have been gratified with how many times
his name (and image) came up in that month's issue, in a series of
features only nominally linked to his work. Even on the editorial page
his name was invoked as *Cavalier* lit into the 'list of gift records for
children published in the [Christmas issue of] the *Saturday Review*':

> That austere and revered periodical lived up to its reputation by
> selecting story records, uplifting classical records and a very few folk
> records that were suitable for the ears of the young. But nowhere

could one find The Beatles, Rolling Stones, Supremes, Bob Dylan or any others whom the kids really listen to. None of the music recommended had anything to do with the energy or rhythm of youth. The list was a symptom of the narrow-minded and arbitrary taste-making that affects many of our Kulchur-istic magazines. … Which brings us to pages 51 through 71 of this issue. We have done Rock. With all the stops out.

On page 51, one finds a full-page colour photo of Dylan at Carnegie Hall brandishing 'the electric guitar that is responsible for a revolution in pop music and a never-ending bash among the pure folkniks'. The ensuing feature on 'The Big Beat of Life'—the cornerstone of this *Cavalier* 'superfab special'—gave Dylan due credit:

> It started when an American group named The Byrds recorded Bob Dylan's 'Tambourine Man', complete with swishy Buddy Holly intonations. Within minutes, there was nothing you were hearing but Bob Dylan—eighty different versions of his songs. And then, in one of those incredible treacherous things that can only happen in America, there was Dylan himself, the pure folk singer … playing an electric guitar with four guys backing him up on organ, drums and other guitars. First he did it at Newport, and then, as if to show he wasn't fooling around, showed up at Forest Hills with all the [same] equipment and all those fellows. And he was brilliant.

There was seemingly nowhere in Pop '65 where Dylan's influence didn't seep. Jackie DeShannon, the nubile pop diva who wrote songs for The Searchers on the side, admitted, 'Dylan twisted my head all around. He made me realize that you didn't have to write only "my boyfriend's gone" songs. You could write things with meaning and emotion.' If Dylan was largely responsible for opening pop's Pandora's box, there was no closing it now.

Dylan was taking all this on board. When the author of said *Cavalier* piece, Jules Siegel, was commissioned to write an entire feature about the folk-rock king for that family favourite, the *Saturday Evening Post*, six weeks after *Cavalier*'s folk-rock issue hit the stands, he was welcomed as an ally in the folk-rock war. But the *Post* swam in an entirely different stream, the same main one inhabited by the predatory *Playboy*, *Cavalier*'s rapacious rival.

The gulf between the two 'gentlemen's magazines' was highlighted a few days after *Cavalier* unveiled its world exclusives—the 'superfab special', an excerpt from Thomas Pynchon's second novel, *The Crying Of Lot 49*, and a couple of artistic nude shots of the Welsh Miss World 1966. Its big brother in the top-shelf section promptly trumped them with a new James Bond short story called *Octopussy* and a 'candid interview' with the man of the moment, presented as his most revealing to date. What it really revealed was a first-class stand-up comic.

The interview that *Playboy* ran that February bore little in common with the one Hentoff had recorded the previous fall. If anything, it came across as a Mr Send-Up script, the same character who once fabricated a nonexistent press conference for a March 1965 *Village Voice* and embellished a fictionalised account of a night on the town for the *New York Herald Tribune*. When it came to gunfire dialogue and associative wordplay, this *Playboy* 'comedy script' could really not be beat:

Bob Dylan: My motto is, never follow anything. I don't know what the motto of the younger generation is, but I would think they'd have to follow their parents. I mean, what would some parent say to his kid if the kid came home with a glass eye, a Charlie Mingus record and a pocketful of feathers? He'd say: 'Who are you following?' And the poor kid would have to stand there with water in his shoes, a bow tie on his ear and soot pouring out of his belly button and say: 'Jazz, Father, I've been following jazz.' …

All this talk about long hair is just a trick. It's been thought up by men and women who look like cigars—the anti-happiness committee. They're all freeloaders and cops. You can tell who they are: they're always carrying calendars, guns or scissors. They're all trying to get into your quicksand … [At Newport, there were] lots of whole families [who] had driven down from Vermont, lots of nurses and their parents, and well, like they just came to hear some relaxing hoedowns, you know, maybe an Indian polka or two. And just when everything's going all right, here I come on, and the whole place turns into a beer factory …

It doesn't matter what kind of nasty names people invent for the music. It could be called arsenic music, or perhaps Phaedra music. I don't think that such a word as folk-rock has anything to do with it. ... The songs used to be about what I felt and saw—nothing of my own rhythmic vomit ever entered into it.

And so on, and so on. Evidence that *Playboy* didn't know it was having its chain pulled came on the first page of the interview, which it illustrated with three-year-old photos of Dylan, fresh-faced from the *Times They Are A-Changin'* photo fit. If this was miles away from the 'straight' interview Dylan had given the previous fall, his straight man insists it was all *Playboy*'s fault:

Nat Hentoff: The final set [of proofs] came to him after they messed with it in Chicago. I don't know what they did but I think they put some words in his mouth. ... I got a call and he was furious. I said, 'Look, tell them to go to hell.' ... And he said, 'No, I got a better idea. I'm gonna make one up.' ... [So] he made up an interview. I helped, I must say. Some of the good straight lines in there are mine, but ... it was run as was with absolutely no indication it was a put-on.

By his own admission, Hentoff had not seen those final proofs. He simply took Dylan at his word. But it seems unlikely that the magazine 'put some words in his mouth'; whereas the twenty-four-year-old was increasingly prone to mood swings and sudden changes of mind. One can't shake the suspicion Dylan simply took the time to read what he had said and realised he had revealed too much. So he draped his original words in barbed wit.

Such was the rat-a-tat of put-downs and put-ons that it was easy to pass over the moments—almost confessional in tone—when a residue of that original interview remained: 'It strikes me funny that people actually have the gall to think that I have some kind of fantastic imagination'; or, 'I don't know about other people's sympathy, but my sympathy runs to the lame and crippled and beautiful things'; or even, 'People have one great blessing—obscurity'.

At the end of this comedic concoction, Hentoff got to ask the one question Dylan usually ducked: 'What do you have to look forward to?' This wandering (and wondering) ex-Jew responded with a word he rarely used, 'Salvation. Just plain salvation.' By now he knew only too well, the road to salvation was 'thick beset with thorns and briers'—and a lot of so-called friends who'd like a piece of him:

Bob Dylan: Sometimes I have the feeling that other people want my soul. If I say to them 'I don't have a soul,' they say, 'I know that. You don't have to tell me that. Not me. How dumb do you think I am? I'm your friend.'

★ ★ ★

Dylan wasn't so sure he had any friends—or old fans—having roundly rejected, in the original interview with Hentoff, those who 'consider themselves ... my old fans. They're not my old fans really. The old fans are [the] 1,228 people that bought my first record ... [or] the 67 people that came into Gerde's. Or the people that went down to the Gaslight ... the people that just hung around the East Side. People I don't even see any more.'

According to his accusers, he had shut himself off from any potential criticism by constructing a world of metaphorical walls. If so, it was the self-defence mechanism of a man called everything from Jeremiah to Judas.[25] Only rarely did he allow inch-thick psychological armour to be breached.

Yet one such instance came the night Dylan bopped down from Columbia's Midtown recording studio to the semi-derelict downtown home of WBAI, a subscription radio station that had consistently championed his music. DJ Bob Fass had first invited the 'distinctive stylist' onto his show back in 1963, and had been pressing for a return match ever since.

When Dylan arrived after midnight on (or about) January 27 1966, he was buzzing. When Fass asked if he had brought 'electricity' with him, Dylan produced the first double-entendre of the evening: 'Turn on the telephone—where is this telephone I've been hearing so much about? ... Your telephone is very infamous.' He was already wired for sound when an early caller to the two-hour show phoned to say he was 'on a psychedelic trip' and wanted suggestions. Dylan's response suggested he had already been there:

---

[25] In the 1980 song 'Yonder Comes Sin', Dylan would directly identify himself with the Old Testament prophet Jeremiah, suggesting 'the critics gave him such bad reviews' as well.

Bob Dylan (*laughing*): If you're on a psychedelic trip, where are you going to? ... How's your gums feel at this point?
Caller 5: It's beginning to hurt! (*Laughs.*)
Bob Dylan: Ah-ha-ha, you see? It wasn't so good after all, was it? ... Well, listen, man, I hope you get where you're going.

Inevitably, opening up a late-night programme to all callers exposed Dylan to anyone with a gripe. Almost immediately, someone wanted to know what his songs *meant*: 'It shouldn't bother you one little bit how I write my songs ... you shouldn't even think about where they come from ... if you like 'em you like 'em, and if you don't, you don't. You don't have to think about 'em.'
Another person was wondering what had happened to the book he had been talking about for the past year. 'It'll be out within two months. I've just been changing it a lot. ... I mean, I just can't let anything go out, right? It's very easy to write a book ... I'm just gonna go over it one more time.'
But it was 'Caller 35' who resolutely refused to take 'Umm' or 'Huh' for an answer. He doggedly stayed on Dylan's case until he finally blew all that carefully cultivated cool and Fass cut the caller off:

Caller 35: I guess you were probably being pretty sincere then, and since then your music has changed ...
Bob Dylan: No, I haven't changed, you've changed. My music hasn't changed. I'm just using other people playing with me. Same music.
Caller 35: Come on, don't goof on me.
Bob Dylan: Other people are just playing with me; the songs are the same! 'With God On Your Side' is contained in two lines of something like 'Desolation Row'. That whole song is in there in two lines. I mean, if you can't pick it out or single it out, that's not my problem.
Caller 35: [So what you're saying is] it's a lot more subtle ...
Bob Dylan: It's not more subtle! It's just more to the point. It doesn't spare you any time to string the thing together.
Caller 35: At the Forest Hills concert, I was there, just after Newport. And most of 'Desolation Row' you had kids screaming and laughing, you know.
Bob Dylan: Well, that's not my problem. I can't worry about what

the audience is gonna do. I mean, who am I to carry the world on my shoulders? ...

Caller 35: [So] when you were writing these more obvious protest [songs], like '[Only A] Pawn In Their Game' ...

Bob Dylan: Well, I did it because that was the thing. That's what I was involved in. There's no big hoax or any kinda secret thing happening, or any kind of plan from the beginning. I [had] played rock'n'roll music when I was sixteen ... I quit doing it because I couldn't make it. ... Old people that smoked cigars and hung around in certain bars uptown, around Tin Pan Alley; well, that used to be the music thing. But it's not that anymore. I don't know what I was thinking about two or three years ago. [Do] I have to explain it to you? It's not so complicated, man. You don't even have to ask why—it's very simple. But I just don't feel like sitting here talking about it right now.

Such criticism had previously bounced off Bobby like rubber bullets. But live on the air, with nowhere to hide, asked directly for an explanation, he reverted to type. As Robert Shelton had perceptively observed in July 1965, 'In a certain sense, he's always been afraid—of fame, of mediocrity, of demands on him, of being stereotyped or pigeonholed, of people with questions he wasn't ready to answer.'

Shelton knew only too well that the guard came up whenever he was asked for *answers*, even from those firmly on his side—which was why 'two highly sympathetic writer friends, Al Aronowitz and Pete Karman, [had] dropped articles they were writing ... because of his expressed contempt for much of what is written about him'.

Shelton's own relationship with the mercurial youth had been strained since the Halloween 1964 show, which he had reviewed in less than glowing terms. His Newport '65 review in *Cavalier* was not much better. Hence, perhaps, why their most recent contact had been at the end of a phone, the weekend before Forest Hills.

That conversation came just a few weeks after his latest *Cavalier* piece, in which the former folk critic expressed concern for Dylan's well-being: 'Like other poets, from Rimbaud to Dylan Thomas ... Dylan has a kindred genius for afflicting his body and health. At 24, he already has a prematurely tired, wizened look. He'll brush aside the concern of his friends, indicating that everybody dies sometime.'

If Dylan seemed to be rationing time spent with a man whose apartment once served as a regular crash pad, he now preferred the company of those bebop fans Hentoff and Gleason. It was to the latter he had been confiding his inner fears ever since his transitional fourth album, about which he wrote to Gleason, 'i've conceded the fact there is no understanding of anything. At best, just winks of the eye an that is all i'm lookin for now.'

And when he found himself way out west in December 1965, bound to the wheel of fire, it was to Gleason that he admitted, 'You have to vomit up everything you know ... I vomited it all up and then went out and saw it all again,' consciously evoking the spirit of Arthur Rimbaud and his quest for the 'unknowable regions'. It was a reference the *Times'* folk critic would probably not have recognised, let alone understood.

Gleason, far wider read, was someone unafraid to assert that he could dial into Dylan's intent. When the singer launched into his electrified 'It Ain't Me Babe' at Berkeley, the *Chronicle* critic insisted it was 'a literal demonstration of how the composer wants his music played, [directly] addressed to the recent pop hit by The Turtles'. And it probably was.

The jazz/beat sensibility Gleason had been writing about for years was something Dylan was looking to consciously embrace, which is why he told Gleason that December, 'All the stuff which I had written before, which wasn't song, was just on a piece of toilet paper. When it comes out like that, that's the kind of stuff I never would sing because people just would not be ready for it.' It was another allusion he knew Gleason would immediately get—to Jack Kerouac's 'toilet roll' scroll of *On The Road*.[26]

Gleason was soon championing Dylan at length in print as the natural successor to the beats. At the same time as *Playboy* and *Cavalier* were running Dylan/folk-rock features in their March 1966 issues, Gleason was publishing a ten-page manifesto for Dylan's importance, 'The Children's Crusade', in West Coast pop-culture magazine *Ramparts*.

With room to really write, Gleason dared to grasp the nettle of Dylan's credentials as a poet, addressing an argument which had

---

[26] When this 'original scroll' of Kerouac's beat odyssey was published in 2007, Dylan's words of praise for the book were used as the front-cover blurb.

been raging ever since an article in the *New York Times* the previous December had asked its readers if he was 'Public Writer Number One?' The article canvassed the opinions of a number of anonymous (and therefore irrelevant) 'anti-Dylan' and 'pro-Dylan' critics. But its author, one Thomas Meehan, also garnered quotes from the likes of Louis Simpson, who had won the Pulitzer Prize for Poetry the previous year (the kiss of death for most writers, Simpson included), Stanley Kunitz and W.H. Auden.

If the one real heavyweight in that trio, Auden, admitted, 'I don't know his work at all,' Simpson proved the sniffiest. Employed to teach poetry to college students for most of his working life, he told Meehan he was 'not surprised ... American college students consider him their favourite poet—they don't know anything about poetry'. Kunitz, to his credit, said he listened 'with pleasure to Bob Dylan', but nonetheless considered him 'a writer of verse rather than of poetry'.

Gleason relayed these comments to the archdeacon of City Lights, Lawrence Ferlinghetti. 'They asked the wrong poets,' he simply observed, before describing Dylan as '*the* poet of the sixties'. Ginsberg, the best-known poet of Ferlinghetti's generation, was equally laudatory: 'Dylan has sold out to God. That is to say, his command was to spread his beauty as wide as possible. It was an artistic challenge to see if great art can be done on a jukebox. And he proved it can.'

Yurchenco, in her *Sound & Fury* piece, also published that March, got a quote from the man who coined the term 'Beat generation', John Clellon Holmes, who was in no doubt Dylan mattered: 'He has the authentic mark of the bard on him, and I think it's safe to say that no one, years hence, will be able to understand just what it was like to live in this time without attending to what this astonishingly gifted young man has already achieved.' The beats, almost to a man, recognised Dylan was carrying their baton.

Jazz & Pop had even thrown its hat into the ring with a two-page 'think' piece in its January 1966 issue by Maurice Capel, 'The Man In The Middle'. Capel, who seemed unable to get past Dylan's cultural value to his music, concluded that the 'mythical element in Dylan's personality ... springs solely from his American context, where any deviation from conformity requires rare courage and gives heroic proportions to the simplest act of defiance'.

It must seem strange to modern readers that such a debate— conducted by jazz and pop critics like Hentoff, Gleason and Capel— raged in gentlemen's magazines like *Cavalier* and *Playboy* and jazz/ pop monthlies like *Sound & Fury* and *Ramparts*. But, as of winter 1966, there were no other obvious outlets to write about Dylan in the context of this crazy little thing called *Rock*.

At this momentous juncture there was simply no genuine US rock press, leaving the likes of Jules Siegel, Paul Nelson, Robert Shelton and Ralph J. Gleason scrabbling to find any forum that would publish their ruminations on folk-rock generally and Dylan in particular. Indeed, the search for outlets to express support for Dylan's new music was probably a factor in the birth of rock criticism in a country that still has never had a weekly music press.

And as of the first week of February 1966, America finally had its first rock music magazine: *Crawdaddy*, founded by Paul Williams, a seventeen-year-old student at Swarthmore College, Pennsylvania. The first print-run of the mimeographed 'zine would run to just five hundred copies, but two of its recipients were Paul Simon, of Simon & Garfunkel, and Bob Dylan, the latter of whom read without resentment Williams's review of *The Sounds Of Silence*—with an ill-considered reference to 'the Dylanesque crime of ten minute songs full of everything but the kitchen sink'.

He probably chuckled at Williams's description of the multi-layered 'I'll Keep It With Mine'—which Judy Collins had just recorded with full folk-rock accompaniment—but which Williams felt 'ended very inconclusively, as though Dylan really didn't have anything to say, just a nice tune to play around with'. Already eighteen months old, 'I'll Keep It With Mine' was a song Dylan had still not given up on, recording a second studio version just three days before *Crawdaddy* #1 was mimeographed.

Where Dylan surely nodded his head in agreement was with Williams's conclusion to his review of the Collins single, a reference to his own 45, 'Can You Please Crawl Out Your Window?':

> The music business geniuses will probably look at the charts, notice how poorly Dylan's own single is doing, and announce: 'Don't play

it, the Dylan trend is over, instrumentals based on TV commercials
are the new trend.' I've never seen a group of prophets so utterly
unable to see the trees for the forest.

Unbeknownst to Williams, Dylan had already recorded an equally
incendiary follow-up 45, 'One Of Us Must Know'; unbeknownst to
Dylan, it would fare even worse in the charts.

Maybe these 'music business geniuses' were smarter than they
seemed. Perhaps the year of Dylan had passed and Tom Paxton's 'folk
rot' prophecy—'It isn't folk, it isn't very good rock … [and] when
it stops paying it will disappear'—was starting to come true. Paying
heed to such concerns, though, was the last thing on Dylan's mind.
He owed Columbia another folk-rock album—one that would codify
his wild mercury period for all time.

5. DOING THE TENNESSEE WALTZ
[January 21–April 8 1966]

Happy Traum: *Did you ever make a song just to be a single?*
Bob Dylan: *Yes I did. But it wasn't very amusing because it took me away from the album. The album commands a different sort of attention than a single does. Singles just pile up and pile up; they're only good for the present. The trend in the old days was that unless you had a hit single, you couldn't do very well with an album. And when you had that album, you just filled it up.*

—SING OUT! INTERVIEW, CONDUCTED JUNE–JULY 1968

Jann Wenner: *How come you never made an album with [The Hawks]?*
Bob Dylan: *We tried. We cut a couple of sides in the old New York Columbia studios. … Right after 'Positively 4th Street', we cut some singles and they didn't really get off the ground. You oughta hear 'em. You know, you could find 'em … They didn't even make it on the charts. Consequently, I've not been back on the charts. … I never did much care for singles, 'cause you have to pay so much attention to them. Unless you make your whole album full of singles, you have to make them separately. So I didn't really think about them too much that way. But playing with The Band was a natural thing. We have a real different sound. Real different. But it wasn't like anything heard. I heard one of the records recently. … It was on a jukebox. 'Please Crawl Out Your Window'.*
Jann Wenner: *That was one of them? What were the others?*
Bob Dylan: *There were some more songs out of that same session [sic] … 'Sooner Or Later'—that was on* Blonde On Blonde. *That's one of my favorite songs.*

—THE ROLLING STONE INTERVIEW, CONDUCTED JUNE 26 1969

By January 21 1966, when Dylan and The Hawks resumed recording 'sides' (which is how songs were termed in Dylan's still-active 1961 contract, as 'sides' of a 78 rpm record), all concerned knew 'Can You Please Crawl Out Your Window?' was not destined to replicate the impact of the two previous singles. Dylan's 1969 explanation for this failure was that it was 'real different … it wasn't like anything heard', which in a sonic sense it was.

But it was also his third consecutive single to poke fun at some poor unfortunate soul swimming in metaphorical lava. Perhaps the audience felt they had been here before—or just longed to hear

Kooper swirling away behind Robert the Rocker. Dylan, though, was just warming up the magma. The viciousness at the core of his lyrics since 'Rolling Stone' seemed to have grown in direct proportion to his fame (and, less coincidentally, his amphetamine use).

As such, when Dylan and co. assembled at Studio A that January day, the first—indeed, the only—order of business was a song so vicious its example sustained Elvis Costello through at least his first three albums:

> She'll be standin' on the bar soon
> With a fish head an' a harpoon
> An' a fake beard plastered on her brow
> You'd better do somethin' quick
> She's your lover now.

Try as they might, they ended up driving her and the lover over the cliff. Fourteen takes with The Hawks failed to finish the song once. After just three takes Dylan's exasperation spilled over in a most uncharacteristic verbal outburst, 'I don't give a fuck if it's good or not, just play it together, make it all together.' But no matter how much The Hawks tried to speed it up, slow it down, build and build, or grind it out, this paranoid speed-freak machine-gun vision of a psychosexual ménage à trois just would not come. And neither would a definitive arrangement.

In the end, someone (probably Grossman) can be heard on the session saying, 'Why don't you take a break?' as Dylan openly admits, 'I can't hear the song any more.' He then takes to the piano where he records a complete solo version, the vocal mournful and slow, the complete opposite of the singer wired to the mains throughout the rest of the session. An exhausted Bob Johnston wonders aloud, 'Last take, right?'

So what went so horribly wrong? Partly, it was Dylan's own methodology, founded on a determination to always record a performance, not make a record. And partly, it was the difference between working with a technician like Tom Wilson and a company man like Bob Johnston. Wilson would surely have insisted they inserted the correct final verse onto the end of a nearly there take 14.

According to the credits on the *Cutting Edge* set, one eyewitness to the session was Michael Bloomfield (presumably the 'Michael John(?)' listed in Michael Krogsgaard's sessionography). I can't hear his distinctive tone, so his contribution was probably confined to thoughts not deeds. A decade later, when interviewed by Larry Sloman about those 1965–66 sessions, his memorable description applied to the *Highway 61* sessions—now seems more suited to a session where he was merely an innocent bystander:

Mike Bloomfield: The producer did not tell people what to play or have a sound in mind. ... I was there, man, I'm telling you it was a result of chucklefucking, of people stepping on each other's dicks until it came out right.

Except in this case it didn't come out right, and bearing the brunt of Bob's rising vexation is the poor drummer, Sandy Konikoff. A suggestion of Robertson's, Konikoff was the intended replacement for Bobby Gregg—who never wanted to be a touring drummer—and it was immediately apparent he was out of his depth. In fact, this would be his first and last session with Dylan, though he would play all the shows over the next two months, until the frontman's *original* choice could be secured. Meanwhile, Bobby Gregg would be recalled when studio work resumed in four days' time.

The main misjudgement was Dylan's. He had arrived at the January 21 session without a Plan B. At previous Columbia sessions, when he got stuck on a song, he would switch to another, returning to the former refreshed and refocused. As Kramer said of the *Bringing It All Back Home* sessions a year earlier, 'If he tried something that didn't go well, he would put it off. ... In this way, he never [got] bogged down—he just kept on going.'

But he had seemingly arrived at Studio A this January day with just the one song to record. No one envisaged it taking all afternoon and evening, and still failing to hit the target. Even the fifteen versions of the song recorded do not tell the full story of the day's work. According to the studio logs, they began work at 2:30 in the afternoon and did not finish until after midnight, which suggests the song was worked up from scratch and a lot of the tutoring went on without Columbia tape rolling.

If the January 21 session was an experience Dylan did not want to repeat—but would, a number of times—the next session, four days later, was also essentially devoted to a single song. This time, though, Dylan *had* hedged his bets, inviting Bobby Gregg, organist Al Kooper, pianist Paul Griffin and jazz bassist William Lee to sit in—or so the AFM (American Federation of Musicians) log sheets suggest. All four had prior experience of Dylan's working methods, though it seems Lee sat out the session and collected his fee, having presumably been summoned there as possible backup. As a result, Danko and Robertson were the only Hawks plugged in when Dylan and the boys warmed up with a straightforward R&B romp, 'Leopard-Skin Pill-Box Hat', which seemingly played to The Hawks' strengths—hence its immediate introduction into the live set, where it remained for the duration, growing ever brassier balls.

After two semi-improvised takes of this lightweight filler, Dylan decided to get down to the serious business of 'One Of Us Must Know'.

Already, it seems, Dylan had earmarked the song for his next single—and maybe for inclusion in the live set. But although 'One Of Us Must Know' seems to have made its live debut on February 5, it disappeared almost as quickly from the shows as from the charts. 'Leopard-Skin Pill-Box Hat' might have made for a better follow-up to 'Can You Please Crawl Out Your Window?'. It was the kind of R&B Dylan had explored thoroughly on *Highway 61 Revisited*; and the lyrics, a hoot from start to finish, might have provided a much-needed shift in the public persona away from a man with a grudge.

To capture 'One Of Us Must Know's untamed self required another marathon all-of-the-day-and-all-of-the-night set of sessions (from 2:30pm to 2:30am, if the studio log can be trusted), and something like twenty-four takes. Capture it they did, but it was a damn close thing.

When Dylan and some other companions of the road arrived at WBAI in the middle of the night with an acetate of the song for DJ Bob Fass to hear, the singer openly admitted, 'It's a rush job. We've just made it. It's a single. We went in to make an album, you know, [but] this one's the only thing we came out with in three days. So [I'm] gonna have to forget about the album for right now.' It was a surprisingly unguarded admission by a clearly frustrated recording artist.

The WBAI appearance may actually have occurred two nights

later—as the reference to 'three days' in the studio suggests—since Dylan returned to Studio A on January 27, even though his heart wasn't in it from the off. Beginning with another one-verse demo, this one called 'Lunatic Princess', he recorded an insert each for 'Leopard-Skin Pill-Box Hat' and 'One Of Us Must Know' and led the band through a single-take busk of 'I'll Keep It With Mine'. Nothing was deemed usable; but rather than revisit 'I'll Keep It With Mine'—this time with an intro and an outro that didn't sound made up on the spot—everyone agreed to call it a night.

And with that decision went any formal role for The Hawks on his forthcoming album. It had taken Dylan four months and a succession of aborted sessions to admit to himself that this combination wasn't working in the studio, no matter how much The Hawks brought to the shows. But admit it he finally did, privately at the end of January and then to Robert Shelton on a flight to Denver in March: 'Oh, I was really down. I mean, in ten recording sessions, man, we didn't get one song … it was the band. But, you see, I didn't know that. I didn't want to think that.'

At least Columbia had another single to keep any commercial momentum going, Grossman having drummed it into Dylan that he was now a pop star and 'unless you had a hit single, you couldn't do very well with an album'. But Dylan soon came to the realisation that he was an album artist, always had been, always would be. 'One Of Us Must Know' would be the second consecutive single that failed to secure a live slot and the last Dylan song ever recorded *as* a single (film soundtracks excepted).

Columbia placed the usual *Billboard* ad and shipped the single to the shops but the non-appearance of 'One Of Us Must Know' in the Hot Hundred remains one of the great chart mysteries. In the country where his face stared out from magazine covers and his concerts continued to sell out, the song never even dented *Billboard*'s lower reaches. Given his public profile, the inevitable radio play and the fact that the song was a hit all over Europe, Britain included, how come it failed so spectacularly Stateside?

Dylan didn't know why, and he couldn't afford to care. The Hawks simply resumed their day job— gigging. Columbia's prized possession would now have to make an album in his rapidly depleting downtime. This time he had decided to visit the home of all country music stations. Although the concert schedule that February/March was again demanding, he needed to find a slot (or two) and head south, not for a winter break but to make his third album in fifteen months.

★ ★ ★

As the tour resumed in early February, the fans still bayed for more (and the ex-fans, less) of the new folk-rock at concerts in Louisville, Westchester, Pittsburgh, Memphis, Richmond and Norfolk, as the Lodestar continued racking up the miles and dissenting voices continued to barrack the band. They resumed rolling in Kentucky only to encounter a dose of southern inhospitality worthy of comment by a local reviewer:

> Near the end of a concert at Convention Center last night, an exuberant fan yelled out, 'We want Bob Dylan!' What made the outburst remarkable was the fact that the man singing on the stage was Dylan himself, the man with the sleepy eyes, Medusa-like hair and gutsy delivery. ... This was 'folk-rock', the mutation of two musical forms. Some, like the collegian who cried out last night for 'Dylan', felt betrayed by the change. Others, particularly teenagers, found in Dylan a new idol. Both varieties of Dylan were on stage last night here. A minority of the fans appeared to favor the folk-singing, or 'real' Dylan.

'Twas another year and another drummer, but the format remained unchanged and the hostility of the few undimmed. As *Louisville Times* reporter Gerald Solomon noted, 'After the intermission, Dylan returned, with two electric guitars, a piano, electric organ and drums—it [was] what the folks came to hear. ... Flashbulbs popped. Police were constantly shooing back into their seats youngsters who rushed to the base of the stage to take pictures of their idol. It was a night for the long-hair set who conform rigidly to the sartorial styles of the rock group.'

Dylan was still the darling of the folk-rock set, even after he made them sit through a fifty-minute acoustic set. At least the sound was good. *Courier-Journal* reviewer Phyllis Funke was listening carefully enough to almost correctly quote two stand-out lines from the unreleased 'Freeze Out': 'Name me one who isn't a parasite and I'll say a prayer for him' and 'Mona Lisa must have had the highway blues from the way she smiles'. But try as she might, she had to admit, 'The words didn't really seem to be the point last night.' Or any other night.

The singer was in more familiar territory the following evening. A gig in Westchester required no plane. Just a commuter-train ride away from Manhattan, the New York suburban set gave Dylan's new music a suitably respectful reception:

> Dylan to today's youth is a guitar-wielding Buddha, a James Joyce of song, a Holden Caulfield of the 60s. One girl said: 'He seems to know the few essentials worth knowing and he goofs so beautifully on the rest.' ... No longer does he stand straight and give voice to the emotional causes of our time. His words are more personal. He sings of alienation, absurdity and unselfrighteous honesty. You mob The Beatles; you sling the works at The Rolling Stones. When Dylan sings you listen silently and inwardly. Saturday night's audience was no different. One long-haired youth in tight jeans, boots and brown suede vest sat sucking his thumb. ... All listened.

A not-so-hardy taper recorded the entire acoustic set in down-a-coalmine mono but only stuck it out for two electric songs, thus missing, apparently, a second outing for 'Leopard-Skin Pill-Box Hat' and a one-off live 'One Of Us Must Know' with The Hawks.

S/he did at least capture the opening song of the electric set. 'Long Distance Operator' had already been discarded. At Westchester there was instead a brand-new original, 'Tell Me, Momma', as opener, compounding any confusion with its deliberately garbled vocal, which, even on multiple soundboards from the world tour, never seemed to resolve its cutup status.

For new drummer Sandy Konikoff, having been obliged to sit out the studio recording of 'Leopard-Skin Pill-Box Hat', it was certainly a baptism of brimstone. By the following night in Pittsburgh, he was struggling to keep up. As Dylan launched into 'Positively 4th Street' and 'Like A Rolling Stone' at the climax of a generally well-received electric set, Konikoff threw himself into the songs with gusto but lagged behind the beat—a sure way to lose Dylan's respect.[27]

---

[27] Konikoff probably had no more than a couple of days' rehearsals, one of which may possibly have been at Studio A on January 31, a supposedly cancelled session date.

Again, a tape-toting ticket holder turned up for a show with only forty-five minutes of cassette tape to spare, and so another opportunity to document a full Hawks set passed by. The Pittsburgh tape at least has the virtue of being the one audio document from the winter 1966 shows that does not make one's ears bleed.

What the two electric songs the Pennsylvania taper did capture confirmed that the Larry Williams who reviewed the Memphis show four days later was not fit to bear the same name as the R&B songwriter responsible for 'Bony Moronie', 'Dizzy, Miss Lizzy' and 'Slow Down'. This Mr Williams thought he heard someone who, were it not 'for the poetry of some of the songs and his mid-Western twang mixing a sardonic wit with a driving electric guitar … might have been Dave Clark. He shouted and showed some of the other tendencies to mumble and substitute beat for content that other rock and rollers have.'

The audience had no such problem 'interpreting' Dylan's music, or joining in the revelries. Such was their enthusiasm that even during the acoustic set, whenever Dylan 'whanged a sad guitar and manipulated a harmonica that wailed like a lonesome whistle—the girls wailed back. And the boys, the ones in Renaissance wigs, whistled and hollered inanities.'

Having been booked to play Memphis on the tenth, and scheduled to start recording in Nashville, two-hundred miles from Memphis, three and a half days later, one might have thought Dylan would take a few days off to work on some songs. Instead, his tour schedule crisscrossed the states of the union, heading west to Virginia for shows in Richmond and Norfolk before returning to base to drop off The Hawks—Robbie Robertson excepted—for a little rest and recreation, then doubling back to Music City, USA.

Dylan arrived in Nashville on February 14 with Robbie Robertson and Al Kooper in tow, hoping to find the key to his next *Highway*. Choosing to record in Nashville was not some whim on his part. Nor was it his response to the cajoling of current producer Bob Johnston, as the latter consistently claimed in later life. It had been an option Dylan had been considering even before Tom Wilson's last session, the previous June—the breakthrough that was 'Like A Rolling Stone'.

The person who first pushed Dylan to try the place out was someone he was far closer to, and respected rather more, than the staff producer with the southern drawl. Johnny Cash had informed an English reporter, the week before 'Like A Rolling Stone' was cut, that he had been talking to his friend in folk, and 'there's a chance he may come to Nashville and let me produce an album with him if the A&R men agree. I've got my own ideas about the Nashville sound and I'd like to try it with Bob.'

Though this intriguing prospect went nowhere, Dylan had acted on the idea, setting up a session in Nashville in November 1965, only for it to be cancelled, probably because he had no new songs he wanted to record. At around the same time, the possibility of Dylan recording his next album in Nashville was being mentioned in a profile by the *Herald Tribune*'s William Bender, drawing on information which can only have come from the Dylan camp:

> Where he'll be this time next year is anybody's guess. ... At the moment he would like to take guitars, harmonicas and 'electricity' to Nashville, Tennessee, to get what is known in the trade as the 'Nashville Sound'—something that has to do with 'presence' of a recording's sound, but that also depends on the superb country-western and rhythm and blues instrumentalists who now gravitate to Nashville for the big record dates.

This was very much inside information. Bender was clearly in the know, to apply the very reasoning that three months later finally brought Bobby to Tennessee: the quality of its session musicians and the 'presence' they introduced to any recording, country, rock, or both.

The musicians also enjoyed a reputation for being laid-back, a trait Dylan was about to sorely test. The songwriter who turned up in mid-February had seemingly completed just one more song in the two and a half weeks since he last tried the patience of musicians, producer and engineers in New York. His second Beatles parody in six months, 'Fourth Time Around', showed he meant it when he told Hentoff his 'sympathy runs to the lame and crippled'. It also provided proof, were it needed, that he wasn't about to change his studio methodology to make life easier for himself. Only a complete live studio performance would do for the Midwest maverick.

The Nashville musicians were happy to be paid double the standard session rate. They had already been told by producer Bob Johnston to keep playing, no matter what. In fact, he told them he would fine any musician who stopped playing before the other Bob did.

What they did not expect was to work from two in the afternoon till 9:30 in the evening on a single song—especially one they nailed on the second take, after a single false start. It was Dylan who loused up the lyrics on the final verse of an otherwise gorgeous, near-perfect performance (for which he apologised profusely afterward). Johnston knew better than to ask Dylan to simply re-do the last verse as an insert. So eighteen more merry-go-round rides were deemed necessary to arrive at the same page.

As day turned to night, a series of sessions on February 14–15 were spent reworking two songs he had already worked over with The Hawks, the first of which was 'Visions Of Johanna', which the band all but nailed first time around and Dylan nailed on the third. This time the words did not get away from him, and the little liar who had claimed, the previous year, he had given up any attempt at perfection achieved it nonetheless.

Just when it seemed everything was falling into place, 'Leopard-Skin Pill-Box Hat', a song that did not really play to these down-home dudes' strengths, singularly failed to find the groove it had in concert even after thirteen attempts.

Remaking these two tracks suggests Dylan had already rejected the New York versions in his mind, though not the songs themselves. But more songs were needed. And fast. When work resumed the following afternoon, the whole session was spent reworking another song recorded at the final New York session. The song in question was nearly two years old, and the version cut nine times was instrumental.

Given Dylan's aversion to overdubs, one can only conclude that he was thinking of including 'I'll Keep It With Mine' as an instrumental on *Blonde On Blonde*. He certainly had a history of recording them, just not of releasing them. Even this gesture would end up a case in point.

The song may have been a way of keeping the band focused while he finished the lyrics to the song he was really looking to record that day—an eleven-minute symphony of sound, 'Sad-Eyed Lady Of The Lowlands'.

To Dylan's great relief he discovered 'in Nashville, people sit around if they want to. If they want to make good records, they just sit around and wait all night till you're ready. But they won't do that in New York, they get bored, and talk, and bring you down some kind of way.' The above comment, made just a couple of months later (to an Australian radio journalist), was the first intimation that these Nashville session-men had got to hone their card-playing skills for a couple of hours while Dylan (re)wrote his next song.

In conversation with Jann Wenner, the songwriter seemed to suggest he never intended the side-four song to be so long, or to get away from him so: 'It started out as just a little thing ... but I got carried away, somewhere along the line. I just sat down at a table and started writing. At the session itself. And I ... couldn't stop. After a period of time, I forgot what it was all about, and I started trying to get back to the beginning.'

With that off-hand comment Dylan triggered a legend—one the union card-carrying, card-shark Nashville cats were happy to vouchsafe (and even embellish) until it entered Southern lore. By 2015, the guitarist that day had turned the story into a synopsis for a whole movie of the mind:

Charlie McCoy: We sat there from 2pm till 4am the next morning and we never played a note. This was unheard of, everybody was on the clock. We couldn't believe it. You're figuring out ways to stay awake because he might decide at any minute that he wanted to record and we wanted to be ready for him. I don't know how many games of ping-pong we must have played. Then at 4am he came up with 'Sad-Eyed Lady Of The Lowlands', an eleven-minute ballad. And everybody's sitting there saying, 'Please don't let me make a mistake.' He just started playing it and kind of left it up to us to decide what to do. Every recording, there was no conversation.

Dylan didn't help matters when he informed Hubert Saal in 1968, 'On *Blonde On Blonde* I wrote out all the songs in the studio. The musicians played cards, I wrote out a song, we'd do it, they'd go back to their game and I'd write out another song.' In fact, the only lyric he worked on extensively at the sessions *before* recording even commenced was 'Sad-Eyed Lady Of The Lowlands'. On this occasion it proved a rather good idea, because the song was recorded in three takes—all of them complete, and near indistinguishable in quality—with a brief rehearsal of the basic structure between takes one and two.

But if the musicians thought the New York artist was about to embrace a different working methodology, they were mistaken. The *recording* of 'Stuck Inside Of Mobile' on the third and final day would occupy them all from six in the evening till seven the following morning, without any sustained breaks for a rewrite and a game or two of draw.

Again, it was mainly Dylan who stumbled and fell fifteen out of eighteen times they tried to get a take, but in the end they arrived at an eighteenth take (logged as take 15) that almost replicated the perfection of 'Visions' seventy-two hours earlier. It had been a long hard grind at times but at seven on the seventeenth Dylan emerged into the cold light of a fine Music Row morning with an album of long songs in the can, and a no longer worried mind.[28]

★ ★ ★

Whatever the distractions, writing in the studio seems to have unlocked something in the songwriter. After months of accruing images, Dylan was brimming again with ideas for songs. But if the unused New York material had now been jettisoned, a second set of Nashville sessions would be needed. However, the wheel on which he was now bound cut him very little slack. Thankfully, a four-day slot in mid-March would be all that he needed to complete his increasingly grand architectural plan for a *double* album.

Meantime, he had a return date in Connecticut the evening after his all-night Nashville session, before catching some much-needed shuteye as the Lodestar headed north by northwest for shows in Ottawa and Montreal.

North of the border, a Dylan concert was still big news. In both cities the press sent emissaries to report on proceedings. In Montreal, national radio station CBC was also granted a rare boon: a short interview backstage during the interval.

---

[28] Had Dylan released a single album featuring the likes of 'Sad-Eyed Lady', 'Stuck Inside Of Mobile', 'Visions Of Johanna' and 'She's Your Lover Now' in 1966, there would have been very little room for anything else.

The two-part format still afforded Dylan the opportunity to switch personalities with such vim that most reviewers were taken aback. *Ottawa Citizen* reviewer Dennis Foley found out from an attendant that, 'between halves, Dylan rejuvenated himself ... with great quantities of tea larded with honey'. But caffeine alone was not jumpstarting this folk-rocker, and no brand of tea could explain the transformation, here, there and everywhere, which overtook the folk-rock frontman after the interval. It certainly astonished the *Ottawa Journal*'s Sandy Gardiner:

> Dressed in a grey suit and blue-striped shirt Dylan, looking tired and badly in need of a good meal, devoted the first half of his act to the purist folk songs which brought him from obscurity to fame. ... The only song he included that was a success in the pop market was 'Mr Tambourine Man' highlighted by an almost baroque harmonica break. [But] when he returned to the stage after a short intermission on Saturday, he was accompanied by The Hawks, a five-piece Toronto rock'n'roll group who were once Ronnie Hawkins's backing group. To a pounding folk-blues beat Dylan came up to the microphones playing rhythm on an electric guitar and tried to deliver more of his musical messages. And this is where the new Dylan was unveiled 'live' to Ottawa. The Hawks played as though they were the featured attraction. They had a great sound but you can be good without being loud. Dylan didn't seem to mind the racket. Despite all the commotion on stage, he remained nonchalant—a man wrapped up in his music, oblivious of what was around him.

Foley concurred with his rival reviewer regarding Dylan's overt enjoyment of the electric half, while still complaining about 'the traditionally poor [Auditorium] acoustics [which] made reception difficult ... [and] if perception was difficult during the solo stint, it was nigh impossible during the second half of the show with the big sound of The Hawks of Toronto as a backdrop'. Dylan agreed with the Canadian citizen. He even suggested to Jules Siegel that the February Ottawa concert had the worst sound in the world—Vancouver excepted.[29] Plans were soon afoot to get a soundman he could trust on the forthcoming world tour, Richard Alderson

---

[29] On the other hand, when Dylan played two shows in Ottawa in June 1990, the sound was the best I have ever heard at a Dylan concert.

having been responsible for making him sound good as far back as the Gaslight Cafe in 1962.

The Ottawa fans were unfazed by 'the traditionally poor acoustics' and seemed to lap it up. Last November's Toronto shows seemed but a distant memory. If Foley had arrived hoping for the evidence that it was Dylan's 'folk–rock' sound which had 'sparked unkind criticism from folk-song purists', he was to be disappointed. None of the purists seem to have braved the Auditorium's acoustic graveyard to hear half a show. Why would they? By now everyone who actually paid for a ticket knew the given format. So when, in Ottawa, Dylan, 'en route to his dressing room after his first set of songs of protest and affliction … muttered something to someone about announcing that the concert was not over … everyone present seemed to [already] know that there would be more'.

It seemed to be just the media who continued to express surprise (and dismay) when Dylan put all those amps and electrical instruments to use replicating an approximate version of his last album and recent hit singles. Montreal's media would prove equally mystified:

> He offered, during the evening, not one event, but two—so different were the first and second parts of the program. In the beginning he wandered on to the stage, as if he thought he was somewhere else, carrying a folk guitar and a glass of water with a harmonica hanging around his neck. He performed in a wailing voice gentle introspective verse of remarkable literary quality. … Then came the second half. In it he took his burgeoning talent and ground it out under his stamping heel. He did it together with a rock and roll quintet. The Hawks. At first it seemed that the amplifiers on the accompanying instruments had accidentally been turned up too loud. For it was impossible to hear anything he sang, or rather shouted, as if trying to be heard above them. But it seems that he had carefully prepared the balance and the volume at rehearsals during the afternoon. Suddenly, instead of an unexpected phenomenon of new, young poetic self-expression, there was another ye[ah]-ye[ah] group, and not such a very good one at that.

These intemperate thoughts from the *Montreal Gazette*'s Zelda Heller failed to speak to a state capital divided by a common language and a widening generation gap. The *Montreal Star*'s star reporter

Wouter de Wet felt equally out of touch on finding that '95 percent of the audience, many of whom [were] looking a little weird like Dylan himself, were under twenty-five. ... One wonders just how many truly understood the complexity of the artist's intent. ... His are very "in" songs, often about very "out" people, brought forward in an almost surrealist style.' But whereas Heller heard nothing significant in the scaldingly loud second set, de Wet experienced a minor epiphany:

> Dylan is not only a musician—he is also a poet. And I found it a great pity that most of the lyrics were drowned out by the loudness of the music. But one can't have it your own way all the way, because a very essential part of Dylan's genius is the way in which he uses electrically boosted music to add impact to his performance. I have long been a sworn enemy of any music that depends for its effectiveness on electric boosting. ... But somehow he has managed to turn these essentially vulgar media into something vital and exciting.

De Wet was not the only Montreal media-hound to have viewed his assignment that night with trepidation but emerged pleasantly surprised. Also there under duress, uninformed and unhappy, was CBC reporter Martin Bronstein, who arrived 'on this freezing Sunday afternoon' to find the stage door 'mobbed. In three years of interviewing performers from various disciplines, I had never witnessed such stage door hysteria.'

Drafted in at the last minute to interview the folk-rock star, Bronstein by his own admission was 'a dedicated jazz fan, weaned on Louis Armstrong ... Duke Ellington, Dizzy Gillespie and Oscar Peterson. When I listened to singers, they were Lena Horne, Sarah Vaughan ... and Nina Simone.' For such a 'dedicated jazz fan', even the rare privilege of watching Dylan from the wings went unappreciated as he considered the acoustic half beyond the pale:

> A new aural experience is the kind way to describe the sound that met my ears backstage. Caterwauling is a little closer to my true feelings. I walked to the wings to see what catastrophe had occurred immediately prior to my arrival. Center stage, bathed in a strong white spotlight, was this skinny Jewish kid with an Afro playing a guitar and producing a nasal ululation. There were

lyrics—he was, after all, the poet of the New Generation—but the accent, enunciation and repetitive undulation of the 'tune' made them impossible to make out. And then he would breathe into this thing strapped around his neck, creating a sort of musical asthma. I suddenly had the feeling that this was all a put-on, a huge practical joke. But then the song ended, and the audience reaction reached a decibel level that would have drowned out several Concordes. This was real; this was something, in its own way, bigger than The Beatles, I was realizing, and somehow it had passed me by.

After the acoustic Dylan was done, Bronstein was ushered into the lion's den, wholly unaware of the singer's reputation as someone who 'enjoyed cutting [journalists] to pieces'. Even before he began 'asking silly questions', he seemed unsure how to pronounce the surname of this someone on everyone's tongues.

Somehow, he was not served up on a platter. Instead, Dylan remained 'extremely courteous' throughout the twelve-minute interview, 'and tried to honestly answer my queries', even after Bronstein asked him whether he had taken his name from Dylan Thomas: 'No, no. That's a rumor made up by people who like to simplify things … I just don't like to refer to myself as a poet because it puts you in a category with a lot of funny people.'

Bronstein relaxed enough to wonder aloud what it was like to cope with the kind of fame he had witnessed at the stage door, and received a surprisingly unguarded reply: 'I never really realized it before six months ago that I couldn't go into a restaurant. I didn't really know it was that bad … It does tricks with your head when you can't go some place … and my whole life I'm used to staying out all night in public places. It's all gone now … [But] I have no right to resent people that come up to me and bother me.'

As Bronstein later wrote, 'I struggled to make the interview last as long as seemed decent.' But he was fast running out of questions, and insights. Finally he asked, 'What particular song would you say you remember as being a breakthrough for you—was it "Blowin' In The Wind"?' Dylan must have rolled his mind's eye at the mention of a protest song he wrote in his minority, gave to another Grossman client, and formally disowned three years earlier. But rather than ridicule the radio veteran, he opened a door in his mind:

Bob Dylan: [When I wrote] 'Blowin' In The Wind' … I was just a kid, you know. … [Then there was] 'Mr Tambourine Man', I was very close to that song. I kept it off my third album just because I felt too close to it … [but] if you're talking about what breakthrough is for me, I would have to say, speaking totally, it would be 'Like A Rolling Stone', because I wrote that after I'd quit. I'd literally quit singing and playing, and I found myself writing this song, this story, this long piece of vomit about twenty pages long, and out of it I took 'Like A Rolling Stone' and made it as a single. And I'd never written anything like that before and it suddenly came to me that that was what I should do, you know. … After writing that, I wasn't interested in writing a novel, or a play or anything.

The unscathed reporter left the dressing room with a remarkable record of the day Dylan decided not to invoke Mr Send-Up. He then 'went back to the studio, did a quick edit ready for the next morning's magazine program. It wasn't used. "The guy was practically inarticulate, couldn't use it," said the producer, a man of my own generation.' The tape would only emerge after Dylan disappeared upstate, having seemingly quit for good.

The sensitive young man Bronstein had encountered backstage must have wondered why he bothered. But bother he did—and he would continue to do so. On the road ahead, he was always looking for a way to communicate to his ever-expanding audience directly, without someone else's sidespin. He even invited the young college kid who had just produced rock's first fanzine, *Crawdaddy*, to come backstage at the first Philadelphia show, four days on from Montreal. He was hoping the boy was emblematic of that audience. It turned out he was:

Paul Williams: I saw a notice in the Philadelphia paper that Bob Dylan would perform at the Academy of Music on February 24 and 25. So I mailed the first two issues to the theater asking for a press ticket to the concerts. As a last minute afterthought, I added a P.S. … asking for an interview with Mr Dylan. … [That] day when I walked into the freshman dorm … another student shouted, 'Hey Williams!! Bob Dylan called you!' I returned the call to … a room in a Philadelphia hotel. His assistant told me the theater had given them my package … and that Bob read the magazines and liked them.

I was invited to come to his hotel room that afternoon. ... Dylan was friendly and open and talkative. At one point he kidded me by pointing to a line in my Simon and Garfunkel review ... and raising an eyebrow questioningly. ... I didn't interview him. I didn't own a tape recorder and I was so pleased by his friendliness and respect for what I was trying to do with my magazine that I didn't want to spoil things by playing 'journalist'. He told me about obscure blues singers I should check out. He mentioned his long-time interest in rock'n'roll as though affirming, and even indicating that he felt affirmed by, my thesis that rock music was as worthy of being talked about seriously as any other musical form.

Though it might frustrate those (including myself) who want details of what the pair talked about that day, Williams was right to trust his instincts and avoid spoiling the moment by playing 'journalist'. For now it was the only reliable way to meet the man with his guard down. As Dylan had informed Margaret Steen the previous November, 'If I met you in a bar somewhere ... we could talk better, I know it. But you're a reporter.'

Such situations always made him wary and inclined to weigh each word in the balance. But the opposite was also true. So when another reporter succeeded in sneaking backstage during the fraught British tour the following May, the fact he was prepared to leave his pencil in his pocket resulted in a memorable conversation from which he gleaned: 'Dylan hates reporters. He won't accept the fact that fame like his makes him a public spectacle ... This wasn't an interview, he emphasized, "We're just gonna have a lil' talkie!" And lil' talkie we had. ... He talked more freely now.' Such was always the way.

In Paul Williams's case, the aspiring rock writer came away with a renewed sense of vocation and a determination to set the world straight on the subject of 'folk-rock', a phrase Dylan doubtless sneered at throughout their hotel room conversation. Sure enough, the following issue of *Crawdaddy* led with an article entitled 'Folk, Rock, and other four-letter words', which invoked Dylan's name repeatedly. One can almost hear Dylan's (non-put-on) voice here:

> The paranoiac need of modern man for a label for anything that comes
> near him resulted ... in the term 'folk-rock' to signify pop music with

strong folk influences. Originally, 'folk-rock' meant pop music that used actual folk material; later, anything folk-influenced that retained a heavy beat, and still later, anything having anything to do with folk that happened to sell in the pop market. The term 'folk-rock' is a silly one, and has grown sillier over the months ... [but] the press and the music trade have ... chosen to believe that folk mixed with r'n'r is the big new trend. There are a lot of 'Folk-rock is a way of life' articles appearing hither and yon, signed by the same old bunch of interpreters who really believe that if you speak the language of the teenager you understand him. The mass media are currently explaining to the mass audience how Bob Dylan, the new pied piper, with his electric flute, is leading the youth of America out of the coffeehouses and into the echo chambers of plugged-in music. Hogwash! ... Folk is folk and rock is rock, and if the twain should meet, and exchange notes, fine. But that's no reason to unite them forever.

But whenever a tape recorder or notepad appeared, caution became his middle name. Even a high-school pupil who had won a *Datebook* contest and was allowed to ask Dylan half a dozen innocuous questions when he came to Miami in early March was not to be trusted; after she asked directly, 'I read that you were secretly married. True or false?' the put-upon Dylan, not imbued with the spirit of George Washington, told the cub reporter, 'False. I don't know where this junk comes from.'

Meanwhile, Sara stayed in her room in the Chelsea Hotel, with their son Jesse and her daughter Maria. Which was probably wise. She and her groom didn't need to stoke the fires of scuttlebutt further. Dylan had doubtless already been warned that a Minneapolis journalist, P.M. Clepper, was looking to publish a 'timely' exposé of the man for the Minneapolis Sunday paper his mother read.

Clepper's March 1966 article proceeded to claim that, when Dylan had played Minneapolis the previous fall, 'His parents came down from Hibbing, but Bob Dylan didn't want the Zimmermans backstage afterwards. He left immediately, got into his private plane and once again fled to the safety of his new self-created image.' This fantasy would reappear in *Variety* four months later, as reported fact.

Not surprisingly, such tall tales, in tandem with the 'powerful medicine' he was taking, were making Dylan ever more paranoid, increasingly hard to gauge and less approachable as the US tour

progressed. The only two bona fide journalists he spoke to that month
had previously championed his new music in print: old friend Bob
Shelton and *Cavalier*'s Jules Siegel.

Though the interviews the pair secured were radically different
in tone—with the old friend receiving the larger number of bum
steers—the pair were afforded one experience in common: the
opportunity to hear the songs Dylan had just recorded in Nashville.
He had finally completed an album made in the shade of *Highway
61*, only to discover the iridescent *Blonde On Blonde* shining just as
brightly and for half as long again.

★ ★ ★

Second time around, Dylan arrived in Tennessee on March 7 bringing
a sheaf of papers containing, as per, partially typed, hand-corrected
drafts for the likes of 'Absolutely Sweet Marie', 'Most Likely You Go
Your Way', 'I Want You' and 'Just Like A Woman', as well as the barest
of outlines for 'Obviously Five Believers' and 'Pledging My Time'.
None of the songs seemed wholly formed, though most of them had
recognizable song structures and a pop sensibility. It was just a case
of juggling lines and writing middle eights, which he had decided to
do in his Nashville motel room, not on Music Row.

Whilst there he lost his motel blues and found his musical mojo,
crafting some of his most memorable melodies when not bussing
his way through a couple of Chess-infused pieces. (The riff-driven
groove of 'Obviously Five Believers' he lifted from Junior Wells's 'You
Don't Love Me Baby', perhaps one of those 'obscure' blues singers
he had suggested Paul Williams 'check out'. But this was no obscure
Vocalion 78: the album it came from, *Hoodoo Man Blues*, had been
out barely three months.)

Dylan had finally worked out a way to make these sessions run a lot
smoother. He would show Al Kooper the basic melody, which Al would
repeat at the piano while he tapped away at the lyrics in the motel:

Al Kooper: This [method] served a double purpose. One, he could
concentrate on writing lyrics and didn't have to mess with playing
the piano; two, I could go to the studio early that night and teach it
to the band before he even got there, so that they could be playing
the song before he even walked through the door.

Dylan was determined to avoid getting stuck in the Tennessee mud a second time. He also seems to have decided to generally stop wasting tape. Rehearsals and run-throughs at these sessions, which ran from the seventh to the tenth, were not always taped. Only first attempts at 'Pledging My Time' and 'Absolutely Sweet Marie' would be logged as 'rehearsal complete', though in the former's case it was not so much a rehearsal as a prototype for a different song, the legendary 'What Can I Do For Your Wigwam, Right?'[30]

The next full take pledged its time, no mistake. For the first time since August 2 1965, the studio Dylan was rollin', rarely tumblin'. 'Leopard-Skin Pill-Box Hat' and the semi-improvised 'Rainy Day Women' were both recorded in single takes; 'Pledging My Time' and 'Most Likely You Go Your Way' received just two full run-throughs, while 'Temporary Like Achilles and 'Absolutely Sweet Marie' needed just three renderings.

The one song that disappeared off the same cliff as 'Fourth Time Around' and 'Stuck Inside Of Mobile', to emerge wiser and stronger, was 'Just Like A Woman', which required some eighteen takes, four of which were logged as complete. There were even a couple of attempts at distinctly different arrangements.

Thankfully, this time Dylan took a leaf from his own studio textbook, taking a break from this important song after four failed attempts while he thought about it. In the interim he recorded another gathering moss blues, 'Pledging My Time', before leading the woman (or androgynous man, if a 1980 onstage rap can be believed) who 'breaks just like a little girl' to the Holy Grail.

These four fertile days gave him a stockpile of potential hit singles with which to renew his assault on the Hot Hundred and replenish the live set, without diverting him from the album process. Of these, 'Just Like A Woman' and 'I Want You' were the most obvious (chart) contenders. But only the former was slotted into the live set, in the acoustic half, stripped bare and bereft of that gorgeous fugue that drives its Nashville engine.

The one he chose as the follow-up single to 'One Of Us Must Know' was as divorced from the live set as could be. A Salvation Army

---

[30] Country musician Pete Rowan attended the session in question, and was interviewed a few weeks later. He recalled this bizarre song title almost verbatim, providing yet another song-title rumour with a disappointingly prosaic explanation in the fullness of time.

revivalist-spoof, 'Rainy Day Women' was cut in a single exuberant take. He had a point he wanted to make and 'Rainy Day Women' not only represented the sound of chart salvation, it showed he had learnt something from listening to Lenny Bruce, who when banned from using the word 'shit' to describe drugs, responded, 'So if you shit in your pants and smoke it, that's cool.'

The double-edged 'everybody must get stoned!' was a hard line to ban—and nobody did. But it prompted a number of inquisitors on the world tour to ask Dylan what the line (and its cryptic title) meant, with the usual hilarious results. In London, *NME*'s Keith Altham was hip to Dylan's jive but still insisted on knowing why this song title bore no connection to the lyric. Dylan fired back: 'Have you ever been down in North Mexico? ... Well, I can't explain it to you then.' In Sweden, he almost gave the game away:

Bob Dylan: 'Rainy Day Women' happens to deal with a minority of cripples and Orientals. ... It's another sort of a North Mexican kind of a thing. And one of the protestiest of all things I ever protested against in my protest years.
Klas Burling: Why that title? It's never mentioned in the song.
Bob Dylan: Well, we never mention things that we love. ... It has to do with God.

And there was something biblical about the song—wholly unrelated to the title, a play on the Book of Proverbs 27:15. But Dylan knew better than to spell it out clearly. He had gotten in enough trouble using the phrase 'Hard Rain' when he meant 'some sorta end that's just gotta happen'. The one time he gave a credible explanation for the rainy refrain was to a caller on the Bob Fass show—but not in January 1966. It was May 1986, and Dylan was in the middle of getting loaded, knocked-out loaded, when Bob Fass rang to wish him a happy forty-fifth birthday and ask if he'd take some more impertinent questions from regular WBAI listeners, one of which wanted to know about that very line:

Bob Dylan: What did I mean [when I sang,] 'Everybody must get stoned'? It's like, when you go against the tide. You might, in different times, find yourself in an unfortunate situation and do what you

believe in. Sometimes people just take offence to that. I mean, you
can look throughout history and find that people have taken offence
to who[ever] come[s] out with a different viewpoint on things. And
being stoned is a way of saying that.

By 1986, Dylan felt he could finally admit that 'Rainy Day
Women' was—at least partly—about being booed every night on
stage. Throughout 1966 it remained a private joke and a way to turn
his verbal bayonet on the barrackers via a million portable radios.
Throwaway or not, 'Rainy Day Women' reversed his singles slump
in spectacular fashion, going Top 10 everywhere and reaching #2 in
America—the same position 'Rolling Stone' stalled at.

Evidence that 'when you go against the tide ... sometimes people
just take offence' continued to be provided nightly. But the song itself
was wholly unsuited to a show straight out of the Book of Revelation.
Indeed, 'Just Like A Woman' and 'Fourth Time Around' were the
only two songs from the February/March sessions now integrated
into the live set, both in acoustic guises. Having fine-tuned the
electric set Stateside, the artist was not for turning.

At least 'Rainy Day Women' gave him some breathing space
commercially. He had decided *not* to fast track his new double album
to ensure it was shipped in time for the start of the world tour. In fact,
he wasn't entirely sure what sequence suited these songs best, nor did
he want to leave the mixing of the album entirely in Johnston's hands.
With the end of the North American leg looming in a fortnight's
time, he put final approval of the album on hold till he got to LA and
could review the tapes one last time.

★ ★ ★

It seems Dylan didn't even have time to get acetates cut at the final
Nashville session (March 10), such was the urgency with which he
needed to split. When, three days later, he found himself in a Denver
hotel room with Robbie Robertson and Robert Shelton, after a
long flight from Lincoln, Nebraska, he had to pick up his guitar
and play the earnest critic two of his most recent love songs, 'Just
Like A Woman' and 'Sad-Eyed Lady Of The Lowlands'. The show
Shelton had seen that evening was another 'jangled echo', but this
was something deeply intimate.

There was more, too, as Shelton saw Dylan disappear for the last time into 'unknowable regions'. Still riding the crest of a creative wave, he permitted Shelton to witness one of those spontaneous 'writing/jamming' sessions he'd mentioned at the December 1965 San Francisco press conference, when he and Robertson would 'be just sitting around playing, so I can write up some words'.

Shelton was concerned that Dylan was pushing body and mind unto the brink. Nor can he have been put at ease by Dylan's confession, in mid-air, 'It takes a lot of medicine to keep up this pace.'

But even with a full medicine cabinet, he couldn't go on this way. Grossman had scheduled two shows close to the Mexican border, one in Albuquerque and one in El Paso, but at the last minute both shows were cancelled. The official reason was that Dylan had a virus and had been advised not to perform, but the truth was he was dog-tired. Wiped out.

The commitments just kept piling up, demanding all of his precious time. He knew he could not afford to put off shows in Seattle and Vancouver at month's-end, as he found himself back in Canada at the PNE Agrodome (on the twenty-sixth) for his final North American mainland show of the year—and, guest appearances aside, his last for eight long years.

Along for the ride was Jules Siegel, who was constructing a *Saturday Evening Post* profile of the man and his music. Unfortunately, he left none the wiser as to Dylan's new music after another show which, in Siegel's own words, was 'an acoustical disaster':

> The arena ... was perfectly round, with a flat dome that produced seven echoes from a sharp handclap in the center, and large open gates which let sound leak out of the hall as easily as if the concert were held in the open air. Although Dylan's $30,000 custom-designed sound system filled eight large crates with equipment, it could never fill this gigantic echo chamber with clear sound. To add to the problem, one of the small monitor speakers, placed on stage to enable the musicians to hear themselves play, was not working ... [which meant that] in the second half ... the music was a garble of reverberation, and Dylan's voice was totally scrambled by the echo. The sound man sweated and twirled his knobs, but it was no use.

The *Vancouver Sun* assigned reviewer William Littler, who made no such allowance for his city's lousy venue, having come to the Agrodome with '3,123 other people' and a huge chip on his shoulder. The man he 'had grown to believe ... represented the most creative force in contemporary folk music', though he 'ignores grammar, rhymes tritely, composes crudely, sings gratingly and plays a rudimentary flat-pick guitar', displayed yet more flaws to fulminate about in the second half. The experience, which prompted the headline 'Electric Dylan Turns To Banality', convinced Littler the former folksinger had been killed by a jukebox spinning out of control:

> Gone was the guitar and in its place Dylan held an electric guitar. Instead of performing alone, he was joined by two more electric guitar players, a drummer, an organist and a pianist. Most significant of all, his music has changed. No longer was he singing folk; now it was folk-rock, a hybrid uniting some of the simplicity and message of folk with a weakened rock beat. And in spite of the suddenly increased enthusiasm of his shaggy young audience, I didn't like it. For one thing I didn't like the way Dylan allowed the sheer sound of his combo to obscure the greatest asset of his songs: their lyrics. Nor did I like the narrowly personal and sometimes nasty tone of some of these lyrics, the commercial banality of the music and the erratic quality of Dylan's own performances.

This familiar whine of complaint did not stop Dylan from having a good time, waving his arms about or, in the middle of 'Baby Let Me Follow You Down', executing a skip and a jump. Littler paid such little attention he failed to mention the frontman had prefaced two songs in the electric set with spoken introductions, both audible enough for English fan Simon Gee, sat way up in the 'gods', to write them down.

The first of these came before 'Just Like Tom Thumb's Blues', which Dylan explained was 'about a painter—not too many songs are about a painter. This one lived in Mexico City. I know it's a long way away but some of you might have been there some time. He lived with Indians in the jungle, and lived to a ripe old age, and was famous in his era. Like other painters he had his periods. This is about his blue period. It's called "Tom Thumb's Blues".' (A variant of this rap would reappear a number of times on the world tour.)

More of a one-off was the other preface which suggested that Mr Jones 'lives in Lincoln, Nebraska—to prove I don't make these things up. He hangs around bowling alleys there ... but we don't talk about that when we're in Nebraska. We just let Mr Jones have his little way.' Dylan was gearing up for audiences divided by a common language.

The Vancouver show closed with the now-obligatory 'Like A Rolling Stone' and Dylan boarded his own jet for one last ride to LA. Scheduled flights would be the order of the day for the exhausting six week round-the-world schedule that beckoned.

★ ★ ★

Dylan's raw nerves were becoming increasingly exposed. As he told ex-*Cavalier* critic Jules Siegel, sharing some thoughts on this goldfish-bowl existence, 'I see things that other people don't see. I feel things other people don't feel. It's terrible. They laugh. I felt like that my whole life.' He was all the while insisting that all he had ever done 'was write and sing, paint little pictures on paper [and] dissolve myself into situations where I was invisible'.

But Siegel was disinclined to cut Dylan the same slack he gave Brian Wilson later in the year, when witnessing the ineluctable disintegration of Wilson's 'conceptual masterpiece', *Smile*. In fact, Siegel showed surprisingly little tolerance for Dylan's word-games, as evidenced by his *Post* profile, published in July:

> Even in the most ordinary conversation, Dylan can be almost impossible to understand. He is often vague, poetic, repetitive, confusing. But his flow of imagery can be startlingly precise and original, and the line of his thought brilliantly adventurous, funny and penetrating. So, in describing his music he will say, 'It's all math, simple math, involved in mathematics. There's a definite number of Colt 45's that make up Marlene Dietrich, and you can find that out if you want to.' This kind of talk is not useful for more than a few situations. Nonetheless, it is the way Dylan speaks to fans, disk jockeys, reporters, acquaintances and, frequently, friends. It is not the way he speaks to Grossman. Then his voice often goes into a kind of piping whine, the voice of a little boy complaining to his father.

Back in Los Angeles, Dylan had allowed himself barely ten days in which to make any last-minute changes to *Blonde On Blonde* and approve it for release; ditto *Tarantula*, whose pristine galleys he had been carrying around for months. He also needed to find the time to sit and watch a rough cut of the 1965 tour documentary D.A. Pennebaker had now completed, awaiting his approval.

At the same time he needed to rehearse his fourth drummer in less than six months; and, in the minutes and hours left, say a fond farewell to his wife whom he was abandoning for six weeks to go see the world, even as the weight of the world continued being winched on to his shoulders.

If the suspicious Siegel had been allowed to witness a Dylan belittled by doubts, they were never about the music he had made in Nashville. When he played Siegel 'Sad-Eyed Lady Of The Lowlands', after getting the mix he wanted from a couple of days' work at LA's Gold Star, he proclaimed, 'That is religious carnival music. I just got that real old-time religious carnival sound there, didn't I?'

He was less enthused about the 'book of words' Macmillan was planning to publish that summer in his name, Siegel later recalling, 'He couldn't bring himself to publish it. He was afraid. Afraid he'd be attacked by the critics. Ginsberg had told him the academic people were laying for him, and he said I was part of the academic community.'

Those fears were real, delaying the book's publication for five years. Two years later, before bookleg editions finally forced Dylan's hand, he would tell another profile-writer, 'The trouble with it is it had no story. I'd been reading all these trash books, works suffering from sex and excitement and foolish things which only happen in a man's mind.'

A more lucid explanation of his concerns was offered at a 2001 press conference, placing the blame squarely at the late Grossman's door:

Bob Dylan: At that time in my life, things were really taking off all over the place. Lennon had put a book out. … My manager at that time had had some offers and he was the one that kind of pushed me into it. … He arranged everything, fixed the publication date and then told me that I had to write it. I managed to do it very quickly. He did that two or three times. Once he set me up as an actor in a TV

show and I knew nothing about it till the day it happened. I thought
I was going [there] to sing.

Back in April 1966, though, Dylan was still placing his trust in
Grossman, whom he relied on to play 'bad cop' if necessary. But his
manager's main task was to keep an eye on those who, as Dylan put
it to Hentoff, 'watch my money ... they're supposed to be very smart
when it comes to money. They know just what to do with my money.
I pay them a lot of it.' (How much of a cut 'they' were taking he didn't
yet know. When he found out, he would hit the roof before pulling
the rug out from under Grossman.)

One of the people Grossman had originally vouched for was
filmmaker D.A. Pennebaker, who had just finished editing the tour
documentary he had shot the previous spring. But when Dylan saw
that 'final' cut in LA, he was not happy. As Siegel, who attended the
screening, noted, 'Baez was everywhere on the film, in the limousine,
at the airport, singing in the hotel room. After the screening, Dylan
said ... "We'll have to take all that stuff of Joan out. It looks as if she
was the whole thing. She was only there a few days. We'll have to
cut it down."'

Perhaps Dylan was worried about what Sara might think (not that
his bride was under any illusions as to the man she had married).
Pennebaker, on the other hand, desperately needed a print he could
take to Cannes in May and was running out of time—especially as he
had just agreed to act as the cinematic 'eye' for a one-hour TV special
Dylan had 'volunteered' to shoot on his forthcoming European trip.
(Was this another 'TV show' Dylan 'knew nothing about ... till the
day' Grossman told him about it?)

Fortunately Dylan, ever a creature of whim—particularly after
a trip to the medicine cabinet—sat through a second screening the
following day only to decide the film was fine as it was. Pennebaker
could relax. He would have three weeks to get prints before flying
to Stockholm to meet up with Dylan, to shoot the sometime-piano
player whilst the entire British Isles was gunning for him.

Surrender was not on Dylan's mind. The Hawks had started to
'find this music' even before Dylan bequeathed them the one phantom
engineer they needed to make the whole thing go with a bang.
Mickey Jones was a drummer who did more than keep the beat: he

propelled the sound skyward, holding it there by sheer force of will. This bulldog with a beat had been playing with Johnny Rivers for the past year, but was finally a free man. And this time Dylan was not about to take no for an answer.

He had been pursuing the drummer since the previous summer. He later told Jann Wenner that the band he had in mind *pre*-Hawks would have featured guitarist James Burton, Joe Osborne on bass, and Jones: 'I knew Mickey Jones, he was playing with Johnny Rivers. They were all in California, though. And there was some difficulty in making that group connect. … Mickey couldn't make it immediately and I think Jim Burton was playing with a television group at that time.' The Hawks had evidently been a last-minute replacement waiting to happen.

As far as Dylan was concerned, the drums were (and are) the veritable crux of his live sound—not Robertson, not himself. As he told a London press gathering in 1997, 'My guitar playing just plays with the drums. In my group, the drummer is the lead guitar player. I play on the structure of where the drum plays, and that's all I do.'

Jones's addition to the ranks gave Dylan a bedrock it would take a diamond drill to cut through. They just needed to find the time for a few rehearsals. According to Jones, these 'took place at the Columbia Recording Studios on Sunset Boulevard in Hollywood. As Bob was with Columbia Records, I suspect that the studio time was either free or at a great rate.' The first rehearsal took place on March 30; the final one was slotted in on April 8, when Jones told Dylan about a soul singer he had just met that day:

Mickey Jones: We took a break around 10pm. Bob and I were sitting in the break room … at the studio and I mentioned that I had met Otis Redding today. Bob said, 'Man, I would give anything to meet Otis Redding.' … I told him that Otis was opening that night at the Whisky and I could call the owner. … I called Elmer Valentine … and told him I was bringing Bob Dylan in for the midnight show. He didn't believe me. … After the show, I took everyone up to Otis's dressing-room … Bob told Otis, 'Man, I've got a song that's perfect for you.' At that point Bob picked up a guitar and played Otis 'Just Like A Woman'. Otis loved the song and told Bob that he would love to record it.

According to Dylan, however, it was Otis doing the pitching for songs on this fabled occasion, and there wasn't a guitar in sight: 'He asked me if I had any material. It just so happened that I had the dubs from my new album. So we went over and played it [to him]. I think he took a dub' of the song.[31] An attendant D.A. Pennebaker affirms that Redding was especially anxious to ride the Dylan wave: 'Otis wanted to get Dylan … Dylan was the magic thing, and anything that connected with Dylan [he] would have done at the drop of a hat.'

Dylan was due to catch a flight the following morning for a show at the Honolulu International Center Arena, having delayed his trip to Hawaii 'to do extra work on a long-playing album'. That work involved both selection and a sequence. In the end, everything that would make up the double album, save for the previously released 'One Of Us Must Know', would come from the Nashville sessions. The likes of 'I Wanna Be Your Lover', 'She's Your Lover Now', 'Number One' and 'Medicine Sunday'—all of which would circulate in the early seventies on a tape dubbed *The LA Band Session*—never made it to a working sequence for what would be another seminal work.

Whatever 'dub' of 'Just Like A Woman' Dylan gave Redding that night was a 'spare'. He certainly had a full set of *Blonde On Blonde* acetates with him when he boarded that Pacific flight. With the drummer he'd always wanted covering his back, the Australians and Europeans wouldn't know what hit 'em. What until now had been an all-American sport—Dylanbaiting—was about to become a whole other ball game.

---

[31] Robertson has confirmed it was an acetate Redding heard, not a private performance.

PART TWO

REAPING THE WHIRLWIND

From the very start Dylan blotted his image in Australia. His fans were shocked to read press reports of his arrival in Sydney that he 'wouldn't write for negroes if you paid me $1,000'. ... Undoubtedly, these news reports kept some of his fans away from his concerts, as here in Melbourne the Festival Hall has been about 60% full. And of those fans that did brave his concerts, quite a few were disappointed. Some walked out in disgust before the end. ... Alone on stage for an hour duration [sic] of the first half ... Dylan monotonously and untunefully slowly belted out his numbers, accompanying himself on guitar and harmonica. The harmonica playing was the best part of his act ... [When,] in the second half, Dylan was accompanied by an unprogrammed quintet. ... Dylan's voice, half drowned by the backing, didn't seem so bad.

—STAN [?ROFE], 'BOB DYLAN DESTROYS HIS LEGEND IN MELBOURNE: CONCERT STRICTLY DULLSVILLE', *VARIETY*, APRIL 27 1966

Bless Dylan, our ambassador of the put-on. When he arrived in Australia on his recent 'round-the-world tour, he was met with the usual mob of square reporters with the usual nowhere questions. They asked him, 'What is your opinion of the horror of young boys being killed in wars?' which is a very insulting question for a cat like Bobby. Dylan assumes by now everyone is supposed to know what he thinks of 'Horror, Killed, War.' And if you don't know, then it means you have no idea of where Dylan is at in the first place. So these reporters make this great fuss over his arrival, then they come on like they've been living in caves for three years. What does Dylan do? He puts them on; he answers, 'This doesn't disturb me at all. I'm quite happy about the state of the world.' Well, they believed him, and they went and wrote these stories saying 'DYLAN NOT OPPOSED TO KILLING AND WAR'. So Dylan's Australian fans read this, and they think Dylan has let them down, Dylan has become evil, and they stay away from his concerts. (Not entirely, he filled 60 percent of the theater, but everyone expected capacity crowds.) Now Bobby is affected by this whole misunderstanding—it brings him down. He gives a slow concert, and acts as if he couldn't care less about pleasing his audience. The show is such a drag that even his hippest Australian fans (who knew what he was doing at those press interviews) are turned off and disappointed.

—DATEBOOK, JULY 1966

Last week Bob Dylan quit Australia after his final concert ... leaving people somewhat confused. A string of press conferences across the country uncovered little about the person who has been claimed by many to be America's number one poet of the 60s. The mask was always down ... Five minutes of the conference here, the instant-born hostility with which reporters greeted his way-out, bare-foot appearance, told me why Bob Dylan was not giving anything away.

—ROSEMARY GERRETTE, 'MAN IN A MASK', *CANBERRA TIMES*, MAY 7 1966

6. THE COURAGE OF
ONE'S CONVICTIONS
[April 9–25 1966]

AZTEC SERVICES Pty. Ltd. and STADIUMS Pty. Ltd.
(KENN BRODZIAK, Managing Director)   (RICHARD LEAN, General Manager)

in association with

ASHES & SAND Inc. of New York

present

The First Australian Tour — April 1966 — of

BOB DYLAN

SYDNEY
Stadium
April 13 & 16

•

BRISBANE
Festival Hall
April 15

•

MELBOURNE
Festival Hall
April 19 & 20

•

ADELAIDE
Palais Royal
April 22

•

PERTH
Capitol Theatre
April 23

The taking of photographs and the recording of any part of the performance is strictly prohibited
without the written authority of the Management.

I was trying to make the two things go together when I was on those concerts. I played the first half acoustically, second half with a band, somehow thinking that it was going to be two kinds of music.

— DYLAN TO JOHN COHEN, *SING OUT!* JUNE–JULY 1968

People in those days—that was the establishment press we were talking to. They didn't understand what was going on in the musical arena ... [These] people were [not even] relating to me ... they would just coldly ask me these things: 'What's this phenomenon that's being created? What does that song mean?' ... How was I to explain to them what the song meant?

— DYLAN TO RANDY ANDERSON, FEBRUARY 1978

The moment Dylan left his home shores he was cut adrift from all he had previously known. Playing to audiences in Australia, Sweden, Denmark, Scotland, Ireland and France would be an entirely new experience to him. At least in England, where the bulk of the shows that spring were scheduled, he was already a pop phenomenon. All of it was new to the band, Mickey Jones included. The production of the songs, though, remained the same. And the now-familiar two-set format was still enough to drive *Advertiser* reporter Bruce Cook, attending a stopover show in Honolulu, to despair:

Man, I say there's only one way to describe an evening with Bob Dylan: wasted. ... During the first half ... Dylan sang seven songs in forty minutes. Between songs he tuned his guitar, changed harmonicas and coughed a lot. In the second half—which the bulk of the crowd was waiting for—Dylan came out with electric guitar and an organ-piano-drums-guitar quintet called The Hawks, a run-of-the-mill rock group from Toronto. He wailed seven more songs [sic], including one of his biggest hits, 'Like A Rolling Stone'. Dylan did all the singing. The Hawks just helped make noise. Other than an occasional catcall, whistle and giggle, the crowd was reserved. There was none of the footstomping, screaming chaos that has accompanied some past Dylan performances. When Dylan laid down his guitar and walked off the stage at the end, there were few shouts for an encore.

At least the Hawaii show (and review) gave the new drummer and the new soundman a flavour of what lay ahead, bedding in with the all-Canadian bar band. Richard Alderson already knew Dylan's, and Grossman's, working methods. He also knew something of The Hawks, after Grossman 'brought the band to me, [and] asked me if I wanted to produce them—before they signed them [up]. They weren't really great—they didn't have any original songs. [It was] a year before we did the tour.' Asked to assemble a new PA after the problems in North America, the man who first taped Dylan at the Gaslight in 1962 had put a whole new PA together for the tour, after Dylan had briefed him as to what he had in mind:

Richard Alderson: [Dylan's] whole idea on that tour was to hit everybody over the head with the loudest rock'n'roll band that he could do. ... People were not understanding what he was doing. So he figured he would pound them over the head. That's why he took the ... drummer. Because he was loud ... and aggressive. ... Mickey was just too much of a redneck to give a shit. It made for great music.

Things were gonna get a lot crazier Down Under, where Dylan was playing every pit stop on the Australian mainland that boasted a test ground: Sydney, Brisbane, Melbourne, Adelaide and Perth; and big places, too. Sydney Stadium, where Dylan was booked for two shows, held close to ten thousand. Australian promoter Kenn Brodziak was taking a substantial financial gamble, reflected in the fact that a number of shows had not sold out by the time of Dylan's arrival.

As a result, not simply to explain his alien presence to a country still excited by the latest Elvis movie but to shift tickets, Dylan found himself obliged to give press conferences every time he landed at another Aussie airport. The travelling circus arrived in Sydney at 7:15 in the morning on April 12, a little time-zoned out from a two-day flight, to discover every uncomprehending hack from LA had an Antipodean pen pal who was just as clueless.

Q: Are you a protest singer?

A: I haven't heard that word for a long time. Everybody knows there are no protest songs any longer—it's just songs. … My songs don't deal about colour discrimination or the horror of young boys being killed in wars. This doesn't disturb me at all. In fact, I'm quite happy about the state of the world. I don't want to change it.

Q: Why have you started playing rock'n'roll?

A: Is that what they call it?

Q: Why have you gone commercial?

A: I have not gone commercial. I deny it [*with Bible-swearing hand upraised*]. Commercial—that's a word that describes old grandmothers that have no place to go.

Q: What does your family think of you?

A: I don't see my family anymore—they're out in the Midwest.

Q: Why don't you see them?

A: Well, I would never be able to find them.

Q: Is there any general theme behind your songs?

A: Yes. They're all about the Second Coming.

Q: When do you expect that?

A: When people don't wear clothes any more.

Q: How would you describe yourself?

A: I don't describe myself. How do you describe yourself?

Q: I have no idea, but I don't have to sell your talent.

A: Neither do I. Write whatever you like.

And that is exactly what the Australian press chose to do: write whatever they wanted. Mostly lies. Australian actor and Dylan fan Lex Marinos, an eyewitness to the airport proceedings, later described the endemic incomprehension that greeted the American artist: 'Dylan's defiant anti-publicity stance … bewildered and outraged the local chapter of the fourth estate. At the time, the roles of interviewer and interviewee were well defined and … suddenly this little smartarse decided to change the rules [as] he constructed and deconstructed and reconstructed his image himself.'

On the day, the Dylan camp were nonetheless on the lookout for allies in that arrival lounge. They found one in Craig McGregor, a young writer for the *Sydney Morning Herald*, who would later edit the first important anthology of Dylan interviews and features (*Dylan: A Retrospective*). The introduction to that influential 1972 collection expanded on McGregor's comments at the time, revisiting that first Australian press conference with a realisation that he had witnessed something historic:

> He settled himself down on a sofa for the Press conference. The arc lights switched on … downcast eyes, hooked Jewish nose. The crucifixion was about to begin. It was soon obvious that nearly everyone there had already made up his mind about Dylan. Or their editors had. He was either a Protest Singer, or a Phony, or preferably both; and they weren't going to be put off by any of that shit about him just being someone who wrote songs. Nobody welcomed him: the first questions were hostile, brutal, stupid. Dylan tried to answer seriously at first, but it was a lost cause. … Dylan kept his cool throughout, answering each question in a mumbled hip patois, and had a gracious word for everyone. … I asked a couple of questions, but they got swamped in the torrent of hostility. Dylan didn't need any help. In the end I got up and walked across to the side of the pressroom, where Grossman and the band were standing, watching the circus. 'They don't even realize he's putting them down,' I said to Grossman. He grinned.

While the others shuffled out of the lounge to file their reports, McGregor stayed behind long enough to witness another Dylan press conference: one solely for the in-crowd. As the singer 'stretched out on a settee, with Albert Grossman, the five members of the band and a last cameraman', Grossman suggested, 'Why don't you interview yourself?' To McGregor's absolute delight, Dylan promptly improvised a press conference on the spot:

> **Q**: How long is it since you saw your mother?
> **A**: About three months.
> **Q**: Why don't you see her more often? Doesn't she approve of your music?
> **A**: Well, my mother doesn't approve of it, but my grandmother does …

McGregor now had his headline, 'Bob Dylan's Anti-Interview', and a first paragraph: 'Looking rather like an extra from *The Ten Commandments*, Mr Dylan arrived in Sydney yesterday and within half an hour had conducted an anti-interview, put down the Press—and parodied the whole performance.'

But Dylan was not done with press duties, nor free of being typecast. Barely had he settled into his Kings Cross hotel than he was expected to conduct a second series of interviews, to more selective gatherings.[32] One fan who found himself in the room as Dylan went one-on-one with a female reporter remembers, 'Bob asked the reporter who she was writing for and then said words to the effect of, "Well, five years ago when I started all this, they asked me all these questions and I answered everything honestly. Next day when I read the story, the press had completely changed it around. So now I just play up to them."' Which is exactly what he now proceeded to do.

The *Sydney Daily Mirror*'s Ron Saw wanted to put the rich immigrant under the microscope, if he would only just cooperate. But the author of 'All I Really Wanna Do' informed Saw that he did not need to 'come under some classification ... I don't have to, so I don't'. Saw further failed to notice how, when confronted with a particularly dumb question, Dylan would adopt third-person plural when he meant second-person singular:

> I don't sing songs with a message. A message is an insulting way
> of trying to put your paranoia across. Everybody asks me about
> messages. In England they asked me about messages. I'm here in
> Australia to sing songs and they ask me about messages. I don't think
> they know too well what I do.

These up-close exchanges were even more fractious than the airport gathering. This time a couple of the attendees were savvy enough to realise they were being sent up, and responded in kind. Much of what appeared in the Australian press over the next two weeks would mirror the incomprehension of so-called Sydney sophisticates like *Sydney Telegraph* feature-writer Roy Castle, who called Dylan a 'singer with a message' in his piece from the hotel. Clearly he hadn't been listening for some time:

---

[32] It is not clear how many were in Dylan's hotel room at any given time, or indeed whether there was a second press conference followed by a series of one-on-one interviews or a rolling series of interviews in which Dylan parried questions from reporters in turn.

The phrases are slurred from the baby-soft mouth as Bob Dylan groped to find the words that bite and sear their way through his protest songs. 'I'm no poet. I just write songs and sing,' he told his tormentors from the Press, swinging a black velvet high-heeled boot above the carpet of his Elizabeth Bay hotel room. He rocks back and forth in his chair, and fixed a stony eye on me. ... 'Write what you like. I'm a tree surgeon if you like.' 'No. I'm not anti-war,' he cried. 'My songs are not anti-war. Do you listen to my songs?'

The singer with a message does not react kindly to press interviews. He is terse to the point of being inarticulate ... [and] caustic on the subject of poets: 'Carl Sandburg and T.S. Eliot aren't poets. Their words don't sing. They don't come off the paper. They're just super-romantic refugees, who would like to live in the past. I never did admire them.' ...

Who does he admire? 'A songwriter called Shelton Ornoqity— his songs are the words that you say without knowing it. And Rory Calhoun.' As you may have guessed, Bob Dylan can be more than slightly paradoxical. Perhaps I'll go to the Stadium tonight to get the message.

One rather doubts that Mr Castle delivered on his threat to attend the actual concert and hear what all the fuss was about. (His paper sent Joe Cizzio instead.) But articles like Castle's generated the greater currency, acting as a permanent backdrop to Dylan's prickly press reception down under.

Uli Schmetzer, a twenty-five-year-old columnist who took himself awfully seriously at the time, ladled his *Sun* account of his mini-conference with so much sarcasm he barely left room to report any conversation—save for Dylan's familiar claim that he had been a thief but was caught one day by a priest who converted him, so he 'became a folksinger'. Each of Schmetzer's impressions, if delivered on a cricket pitch, would have been called wide:

Pigmy-sized [sic], pallid-faced, with long fluffy hair, Bob Dylan is the latest and strangest of the new breed of mop-haired anti-socialite, non-conformist, pseudo-beatnik comedians to invade Sydney. And although his songs, raved and written about as brilliant, have a message to mankind, little Bobby had startlingly little to say. In fact, he bore the expression of a man being wheeled out of the operating theatre still partly under an anaesthetic. Throughout the forty-five minutes of nonsensical spluttering, ho-hum mumbling and vague gabbling, I received the distinct impression he was trying to say something, but didn't know what. In the end I chucked in the towel in my search for a person beneath the empty shell, since it appeared to be like fossicking for a pin in Sydney Harbour.

Schmetzer didn't have to wait too long to discover what Dylan's legion of female fans thought of his portrait: 'I was furious Dylan did not take me serious[ly] but made fun of all my questions. He was probably high on something or other. … [But] next day a delegation of Dylan fans, all girls, turned up at the *Sun* office, where I talked them out of thrashing me.'

Dylan also took in what Schmetzer had written. Indeed, for all his studied indifference in person, he would read every single report in the Sydney daily papers the following morning, searching for the slightest sign of 'a recognition of me in you, and the enemy, time, in us all', Tennessee Williams lines he would (mis-)quote from the stage on his next-but-one Antipodean tour in 1986. The only place he found it was in McGregor's piece in the *Herald*, even after 'the sub-editors cut [it] … in half'. McGregor was still at home when Dylan's road manager called to ask if he was going to the show that night: 'Hell, yes, I'm going to review it.' Well, Dylan wanted to meet him. During the interval.

Before that propitious moment, McGregor needed to make his own way to Sydney Stadium, joining a large, expectant crowd in this most unmusical of settings. The memory of this surreal experience lingered with Dylan, who reminded McGregor twelve years later, 'We came before any of the big groups came, before the sound was sophisticated; they put us in boxing arenas and wrestling arenas, in one place we followed, I think, Gorgeous George into an arena where the stage moved.' He meant the stadium, whose stage swivelled a quarter turn between songs, making the all-American alien boy's singular appearance doubly disorienting.[33]

With something on his mind, McGregor had very little to say about that first half in his *Herald* review, save to note how Dylan was

---

[33] It could have been worse. At earlier concert performances at the Stadium, the stage revolved continuously.

'accompanied only by his guitar and virtuoso harmonica blowing'. He did nonetheless notice how the 'mood was pervasively elegiac, a sad celebration of all emotions, even pain'. For him, its best expression was to be found in 'It's All Over Now Baby Blue', destined to receive perhaps its definitive rendering in Melbourne a week later. The audience remained respectful throughout, split between those there to hang on every acoustic word and those anxiously awaiting folk-rock. The *Australian*'s Edgar Waters, a folklorist of some repute and as such an outsider looking in, felt distinctly separated from both constituencies:

> When Bob Dylan gave his first Australian concert in Sydney last Wednesday, I took a curious look at the audience for the inventor of folk-rock. It did not look at all like the kind of audience I had seen at the big folk song concerts in Sydney a year or so ago, though there was a good sprinkling of well-known 'folk-nik' faces. Still less did it look like the usual audience for rock'n'roll, or such legitimate offspring of rock'n'roll as The Beatles.

As for the 'virtuoso harmonica blowing' that so impressed McGregor, Waters felt that 'some over-ambitious blowing' from Dylan somehow proved that 'there are great limitations to what you can do with the mouth organ when you cannot cup your hands around it'. In fact there was no limit, Dylan punctuating his mic-popping vocals with the most heavenly harp playing.[34]

With that swooping harmonica still ringing in his ears, McGregor headed nervously backstage for his meet'n'greet with the man behind the mask, now gearing up for his first all-electric assault on Australian ears. McGregor quickly realised Dylan was in a chemically enhanced state, bracing himself for any kind of reaction that might come his way and not at all focused on what reading matter he perused that morning:

> He is squatting down on his heels on the floor, electric guitar already around his neck. ... Dylan mumbles hello. Yeah, he dug what I wrote. People don't understand what he's into. He's got the band because the songs needed it; he wanted something to fill in

[34] The emergence in the 1990s of a complete PA tape from the first Sydney show definitively settled the argument in McGregor's (and Dylan's) favour. By then, the harmonica work at these shows had become the stuff of legends, and Waters's critical reputation had gone down the drain.

the spaces between the words. He is jumpy, nervous, unable to keep still. … It occurs to me, for the first time, that he is stoned, and not on grass: he isn't anything like the calm, self-possessed guy I saw at the airport … [but rather] edgy, twitchy, hyperactive: 'Hey, come up to [the] hotel room after tomorrow's show [sic], huh?' He's got the acetates on his next album, he wants me to hear them.

McGregor nodded his assent and headed back to his seat for the second half, just in time to see Dylan reappear 'with his five-man group' and launch into what the reporter described as 'a rollicking version of "Tell Me, My Love, What's Wrong With You This Time" ['Tell Me, Momma'], which deserved the applause it got … "Tom Thumb Blues" … jazzier and more Bert Thrustful now than on record, continued on where some of the earlier songs left off.'

Anyone who read both Waters and McGregor's reviews would have concluded that they had attended two different shows—one real and one not. Waters, having heard nothing remotely folkloric in the first set, failed to get beyond the sheer volume of Dylan's band in the second, a state of affairs for which he primarily blamed Jones:

> The drummer is odd man out in the rock group … He bashed away at drum and cymbal with a solid left and a solid right, as though he hated his instruments. He makes Ringo Starr seem to have, by comparison, the subtlety of an Indian tabla player. The guitarists were with the drummer in spirit, and so was the sound control man, who stood a few feet away from where I sat, with the pleasure shining through his attempts to keep a dead-pan face, as the solid waves of sound battered at my ear-drums until they throbbed and ached (and went on throbbing for half-an-hour after it was all over). It was an ugly, factory noise set to a factory rhythm; and Dylan's voice took on a new quality, as though he were shouting—though I suppose he was not actually shouting—to make himself heard above the mechanical din.

Once again, a reviewer could not get past the volume to the actual content. The whole experience was so completely alien to those who thought rock and folk were on opposite sides of the picket fence. Waters was not alone. Others, too, found the volume an almost insurmountable obstacle to musical appreciation. George Westbrook, a willing attendee, found it 'much louder than anything else I'd heard in concert. The PA system was much larger and more potent than anything seen or heard in Australia before. There's no doubt that the volume took the audience by surprise. ... [Some]one said, "I'd like to kill that drummer."'

If Mickey Jones sounds on the soundboard tape like he is already finding his way, the audience had certainly never heard anything like this from any 'legitimate offspring of rock'n'roll'. It was, to use Paul Cable's deft description of the world-tour shows, *sui generis*, 'totally integrated, inspired rock music. In no way could Dylan or The Band be accused of specifically copying anybody. The sound is very different from most of the music on the scene at the time; apart from the fact that none of The Band's instruments is restricted to a background function, it has a much more fundamentally rock beat than was generally being used around '66, yet at the same time it has a very high melodic content.'

Even Joe Cizzio, there on the *Sydney Telegraph*'s behalf, was conflicted by all he heard. Having found Dylan in the first half 'withdrawn, unresponsive, even monotonous ... yet there was a magic about him', he needed no halftime tête-à-tête to notice 'a complete change of personality during the second half, when he sang against a background of a five-piece rock'n'roll band'. Initially disorientated by 'the volume of sound [which] swamped the sense of his lyrics', Cizzio came to realise that 'each instrumentalist was good and the arrangements pleasing'. Others were less pleased, obliging him to report that 'some people, apparently in protest at this apostasy from pure folk, walked out. ... Dylan appeared indifferent'.

Those who walked out did so remarkably quietly, perhaps because many stayed put to mutely protest. As Peter Michelmore of Sydney's *Sun* reported, 'A thousand or so people in his audience shifted restlessly [but only] a few went home. The ushers and police complained that Dylan was driving them up the wall with his plaintive nasal singing. But the blue-jeaned 4,000, mostly university students, listened in rapt attention.' Soundman Alderson recollects, 'The concerts were better received in Australia for the most part. There wasn't all the hooting and hollering.'

There is certainly not a hint of animosity from the audience on the PA tape, though such a tape, being essentially a 'dry' mix of what is coming out of the public address system, was only ever picking up the most vociferous—and close—fan through Dylan's vocal mic. One particularly persistent soul, though, wants to hear 'A Hard Rain's A-Gonna Fall'. According to another attendee's recollections, the requester was part of a highly organised, heavily outnumbered dissident group:

David Pepperell: The booing and catcalling was … vicious during the second set. … I was shocked. … It was a rump of a couple of hundred people, enough to make it unpleasant for everyone. It was organised. They were all sitting in the same place … it wasn't spontaneous. As soon as he walked out with the band they started yelling and booing. … Someone kept yelling for 'Hard Rain'. Others in the crowd were trying to drown them out. … The [known] recording is quite deceptive to what was going on.

Those who tried to 'drown them out' and enjoy Dylan's new music were rewarded with a welcome 'Positively 4th Street' in place of 'Like A Rolling Stone'—probably for the last time.[35]

★ ★ ★

The first Sydney show having passed off with only the usual discontented minority out of sorts, Dylan decided to take up an invite to a party at local academic Don Henderson's house. Henderson's partner, Margaret Kitamura, remembered how 'Dylan just turned up with his band and his damaged acoustic guitar. He asked us straight away, "How was it? How was it?" We said, "It was great." Then he said, "Too loud, though, huh? Too loud."'

When someone else at the party, a member of local band The Id, walked up to Dylan and asked him, 'Do you consider yourself to be a folksinger?' Dylan just shook his head and headed off to find someone who could repair his broken guitar—a constant undercurrent on the tour to come. Even after it got fixed, it was never quite right again.

On his first day off, Dylan managed to sleep till the afternoon, when he got up to read the reviews. Unfortunately for Dylan, he had another appointment that evening. When he arrived at the TV

[35] A rumoured performance of 'Positively 4th Street' in Stockholm later in the month is almost certainly erroneous.

studio for a live interview, producer Harry Griffiths later noted, 'he was "floating" and didn't know which way he was walking'.

The demands now being made on the American singer reflected his new 'superstar' status. One of these was a rare TV interview, the evening after the first Sydney show, on primetime national TV, for Don Lane's *Tonight Show*. The ever-optimistic Australian promoter had already booked a return bout at the 'boxing arena' three days later, and it was time Dylan helped to put some Antipodean bums on Stadium seats.

Unfortunately, Lane was ill-prepped to cope with a man who, when he asked him what his music was about, replied, 'Clocks and watermelons.' It became a battle of wills that Lane tried his best to win, rather than doing his job of putting a 'difficult' artist at ease.

The following week, a letter apologising for Lane's behaviour was published in the local *Sun* paper, headlined, 'Sorry Mr Dylan' and signed 'Mother of Three'. This was because, having lost his verbal joust with Dylan, Lane attempted to send up the singer in a lame sketch the following evening, when Dylan was already in Brisbane, where he was greeted by another local TV reporter, Don Seccombe, and reporters from the local radio stations, 4BK and 4IP, none of whom made any greater headway with the taciturn troubadour, as one local photographer–journalist recalls:

Frank Neilsen: One reporter was a very conservative, straight-looking guy and rambled [on with] a convoluted question that went on for four minutes, with Dylan ignoring him throughout. At the end of the question, the reporter said, 'And what do you think of that, Mr Dylan?' Bob just responded by saying, 'Huh?' The station ... played the whole four-minute question followed by Bob's one-word answer.

Coming to a place like Brisbane, a thousand kilometres from Sydney and another decade behind in pop-culture terms, Dylan arrived with very little idea what to expect—and nor did the locals. The one local journalist who reviewed the show for the *Brisbane Telegraph*, 'B.W.', rather wished that rock'n'roll had never been invented, or at the very least that Dylan had never heard (of) it:

After two hours of Bob Dylan at the Festival Hall last night, one could only be sorry that this fine songwriter and impressive artist ever discovered rock. Not that we have anything against rock, as long as it is good rock. But Dylan-style rock (or as he likes to style it 'folk-rock') is not good rock. Before intermission ... Dylan sang unaccompanied, and he was good enough to make us see why he has become a leading voice of the mid-1960s. ... But after [the] interval, Dylan plugged in ... brought on a five-piece only-fair rock group, and the concert deteriorated rapidly. ... We hopefully forecast an early death to 'folk-rock'.

For B.W., the highlight of 'the folk-rock section of the show' was 'Leopard-Skin Pill-Box Hat', which emboldened him to suggest 'Dylan should stick to R&B if he insists on playing rock'. One doubts whether Dylan even saw B.W.'s review, which only appeared in the early editions of the paper, but he certainly shared the pen-wielding malcontent's hope that 'folk-rock' would die an early death. No other contemporary report or recording allows an insight into what went down in Brisbane, but a number of eyewitnesses interviewed by the indefatigable Zac Trader in 2016 have regaled him with accounts that suggest a 'Manchester-like' hatred of the new sound:

Paul Smith: At the intermission, the band members were down in the front rows of the crowd chatting with people and mingling. It was very relaxed ... but the moment they actually walked on stage, it was [full] on. ... In 'Ballad Of A Thin Man' he was singing the lyrics as if they were directed at the crowd ... looking to the left, looking to the right ... when people were booing.

Raymond Evans: As soon as the band had started to walk out with their guitars, some started booing and yelling out derogatory things, like, 'We don't want this!', 'Rubbish,' 'Crap', 'Get off' [etc.] ... these other people were all sitting behind me over to the right. ... The confrontation in Brisbane was on a par with Manchester, maybe more so, because Brisbane people don't hold back once they start.

Frank Neilsen: There was a large contingent of ardent folk addicts, part of the Folk Centre. ... They showed their conservatism, really

... there was a lot of booing, catcalling and ridiculous behaviour. And people like us were yelling 'Shut up'. ... It was almost fisticuffs ... the dissent all came from one direction behind us, one big group.

The Brisbane brouhaha was a strictly local affair—and the second Sydney concert attracted little in the way of comment (except, maybe, a letter to the local *Herald*, which suggested how 'in the first part ... [Dylan] seemed a forlorn and joyless figure, alone on the stage and hating his loneliness [but] he perked up in the second half when singing with his "folk-rock" group').

On his last night in Sydney, he again allowed himself to get recreationally wasted, which is how Craig McGregor found him when he took up Dylan's previously proffered invite to join a listening party. The still-starstruck scribe later described the scene he stumbled on in telling detail:

> I walk into the main suite. It is a big room. Grossman is there. And most of the band. They are lounging back on sofas, untalking. Bob is slumped in an easy chair, motionless. He is wearing shades. Head propped against the back of the chair; staring up towards the ceiling. He doesn't notice me enter. Grossman motions to Robertson. 'What're we gonna do?' says Robbie. The others are looking at me. 'Bob wants to play 'em to him, so play 'em,' says Grossman. Robertson shrugs, gets out an acetate, puts it on the portable record player. ... I sit on the floor, propped against the bed. It is a bad scene. I concentrate on the music.

Unbeknownst to McGregor, he had entered a scene weird enough to be repeated a few times on the road ahead. Although the acetates he got to hear were in pristine condition when he heard them on April 16, six weeks later they were still being put to service in London, when Dylan took it in turns with Paul McCartney, hoping to trump him musically. In a contest with 'Tomorrow Never Knows', Dylan's mercurial music continued to shine through. In between, journalists and musicians aplenty were privy to such previews.

Hearing the *Blonde On Blonde* songs in such a disorienting setting would have challenged even the most attuned armchair critic. When McGregor said he liked the sound, Dylan nodded, perhaps in recognition, perhaps not. The Australian wasn't sure. He had nonetheless performed a valuable service—honest feedback.

Such honest feedback was in short supply in Sydney—and Melbourne, where the man's touchdown at the airport at 2:15 on the afternoon of the seventeenth, for two shows at its Festival Hall, generated almost as much of a media storm as Sydney.

The Melbourne press conference suggested the circus was back in town, with Dylan again expected to play ringmaster. By now *he* knew what to expect, even when the Victoria press acted like it was his first such conflagration. As the *Age* correspondent noted, 'Some of the queries he threw back at the questioners, others he shrugged off as if they weren't worth the physical effort of answering, and for a few he wove long answers of fairyland fancy from the beat world—nonsensical, but sharply amusing.'

To give a flavour:

Q: Why did you come to Australia, Mr Dylan?
A: Well, ever since I was a little boy I had read about Australia. And I had this feeling of animosity and curiosity, you know? And I once had a friend who had an uncle whose cousin had a brother who knew someone who had heard of Australia, so I decided to come and see for myself.
Q: Do you watch television, Bob?
A: Yes, I watch Roy Rodgers.
Q: Isn't that a bit below the intellect?
A: It's not below mine. It might be below yours.
Q: Are you changing your image?
A: Yes. I'm sitting right here changing my image.
Q: Did you try to run away from home?
A: No, it's been exaggerated.
Q: Are you still running away?
A: I'm still here, aren't I?
Q: Do you like travelling? You have said you like meeting people; surely you do this by travel?
A: Oh no. You can sit in a room with four walls, and look at the walls, and know exactly what everybody's doing everywhere.
Q: How important to your image are your clothes?
A: My clothes and my hair are very conservative where I come from.
Q: What is your greatest ambition?

A: To become a meat cutter.

Q: Do you see pop music undergoing a synthesis in the same direction as pop art has …

A [*interrupting the questioner*]: Pop art? Pop art does not exist anymore. Pop art lasted only three months.

Q: What happened to it after three months?

A: After three months people stopped painting soup-can labels. After three months people stopped buying paintings of soup-can labels. After three months people stopped buying soup! In fact, they picketed the supermarkets. I know, 'cause I was there.

Q: Did you join the pickets, Bob?

A: No, I was across the road buying a pack of cards.

Q: What cards do you like, Bob?

A: Oh, jack of diamonds, ace of spades.

Q: Do you wish to see any kangaroos?

A: Yes, as many as I can between playing in Adenoid and Berth.

Q: Are you interested in answers?

A: No, I'm not interested in answers. I'm a storyteller, that's all.

After the Melbourne media had finally got their fill, promoter Kenn Brodziak, experiencing his third airport press conference in a week, exclaimed, 'Thank goodness he kept his patience.' Brodziak, who owned the only large indoor venues in Sydney, Brisbane and Melbourne, had gone to some pains to convince Grossman that Dylan could fill these places. He may have not entirely spelt out how much media Dylan would need to face in order to fill the Festival Hall twice over.

At least by now Dylan's burgeoning reputation for being 'difficult' had convinced the likes of Channel Zero's TV presenter Tim Skinner to bring 'along an enlightened record salesperson [Michael Kinnear] to prompt him in his questioning'. It also prompted another soul 'from the beat world'—poet Adrian Rawlins—to attend, fearing the worst.

Rawlins had already heard firsthand about the Sydney shootout (presumably from McGregor); in which 'they [had] misquoted his serious answers. … They didn't laugh, they ignored his answers. It was finally obvious that all they wanted was some sort of easy sound. The truth didn't enter into it.' Another letter to the Melbourne-based *Go-Set* the following week complained about how 'the Australian daily press has shown themselves to be parochial and downright stupid. The press reports in the Sydney papers showed a total lack of understanding of the Folk Seen [sic] and its artists. Bob Dylan was … asked the most stupid and irrelevant questions.'

It was in just such a context that Rawlins and *Go-Set*'s own blues columnist, Chris Hector, had arrived at the airport wondering whether the Melbourne media would give Dylan a similarly hard time. Hector watched in bemusement, and then afterward went up and 'talked to Dylan for another twenty minutes before Grossman broke up the party. Dylan spoke to me freely as he would to anyone not trying to send him up.'

Rawlins was more intimidated. As he later wrote, 'I tried to ask Bob a couple of questions but became tongue-tied because of the context and then fell silent.' While a foolish few continued to fire their verbal arrows, the poet decided to detach himself from the herd and make himself known to Dylan's inner circle:

> While the uncommunication continued, I turned my attention to the members of Dylan's band, who looked … informal and casual, and just a little rumpled from the flight. My attention became riveted on one man … who, at times, showed the slightest signs of annoyance at the decidedly ungroovy trend of the interview. He finally seated himself away from the main crowd. I sat beside him, offered him a cigarette, which he graciously accepted, told him who I was and asked if I could speak with the leader of the band. … He introduced himself to me as Robbie Robertson and asked me to ring him at the hotel later in the afternoon. By this time the management were clearing people out.

Rawlins seized the opportunity to hand the guitarist a poem he had written about Dylan six months earlier, 'Ten Statements re Bob Dylan', published by the *Age*; he hoped it might find its way to its subject. He subsequently arranged to meet up with Robertson the following lunchtime and show him around town. He evidently passed some test, because, as he later wrote, 'Dylan joined us at the end of the meal and, though nervous, was courteous and gracious … He wanted to see Melbourne's slums. … It was decided I should come along as a sort of Arab guide.'

The poet and the driver 'concurred that Fitzroy was the slummiest part of Melbourne, so we drove around Gertrude Street and George Street and Gore Street and Bob said, "Is this the worst place in Melbourne?"' When the Aussie poet replied in the affirmative, Dylan remarked, 'Maybe nobody here has got it all, but [equally] obviously, nobody's got nuthin'.'

Anxious to retain Dylan's waning interest, Rawlins suggested they headed for the university, reminding him about 'that girl yesterday. She's a university student. Maybe we could find her.' (Dylan's Australian publicist, John Collins, had taken it upon himself to eject two attractive blondes from the press conference the previous day because they lacked accreditation.) The perky student/s, according to Rawlins, 'wanted to write something for [the] Monash University newspaper. Dylan wanted them to write [something]. In fact, Dylan wanted to write [an] article for them.' Which is one way of putting it. The girl Dylan was particularly struck by was a nineteen-year-old blonde—just his type.

At Rawlins's suggestion, they trawled Elgin Street for a pinball machine and the university grounds for this girl.[36] Rawlins recounted this campus visit in detail for a December 1966 *Music Maker* article:

> As the cab slowed [down], Bob noticed a sign chalked to a tree which read 'SAENGER loves trees'. This tickled his fancy ... Bob kept leaning out of the window asking people, mainly girls who happened to be passing, who Saenger was and did he really LOVE trees? None of them knew, or hurried away in a state of flap. One girl tried to avoid us and I kept beckoning her over in my most cajolatory manner. ... Bob wanted her, naturally, to come to his [window], and leant further and further out, waving over the roof, till he almost climbed right out. ... Bob was having a whale of a time clinging to the roof and waving wildly ... and [then] I noticed that the windows [of the Architecture School] were filled with (largely male) faces, waving, gawking, laughing, inviting Bob to come up and talk with them. He continued to wave till it bored him. ... It was getting late so we headed back to town. ... During the car trip back to the hotel, Bob ... had passed a comment about the city. [He] thought Melbourne a better-looking place than Sydney. Bob thought Sydney vulgar.

---

[36] As it happens, they were looking in the wrong university. The girl in question was at Monash, not Melbourne.

Without the same sightseeing options Sydney offered—and bereft of anything as grand as Terry Stanton's yacht, on which he had previously enjoyed a midnight cruise in Sydney Harbour—Dylan returned to the Melbourne hotel. He had done enough sightseeing for the day, retiring to his suite for a private powwow with Mike Kinnear, the record salesperson who had helped to feed the media soundbites the previous afternoon. According to Kinnear, they talked 'about poetry, music, the blues, poets, songwriters and all that kind of stuff'.

The following day was showtime, Dylan only emerging from the hotel for the gig itself. John Collins had arranged for a local radio station to record the second Melbourne acoustic set, perhaps feeling that to broadcast the electric set was asking for trouble. (The fact it was the second show which was recorded for radio and TV was only recently confirmed by the emergence of a partial audience tape of the first show, made by Michael Kinnear. Dylan had informed him he would be playing some unreleased songs.) The *Lot's Wife* reviewer, Mick Counihan from Monash University, was the one hardy reporter to catch both shows, and he refers to the 'tuning problems' at the second show that appear on the radio tape:

Dylan's husky voice has an exciting, intriguing tonal quality and his singing was very expressive. His guitar playing was simple but effective, but his performance as a whole was marred by a number of irritatingly long and meaningless mouth harp breaks. The Wednesday concert was altogether shabbier. Dylan was in poorer shape and was troubled with tuning problems and a dry throat.

On that first magnetic night, reviewer Howard Palmer of the Melbourne *Sun* found, 'In the first half of the program … you can hear everything, for the silence is so intense as to be felt. Only Brubeck had this silence.' Equally impressed was *Go-Set*'s Robert Westfield: 'The first half of his show was just Dylan, guitar, and a voice infinitely more beautiful than the one you hear on record. It was a surprise to hear it and realise that Dylan can sing.'

Another local writer hoping to be up close had arrived at the Festival Hall to find no sign of the 'comp' ticket Dylan's guitarist had assured him would be waiting for him. Reluctantly, Rawlins 'bought a ticket and sat, feeling awfully alone, the sole occupant of the second back row'. Even from here, 'Dylan looked very fragile and really scared and vulnerable, incredibly vulnerable. He didn't actually fall off the stage, but he did kind of stumble.'

Another attendee that first night, Andie Pasqualini, remembers how 'when he spoke between songs, his speech was ... slurred and he sounded out of it. But when he sang, he was completely in control, absolutely spot on all the time.' For Nicolas Ribush, his abiding memory is of Dylan 'tuning up his guitar and swaying unsteadily'.

Yet this was not the show preserved on the fabled 1974 bootleg, on which it does rather sound like Dylan is about to slump off the stage any second now. But he doesn't. He keeps going, weaving skipping reels of rhyme with that gossamer-thin voice and harp breaks that echo round the Festival Hall. (As Paul Cable wrote regarding the radio tape in his 1978 study of Dylan's unreleased recordings, 'The performances are superb. Dylan sounds exhausted mentally and physically and does a lot of coughing, but the songs gain rather than lose from this.')

For now, the folk fans at the Festival Hall kept any lingering doubts to themselves. But that all changed in the second half. The reaction on night one—if Rawlin's memory still served him well in 1981— suggests that Melbourne fans of the acoustic Dylan were as organised as Sydney's: 'After the interval Bob strode to the mike, strapping on an electric guitar ... [but] before they could [start to] play, a section of the audience, at least 20 percent, maybe more, erupted in fury and outrage. They booed; they screamed; they shouted "traitor"; they held up prepared placards reading TRAITOR and COP OUT.'[37]

The first Melbourne show was certainly widely reviewed, but neither those overawed nor those underwhelmed by the electric set mention a staged protest. Mick Counihan provides by far the most detailed and the most sympathetic account of the electric set—for both nights—noting in passing that the first night 'was decidedly better', before giving an almost blow-by-blow report of the electrifying experience:

> The second half opened with Dylan ... plus band. ... The group was hard working and more than adequate (though not as good as the backing on Dylan's last two records). ... The 'sound' was harsh, unpleasantly aggressive and nowhere near as musically

[37] Photographer John Gollings, a friend of Rawlins, says he doesn't 'remember anyone with placards ... but there was a fuss'.

interesting as on his records. The songs included 'Tom Thumb's Blues', a wild rocking version of the traditional blues 'Baby Let Me Follow You Down', 'One Too Many Mornings' (the rock version proved too much for many folk Dylan fans), 'Ballad Of A Thin Man' (on Tuesday dedicated to the Taj Mahal, on Wednesday to a Mrs Spinks—it being about her husband 'who's not a bad sort but he gets in the way a lot'[38]), a hilariously comic satire called 'I See You've Got Your Brand New Leopardskin Pillboxhat' and finally 'Like A Rolling Stone'. This last provided a spine chilling fantastic climax to an evening. Dylan, against a surging rhythm and wailing organ, screamed the ultimate challenge, through cupped hands, at the battered pulverized audience ... He then finished up, mumbled incomprehensible thank you's, twitched and grimaced at the audience and minced off. I left feeling momentarily, physically and mentally empty.

The *Go-Set* reviewer was also quick to notice a newly enthused Dylan, Robert Westfield noting how 'it was obvious that ... the tiny frail figure was ENJOYING himself' while remaining somewhat dismissive of the 'solid Dylan-style rock show, with his fifties-style band providing loud but mediocre backing'.

If the *Sun*'s Howard Palmer found what was happening 'all din', the reporter from the *Age* was also struck by the change in Dylan's demeanour: 'In sharp contrast to the first half, his second half of the programme introduced Melbourne to his invention, folk-rock, with a great blast of noise. Like a marionette, his now-mobile face framed by all that fine hair, Dylan strutted and stomped and obviously enjoyed himself despite the hostility he poured out, particularly when he took to the piano for "Something's Happening And You Don't Know What It Is, Do You Mr Jones?"'

Any positive review—even an uncomprehending one—was welcome in Melbourne because—in another fit of overconfidence— the promoter had booked two shows there. Sales for the second show had been slower than he had hoped, meaning Dylan would be playing to a half-empty hall. The singer's mood was not greatly improved when he was informed that GTV-9 was going to be filming the electric set for later broadcast, prompting Rawlins to suggest it was

[38] It would appear that Dylan actually dedicated the song to Mrs Sphinx, which at least connects it to the Taj Mahal introduction.

somehow *their* fault that 'the second half was pretty awful. Channel Ten [sic] had cameras all over the place and Bob played the entire set with his back to them.'

The meaning of Dylan's repeated back-turning was apparently lost on the middling Melbourne audience. According to one review, 'He annoyed the audience by taking time to tune up on the guitar so that on two occasions he received a slow handclap.' Perhaps this was the moment when Dylan decided to gauge the temper of an audience by turning to Robertson and talking tactics, a regular feature of later shows whenever disapprobation loomed large.

The TV station still managed to film three songs good enough to broadcast—'Tell Me, Momma', 'Baby Let Me Follow You Down' and 'Just Like Tom Thumb's Blues'—though it seems that they missed what sounds like the spoken intro to the first of these. According to Counihan, Dylan prefaced one song with 'Here's a folk song now. We play all types of music here' during his second Melbourne concert. 'He was replying to the various boos and yells for "Folk-Dylan" which occasionally interrupted the "rock half" of his program.'

Unfortunately, Counihan's was not the account that made it back to the USA. Another review, of a different hue, appeared in *Variety* barely a week after the show, providing Dylan's fans back home with their only report of the world tour in real time (see the opening quote of the section). This poison-pen review—which ran under the slanderous headline 'Bob Dylan Destroys His Legend In Melbourne: Concert Strictly Dullsville'—suggested that, 'of those fans [who] did brave his concerts [sic], quite a few were disappointed. Some walked out in disgust before the end.'

Credited to 'Stan', the piece was probably sent to the US paper by Melbourne DJ Stan Rofe, who also inserted his own questions into a radio tape of Dylan being interviewed at the airport, which probably says it all regarding his concerns for fidelity and accuracy. But there were clearly still some fans turning up to boo the electric Bob. According to Rawlins, Dylan was greatly hurt by the audience reaction at *both* the Melbourne shows:

His two Melbourne concerts at Festival Hall were not successful on his terms (which alone obtain) because the audience in the main could not grasp the meaning of his words and were unfamiliar with this particular sound (though he has issued two LPs in this mode). Dylan, I know, painfully took this as rejection; it was simply non-culpable ignorance. But the audience which could have simply let the exciting, fresh, stimulating sound wash over it and thereby got what Dylan's liberating art is all about, preferred to, as it were, hold back, stand back and frown.

Yet despite Dylan ending up 'turned off and disappointed' by the reaction, on the substantive evidence of three distinct recordings, both audiences sound largely enthusiastic. Indeed, the introduction to 'Tom Thumb's Blues' on the second night is met by pubescent screams of joy. If there was a difference between the two nights it was that Dylan seemed overcome with a new negativity on that second night—immersed in a fug from which he did not fully emerge for the remainder of the Australian leg. The cause of this would not be divulged for some years.

★ ★ ★

After the first show, Dylan, who seemed if anything on something of a high, had decided to make a night of it. He had finally (been) tracked down (by) the two blonde girls who had made such an impression on him at the press conference, who joined him in driving around town trying to find Adrian. When he returned to the hotel, blonde on blonde in tow, Rawlins was already there, talking to road manager Bill Avis: "'Oh, there you are, Adrian!" he said with a half smile. "Where the fuck have you been? We've been searching for you for hours! ... Shall we go upstairs an' talk?'" It was to be a life-changing evening for Rawlins, who would write a detailed account of it:

> He taught us to smoke hashish pure, over silver foil over whisky; we drank whisky, then tea (brought in elaborate silver service), then coca cola, then water. Dylan and I talked for over six hours. ... He talked and talked, telling me intimate details about his childhood, about his cultural affiliations, about his worldview: he mentioned visiting Henry Miller at his home in Pacific Palisades; how he felt that the older writer mocked him; he mumbled, 'I don't like Ernest Hemingway ... I don't like *Time* magazine, prefer *Newsweek*.' ...
>
> About six thirty in the morning he said he had a song he wanted me to hear. He took the borrowed guitar and played 'Sad-Eyed Lady

Of The Lowlands'. Obviously it was a love song. But, at a deeper
level, it seemed a song for all mankind. 'What'd'ya think of that?'
he asked in utter humility. 'It's a hymn for all mankind,' I stuttered.
... 'Yeah,' he mumbled, 'That's what Allen says.' His mood was one
of extreme shyness and deep humility. He wasn't putting me on ...
'You wanna hear some more songs from my next album?' So he
played me 'Tombstone Blues' [probably 'Obviously Five Believers'],
'Stuck Inside Of Mobile' and two other tracks from *Blonde On
Blonde*. It all sounded crude to me—the playing, I mean ... Dylan
told me that his mother was a Red Indian named Dillon. 'I don't
accept that Zimmerman's my father ...' he muttered with something
like venom. ... He was most loquacious about 'Desolation Row',
a still epochal song inspired by Jack Kerouac's *Desolation Angels*.
Initially, the song began as sixteen pages of lyrics. Bob set himself
the task of reducing this body of work to four pages without any
loss of meaning. ... I asked Bob whether he had actually read Pound
and Eliot. 'Yeah, man, Allen gave me the books. I read three pages
... that's not where it's at!' ... Around 7:30am Bob and I moved on
to the balcony to watch the dawn come up over Treasury Gardens.
... [Then he] went inside to reread the reviews.

If this was not a typical night, neither was it atypical. At various
junctures, Dylan was known to welcome outsiders into the inner
sanctum, yearning for a little conversation about music making, with
a little drug taking for good measure. On such occasions he would
encourage honest feedback—mutual communication—from those he
perceived to be on a similar wavelength.

Once again, he took this opportunity to play the *Blonde On
Blonde* acetates. Again, the listener struggled to get much from the
portable mono setup, so much so that Dylan finally played his fellow
wordsmith the album-closer, a perfect hashish song-dream, in person.
For Rawlins, the experience 'was like hearing a Bach chorale for the
first time'.

The near-nocturnal lifestyle was Dylan's way of shifting his body
clock so that he was engaged to the max when the evening came
around and a second performance expected; it could be a punishing
regime. On the morning of the twentieth, barely had Dylan retired
to bed when a most unwelcome set of party-crashers came a-calling.
As Rawlins later wrote, 'Later in the morning the Drug Squad had

called. They [had] knocked on the door. Albert came out and they said, "Are you Bob Dylan? Where is Bob Dylan?" Albert ... took the remaining hash and threw it down the incinerator.'[39]

This was Dylan's worst nightmare. It seems that his road manager, Bill Avis, perhaps with the overt encouragement of Victor Maymudes, who was a sexual predator of the worst kind with a known proclivity for young girls, had unwittingly picked up a girl at the post-gig party who was the daughter of the chief of police. Avis was quickly spirited out of the country, while Maymudes left town, reappearing in Adelaide seemingly unfazed by the experience and as yet unaware that he was on the way out. Soundman Richard Alderson, who was sharing a room with Maymudes on this leg of the tour, had had the presence of mind to flush whatever he had on him down the toilet.

When Rawlins returned to the hotel, mid-afternoon, he found a 'highly agitated' Dylan. Having been challenged by Robertson earlier on about a previous drug bust, Rawlins's leaving the building just before the cops had come to Dylan's door was now held against him.[40] As a result of this disquieting coincidence, there would be no further evenings spent turning Dylan's Melbourne hotel suite into an opium den.

Even Rawlins's glowing review of the two Melbourne shows in the following week's *Farrago*—which suggested 'Dylan and his band are producing a song and sound unit which is better organised, more genuinely exciting, more uplifting, better emotionally balanced, more *absolute* than any other sound in the general "beat" genre'—failed to mend this bridge. When Adrian wrote to Dylan the following month, enclosing the *Farrago* review, the response from Liverpool—after another trying night—cut the Beat poet to the quick: 'I really resent the lame and pleading tone of that piece of shit you sent me.'

Everything—and everyone—that happened in Melbourne, Dylan preferred to stay in Melbourne. When Rawlins tried to speak to him in Perth, the conversation was brief and halting, leaving him feeling

[39] In fact, the raid took place shortly after Rawlins left, which was closer to seven than ten.

[40] 'Robbie asked me [that afternoon] if I was wanted on a drug charge, and I understood the reason for Dylan's nervousness. I was able to assure him that the matter the Australian promoters had obviously warned them about was a very minor affair which had been settled two months previously.' ('Through The Looking Glass', Adrian Rawlins, 1981.)

disconnected. Dylan had moved on. After that dispiriting second show, Dylan did not hang around Melbourne to bestow (or deny) his benediction to the local beat/s.

By the following afternoon he was in Adelaide, slumped on the sofa of another arrival lounge, fending off the enquiries of another set of scribes: batting away condescending questions about his singing ('Most people underestimate my voice, but left alone in an empty room I can sing better than anybody else') and his writing ('I write the same way I drink a glass of water'); all the while refuting any suggestion he had ever bought into the American dream: 'I never was a teenager. I never played football, basketball, soccer. I never went to track meets. I never had good grades in school. I never was in the honor society. I never graduated with high degrees.'

'Twas all to no avail. His main antagonist, Roger Cardwell, was determined to get Dylan to admit (on local radio) he was a fraud or charlatan. The extant part of their on-air interview—interrupted on occasion by other reporters—comes to an abrupt end after Cardwell has the gall to ask, 'Do you sing songs because you can make some money out of this, or do you sing them just because you like to sing the songs, and money doesn't mean anything at all?' Dylan takes righteous umbrage, 'I consider that an insult, sir.'

One wonders if the interview he gave to local TV—which again has not survived—was equally fractious. The show certainly was. The audience in Adelaide was at times as rude and uninformed as its media—an attitude reflected in the university paper *On Dit* by W.K. Parish, who delighted in portraying Dylan as 'The Fallen Idol'. This self-professed 'fan from way back', who preferred songs like 'Goodbye, Baby Blue', felt betrayed by all he heard after the interval:

> As a Dylan fan from way back it was, with considerable trepidation that I went to see him at the Palais last week. The first half—nothing startling, not bad; Dylan, looking bored and ignoring the audience, singing the more obscure numbers from his repertoire (with the notable exceptions of 'Goodbye, Baby Blue' [sic] and 'Desolation Row'). ... However, when I came back from a quick drag at interval, I thought perhaps that I had accidentally stumbled into some gigantic discotheque or a Friday night Princeton club. Dylan was hopping around like an animated marionette, three electrified

guitars were screaming, an electric organ and piano thumping and a greasy-haired rocker pounded the drums. All that was missing was an army of screaming pubescent females. True, it was an exciting sound, but as Dylan wriggled his little bottom around the stage and the amplifying system shook the walls, it was noticeable that the applause had definitely cooled and many embittered persons were leaving.

If Mr Parish convinced himself that 'many embittered persons were leaving', the more level-headed 'A.M.M.', writing for the *Adelaide Advertiser*, suggested it was only 'a few people [who] walked out during the second half, when Dylan was joined by his thunderously loud backing group'.

This local adman provided some much needed balance to the debate, calling Dylan's music 'hard and harsh at times, soft and flowing at others, but always compelling. And the words of contemporary poetry, sometimes spoken, sometimes yelled, pour out of Dylan in such a way that one is forced to listen and try to understand their message. ... With the wild, pulsating beat of drums and amplified guitars, the younger element greeted the close of each number with whistles and calls for more.'

University reporter 'Justine', who attended the earlier press conference and found Dylan 'impertinent in conversation, boorish in manners', chose not to hold it against him, describing him as 'magnificent on stage' while noticing a raft of dissenting voices in the audience the minute Dylan began playing at a volume designed to drown out their orchestrated negativity:

The first half of the show was a feast for his ethnic followers. He devoted this half to his old style. ... With his harmonica wired over his shoulders, he strummed his guitar, and looked distractedly to his right as he sang. ... Occasionally as he stood in front of the microphone he would draw one leg sensually up against the other, and one would wait for the pubescent girls to scream. But there were no screams and whistles. For he was a rocker of a different school. His audience was not a mob of screaming fans, tearing their hair with the passion of the music. They were a subdued group of all ages, listening to the poetry of Dylan, oblivious to the presentation. They were neither insulted by his obvious boredom in the first half, nor disturbed by the volume of his backing sound in the second half. They listened intently to his every word …

The ethnics got a shock at the second half of the show, when Dylan was joined by two guitarists, an aggressive drummer, a pianist and an organist. Clutching his electric guitar, Dylan shouted his poetry over the thunderous rock band, bounding around the stage to the beat of the music. He was like a child with a new toy …

[Yet] there were [still] the few who made their disapproval clearly felt. 'Bring on the Go Go girls,' was one cry that went up from members of the audience, when Dylan appeared with his greasy-haired backing group. 'And he calls himself a folk-singer,' was another comment from a disgusted middle-aged couple as they stormed back up the aisle. Throughout the 'folk-rock' part of the performance the sound of footsteps heading towards the exit was clearly audible. They were the ethnics … the traditional folkies, who had never dreamt that poetry could be conveyed with noise.

If the majority of Adelaide fans who paid for their tickets were in no mood to complain, the collegiate spat in the pages of *On Dit*— between W.K. Parrish and 'Justine'—suggested more dissent than there was. As the final Australian show (and press conference) in Perth loomed, what was really needed was for the voice of the enthused majority to be heard in print.

★ ★ ★

The first such piece that really hinted at what made the man onstage tick would not appear until the first week in May in the *Canberra Times*, written by one lucky advocate invited into the darkness of Dylan's hotel room. The lengthy feature, written by would-be actress Rosemary Gerrette and called 'Dylan—Man In A Mask', was perhaps the most revealing peek behind the shades since Nat Hentoff's *New Yorker* profile. Gerrette found herself spending a great deal of time with Dylan after the Perth concert because, just like The Saints, Dylan now found himself stranded far from home. The scheduled flight to Stockholm the day after Perth had been cancelled, and he and the band were stuck for two whole days on the edge of the known world.

Like McGregor and Rawlins before her, the initial point of contact for Gerrette—who knew both predecessors—was an airport press conference, which she described thus:

Five minutes of the conference here, the instant-born hostility with which reporters greeted his way-out, barefoot appearance, told me why Bob Dylan was not giving anything away. To him, people are valuable. Those with open minds, that is. Time spent with them has to mean something ('I'm Pledging My Time To You'). Reporters who ask ad infinitum questions like what do God, people, life mean to him, get the Dylan cold shoulder. Someone asked what his protest songs meant to him—war, civil rights [etc.]. He answered, 'Nothing.' I said that surely he must have been moved to write them: like when you are hungry, you eat; when you are thirsty, you drink; when you are stirred by something you write about it? He said, 'No, when YOU'RE hungry, YOU eat. When I'm hungry, I write.'

Actually, this brief report of the conference was neither entirely accurate nor authoritative. Gerrette had rather simplified a crucial exchange. Having been asked, **'What do you think of the war in Vietnam?'** Dylan had replied, 'Nothing. It's Australia's war.' When the indignant reporter snorted, 'But Americans are there,' he suggested, 'They're just helping the Australians.' If he had set out to offend, he couldn't have done better. His patience with the Australian press was not wearing thin; it had worn through.

'The instant-born hostility' may have triggered his ill-disguised antipathy, but as the *Music Maker* reporter Murray Jennings detailed in one of the best Australian 1966 Dylan features—sadly not published till the following month—the Perth press conference was a hoot from start to finish:

A: I wouldn't write before eating, and I never write on Fridays and I never write on Tuesday nights.
Q: Why is that?
A: It's a tradition in North Mexico, where I first learned how to write … I follow tradition. I'm a traditional writer.
Q: You don't dress very traditional. Why do you wear your hair long?
A: For the same reason that you wear yours short …
Q: Wouldn't it be warm in this climate?
A: Well, I don't have to be in this climate very long …
Q: Mr Dylan, what interests you apart from songwriting?
A: Nothing.
Q: Nothing at all? So you see your life purely as writing songs?

A: I don't see my life as anything.

Q: Who designs your clothes, Bob?

A: Nobody. I buy them off the rack. If you go over to the States, you'd see they're the typical thing ...

Q: Do you need an audience to be listening to you? Is that the way you prefer it? Or do you prefer to record?

A: Well, I never took recording seriously until the latest record they've got coming out, but I'd rather record in the studio now.

Q: Folk songs are usually written about misery, bombs and racial troubles ...

A: No. Folk songs are not written about that! Not at all! I'm afraid you don't know much about folk songs. You're speaking of topical songs—1930 labour movement songs and stuff like that. Those are not folk songs ...

Q: Well, how would you define a folk song then?

A: Folk songs are traditional songs or ballads. They're not meant to be sung at parties or in crowded rooms where there's noise ...

Q: Would you like to see other people going around the streets dressed like you?

A: I wouldn't want to see anybody doing anything they wouldn't want to do.

Q: Do you follow any fashion or trend?

A: No. I just do what I do, and everybody else can take care of themselves ...

Q: What about Allen Ginsberg? Do you count him among your friends, and an influence?

A: Yes, he's a good friend of mine. I like what he does.

Q: Is he still held in such high esteem as he was when he was first published?

A: Yes. He's a man held in high esteem, but he's not really accepted by the literary world. But he will be in time. He's the best poet, to me, anywhere in the world. He's certainly better than any of the Russian poets or the other European poets. He writes on paper. I'm not a poet, you see. What I do, I feel that to write poetry, it should sing off the paper. I don't have to worry about that because I sing it to myself. So I can't really be classified as a poet ...

Q: Bob, songs like 'Ballad Of A Thin Man' and 'Just Like Tom Thumb's Blues'—do they mean anything to you at all?

A: Yes, 'Just Like Tom Thumb's Blues' is a line I crossed about a year and a half ago, and once I crossed that I didn't have to worry any more. Everything became one. The words and the song itself became one whole thing, while before that it was just plain basic simplicity, you know, songs of the dimension. I wrote them in New York City for specific personal reasons. 'Just Like Tom Thumb's Blues' means more to me than, say, 'Times They Are A-Changin''. Although I don't put down any of these other songs I wrote. I know I wrote them and I know nobody else did write them. There was no market for them when I wrote them. These songs have sold well on record since, but the recordings were made a long time ago when there was no market for them ...

Q: Mr Dylan, what things are important to you?

A: I just answered that question. Nothing is important to me. Nothing. You name it and it's not important to me ...

Q: Bob, have you ever had a job apart from what you're doing now?

A: Yes, I've done odd jobs. But I don't come from a generation that cares to have jobs ...

Q: Bob, why did you change your style to the big beat?

A: No. You don't understand. People in the United States who are my age now have been raised on rock'n'roll music and country & western music. It doesn't come from England. It comes from the United States! It's something I played when I was twelve years old. I was raised on Hank Williams and Lefty Frizzell. That's all I could hear on the radio. [Then] Elvis Presley ... I've played this music all my life. I quit—that's all. I quit when I was seventeen. I started playing folk music. Because it was easier. And the people in it were all very unknown at the time.

The tenor of Jennings's entire feature made it plain he was firmly on Dylan's side at the conference itself, which he described as full of 'questions [that] tried not his intellect, but his patience—and indeed the patience of some locals present at the time [as] devotees and newspapermen intermingled, [and] university-rag writers rubbed shoulders with radio and television men'.

Among this eclectic mixture of the hip and the hapless, it was the newspapermen who had again turned up ill-informed and unprepared. And it was no different the following evening at the final Australian concert, where Kim Lockwood, writing for the *West Australian*, dug himself his own critical ditch by taking umbrage at the very idea that fans had come to see a poet and a philosopher:

In years to come, students of English Literature may point to the
lyrics' subtle symbolism. But I do not think he wrote any of them
with symbolism in mind. I think that when he comes to the end of
the line he writes the first rhyming word that comes into his head.
Mr Dylan has been billed as America's greatest folk-singer. He is
not. He is a competent folk song composer, if we forget the absurd
lyrics, but he is not a singer. … His absurd lyrics and lack of singing
ability became more evident as the concert went on, and some of
the audience left after the first few songs. The folk devotees who
remained gave him a cool reception.

Dylan's 'cool reception' was as nothing to the one which greeted
Lockwood's review. Rede Moulton fired off the first retort, insisting,
'If Mr Lockwood did not see any meaning in "She Belongs To Me"
and "Desolation Row" he should not be reviewing folk music.' He
proceeded to do Lockwood's job for him by reviewing the *actual*
show: 'I thought the audience last Saturday night gave Dylan an
enthusiastic reception for his first half and I certainly did not see
anyone leave after the first few numbers. He probably shocked the
folk element [who] with his second half most probably found his
folk rock too noisy.'

Nor was Mr Moulton alone. In the same letters column five days
later was M. Sydney-Smith, who also decided to give Mr Lockwood
both barrels: 'A reporter covering such a function as Bob Dylan's
show, should, if not a dedicated fan, at least take the trouble to
learn something about the performer and his work. … Perhaps Mr
Lockwood is one of those folk-lovers who like their songs to be sung
beautifully, with a delightful harmony and nice simple lyrics, thereby
reducing the character of folk music from the sincere message of a
people to a mealy-mouthed exercise in music.'

Even though Dylan would try to maintain a Zen-like indifference
to the Lockwoods of this world, the two letters to the *West Australian*
would be part of a growing trend. As controversy continued to dog
his heels, readers' letters from this time forth redress the balance in the
ongoing debate. They also usually provide a more level-headed, nay
objective account of what was going on in these large auditoriums.

As for Dylan, he still continued to show a glimpse of his mind
a-working, but only to those who seemed like-minded. Thus he

displayed no such antagonism toward Gerrette—or at least not until it was time to go and he unexpectedly flew into a rage, ordering her to leave. A friend of Adrian Rawlins's, she had already been mentioned to Dylan—presumably as someone he could look up in Perth. So the summons to his hotel after the concert was not entirely unexpected. Nor can it have come entirely as a shock when Dylan offered to play her his forthcoming album:

> I sat for six hours while Dylan played me his music, a pile of unreleased acetate cuttings, which he carries around with him. 'Like, I've been living music for ever.' But the words seemed to mean more to him than the music because he made me ask at once if I missed a word or its meaning. And although I can forget what somebody said to me yesterday, he knew every word through something like forty songs. He loved those songs. And to me it was six hours of throbbing poetry. Critics here accused him of an unprofessional manner. On stage he didn't seem to be trying. Yet he asked me eagerly what I thought of his concert, did it go well? 'I don't usually ask people that.' He cared ... I sat up with the group until dawn. After four days in Perth [sic] they were leaving for Stockholm for concerts.

A private performance by Dylan and Robertson, though, proved to be a wholly unexpected bonus, enabling Gerrette to provide the only detailed report of what sitting in on 'a composing session' that year was really like:

> They were trying to get tired so they could sleep through the twenty-seven hour flight and I was able to listen to a composing session. Countless cups of tea; none of the group drinks. Things happened, and six new songs were born. The poetry seemed already to have been written. Dylan says, 'Picture one of these cats with a horn, coming over the hill at daybreak. Very Elizabethan, you dig? Wearing garters.' And out of [such] imagery, he and the lead guitarist work on a tune and Dylan's leg beats time with the rhythm, continuously, even when the rhythm is in his own mind. Six a.m. and he asks am I tired? Later he plays a melody to us, a very special one. 'I'll never have it published, recorded. I wrote it for this way-out moon chick. We just sat on the floor on these mattresses ... and

for two hours I spoke to her with my guitar. And she understood.
She'd just say yes, or no, or yes. And I never spoke a word, you dig?
Only of course, this isn't quite like I played it, because it meant
something to me at the time, but now it doesn't.' It was beautiful,
I thought.

What Gerrette, for obvious reasons, did not include in her *Canberra
Times* piece was her private conviction that 'Dylan was on some
kind of drugs. He said it was pot and I said to him I had never had
marijuana ... I don't think he ever met anyone who was so not into
anything.' She also left out the part where Dylan justified his 'truth
attacks' by saying it was his way of 'being honest ... telling things and
expressing things the way you really want to. ... He was saying that
small unkindnesses were not necessary, but when it came to things
that involved your feelings, things you had to *tell* people, then it was
okay to be cruel, if necessary ... He was saying he could be cruel—
we should all be cruel—to show someone what was wrong with [his
or] her life.' It was a worldview that had already inspired some of his
greatest songs. And yet he continued to obsess about the virtues of
'obscurity' a favourite theme of his:

He spoke of obscurity, of the going down, when the good times
will be over. 'People don't value their obscurity. They don't know
what it's like to have it taken away. Not to be able to walk down
the street or sit in the park or dare to go out of your hotel room.
The money I've made means only that when I'm off this kick I'll be
able to protect myself, because I know cats who'll want to tear me
to pieces and I'll have to kill myself. And I don't want to do this.'

Finally, at seven in the morning, Dylan read Rosemary 'pieces from
the book he is writing'. It was a rare expression of faith, although
neither of them was entirely convinced the book made any sense. Her
private view, not expressed to Dylan, or in print, at the time, was, 'It
was unintelligible, avant-garde, like the backs of his record covers.
The boys all thought it was really groovy. I couldn't see why.' Yet
it turned out the world of literature was just one media Dylan was
looking to conquer in the months ahead:

Then there was talk about the film he is going to make—about himself. Dylan the egotist—yet everyone is silent when he speaks … Unexplainable contradiction. Books were strewn around the room. The poetry of Baudelaire, Durrell, *Australian Poetry 1965*, Mackaness's *The Wide Brown Land*, a couple of newer Australian 'magazines', the inevitable *Newsweek* (Dylan story inside, of course). He keeps a very close eye on publicity about himself.

Their confab was interrupted by a phone call from Melbourne, presumably from the disconnected Rawlins, and another one from 'a Sydney journalist whom [Dylan] wants to get to America because he likes him', presumably Craig McGregor. A telegram also arrived, which read, 'Dylan, be free always.'

And still the talking continued. Dylan even revealed something of the thief of fire within by telling the wide-eyed girl from Canberra that 'he was interested in [the] Self … He had come to know that he must go back inside himself, that everything that happens comes out of re-examination. … You go down into the deeper self and go through it all and come out the other side, and then you're going to *know*.' Here was someone who had taken Arthur Rimbaud's 1871 letter to Georges Izambard to heart.[41]

Gerrette, along with many others who encountered Dylan on this historic tour, feared the cost of this pursuit might prove too great. As she was to tell Dylan's first biographer, 'I began to feel that Dylan was sacrificing himself … that he would eventually die or that something horrible would happen to him. I felt it psychically, I felt it strongly … Adrian Rawlins came to that conclusion the same time I did. Other people felt it.' Even a single evening this close to the flames flickering around this Promethean poet had seemingly singed her very soul—as it had the soul of the girl from Monash he had spent the evening with in Melbourne.

Dylan, meanwhile, had no choice but to continue his journey into the unknown. He had a flight to the opposite end of the world

[41] 'The Poet makes himself a seer by a long, gigantic and rational derangement of all the senses. All forms of love, suffering, and madness. He searches himself. He exhausts all poisons in himself and keeps only their quintessences. Unspeakable torture where he needs all his faith, all his super-human strength, where he becomes among all men the great patient, the great criminal, the one accursed—and the supreme Scholar!—Because he reaches the unknown … and when, bewildered, he ends by losing the intelligence of his visions, he has seen them. Let him die as he leaps through unheard of and unnameable things.'

booked. It was time to go. He had exhausted all the poisons Australia
had to offer, and himself into the bargain. Weary to the bone, he
boarded a flight to Stockholm for a month of European shows that
would take him deeper into himself than even the Rimbaud who
ventured into darkest Abyssinia.

It would be left to another *West Australian* commentator, the
perceptive Murray Jennings, to summarise the media incomprehension
that had blighted Dylan's Antipodean visit—and was destined to
continue to spread its miasma of muddled thinking across Europe in
the coming weeks. It concluded his *Music Maker* feature, 'Bob Dylan
Approximately':

> Bob Dylan has returned home. ... He left behind a few memories.
> In the minds of a few ... there will be confusion. Others will
> experience some kind of hatred because he carved them up, even
> though they set about to do just that to him. We have since seen
> newspaper articles and reviews of his concert that demonstrate two
> things. Firstly, newspapermen generally cannot take their own
> medicine. Secondly, newspapers should train their staff to open
> their eyes and ears to what's happening about them. We in Australia
> are isolated enough without having our mass media blinded by this
> isolation.

7. BOY FROM THE NORTH COUNTRY

[April 26–May 1 1966]

Betrügt Bob Dylan seine Fans?

Augen. Er fuhr zurück nach New York. Dort sagte er einem Reporter: Ich habe dieses Publikum in Newport genau angesehen. Es waren zu viele Krankenschwestern mit ihren Eltern dabei. Ein widerliches Anti-Frohsinn-Kommitee!"

Der Mißerfolg von Newport bewog Dylan, sich dem Ausland zuzuwenden. Jahrelang hatte er etwas gegen Tourneen außerhalb Amerikas. Joan Baez und einige andere Freunde überzeugten ihn davon, daß er seine Vorurteile aufgeben müsse. Wochenlang sah man den Protestsong-Manager Charlie Green in der Nähe Dylans. Er war mit seinem 70 000-Mark-Auto aus New Jersey nach Greenwich Village gekommen, um Dylan zu einer Auslands-Tournee zu raten. Er gab den Ausschlag. Ende Mai 1966 ging Dylan auf eine Europa-Tournee. Er kam nach Frankreich, Skandinavien und England. Das Publikum empfing ihn mit großer Neugierde und enthusiastischem Beifall. Nicht so gut war das Echo auf seine Konzerte, bei denen die Fans unter seinen Stimmungen und unter seiner Vorliebe für Whisky zu leiden hatten. Es gab kaum eine Zeitung, die diesen Umstand nicht vermerkte. In der französischen Millio-

nen-Zeitung „Paris Jour" schrieb der Pop-Musik-Kritiker Jaques Bourdette am 27. 5. 1966 über Bob Dylan: „Du hast keine Gelegenheit ausgelassen, uns den Rücken zuzuwenden, deine Gitarre zu stimmen, am Verstärker herumzufummeln, ein Glas Wasser... war es überhaupt Wasser?... zu trinken." Und ein paar Zeilen weiter: „Ich weiß einen Rat für dich, Bob Dylan, kauf dir eine anständige Gitarre und fahr wieder heim!"

In diesen Tagen hält sich mal wieder hartnäckig das Gerücht, daß Dylan im Herbst nach Deutschland kommen will. Wenn er wirklich kommt, sollten ihn seine Fans unvoreingenommen empfangen. Auch ein Star hat ein Anrecht darauf, sich mal zu irren.

Dylan – mit richtigem Namen Robert Zimmermann – hat ungeheuer viel für die Pop-Szene und unsere Musik getan. Er schrieb mit zehn Jahren seinen ersten Text, brachte sich mit zwölf Jahren das Gitarrespielen bei, spielte mit dreizehn Akkordeon und Mundharmonika, erlernte mit fünfzehn ohne Hilfe das Klavierspielen. Dylan ist groß. Er wird als Songschreiber in die Geschichte eingehen. Als Mensch bleibt Dylan das große Rätsel. Er ist undurchschaubar. Vielleicht wird er sich eines Tages auf seine Anfangszeit in einem Kaffeehaus in Greenwich Village besinnen und wieder der große Rebell werden, den seine Fans immer noch in ihm sehen. ■

Das sagt Bob Dylan:

Folk-Musik? Was ist das? Ein Bündel fetter Leute.
(Dylan, Mai 1964 in New York)

Ich habe meine Leute, die auf mein Geld aufpassen. Sie sind alle sehr höflich. Ich bezahle sie gut. Ich spreche nicht viel mit Ihnen. Sie sprechen überhaupt nicht mit mir. So schätze ich, ist alles in Butter.
(Dylan, Juni 1966 in Kopenhagen)

Leute mit kurzen Haaren frieren leicht.
(Dylan, 1965 beim Newport Festival)

Frage: „Immer noch sehen Hunderttausende junger Leute in Ihnen einen Folk-Helden. Fühlen Sie sich ihnen gegenüber irgendwie verantwortlich?"
Antwort: „Nein. Ich bin

wirklich nicht der richtige Mann dafür, durch das Land zu ziehen und Seelen zu retten."
(Dylan, Juni 1966 in London)

Lieder können die Welt nicht retten.
(Dylan, 1965 beim Newport Festival)

Frage: „Einigen Erwachsenen paßt Ihre Kleidung nicht. Sie ist ihnen zu schlampig, zu oberflächlich. Was sagen Sie dazu?"

Antwort: „Ochsenscheiße. Oh, solche Ochsenscheiße! Die Ärzte haben kein Mittel gegen den Krebs, und hier reden ein paar Hinterwäldler darüber, wie wenig sie die Kleidung von jemanden mögen."
(Dylan, Juli 1965 beim Newport Festival)

Impolite, brusque, tired and angry, he came to Sweden, pushing his way through
the photographers at the airport, teased journalists, refused to give them the most
expected answers at the press conference, was given good reviews by those who
appreciated him, but left the country in a fog of misunderstanding, vague words
and attitude.

—ANNETTE KULLENBERG, 'BOB DYLAN: AN AMBIGUOUS PICTURE OF
OUR TIME', *IDUN/VJ*, MAY 13 1966

The Swedish media that greeted the 'curious' Mr Dylan at Stockholm
airport on April 27 1966 came armed with as many preconceptions
as their Australian cousins. Being the first foreign-language reporters
Dylan had encountered to date added an extra barrier to communication,
as well as a touch of comedy to some of their exchanges. If this was
new territory for a man who was, at heart, an American artist—and
until now almost exclusively an Anglo-American phenomenon—he
now had the equipment to capture such a media circus through his
own viewfinder, held there by D.A. Pennebaker.

Scandinavia had held an abiding fascination for him ever since he
befriended his first serious girlfriend, Echo Helstrom, who came from
Swedish stock and instigated Dylan's penchant for northern blondes.
But in five years of unbridled success and steady commercial growth,
having spent time in Italy (in 1963, possibly twice), France, Germany
and Greece (1964) and Portugal (1965), his one and only performance
to a non-English-speaking audience had been a brief, impromptu
appearance at a Rome folk club in January 1963.

At his first European mainland press conference, he seemed a little
out of it, something he blamed on having 'been up all night, taken some
pills and eaten bad food … and been out for hundred-mile-an-hour
car rides'. Despite this, his wandering eye alighted on a sweet pretty
Swede, Pi Ann Murray, who had taken her cue from a distracted Dylan:

He looks tired and bored sitting at the press conference. About fifty
journalists and photographers have gathered to be able to meet by

far the most successful and indecipherable of all folk singers—Bob
Dylan. I sat there, too, trying to build up courage to ask questions—
but it felt somehow unnecessary, everything that the journalists
asked had already appeared in all the papers. Besides, as he always
seemed hounded by press folk, I spoke instead with Mike Rispoli, an
agent for Tito Burns in England whom I had met earlier when the
Stones were last in Stockholm. He promised I could follow him and
Dylan back to their hotel—something I, naturally, gladly accepted!

While Murray was busy networking, Dylan delivered one of his
best sit-down routines since the *Playboy* prank. With all those TV
cameras, microphones and radio station reel-to-reels trained on
him, Dylan kept his mask (and shades) in place and his psychological
armour on. The benign figure evident on the San Francisco press
conference the previous December had sharpened his blade on the
worst Australia could throw at him, and was curious to see if the
Swedes could match him blow for blow in their questioning:

Q: Do you trust reporters?
A: You know I don't. I mean, nobody believes what they read. Even
if you're a reporter, you don't believe what you read.
Q: Do you earn a lot of money?
A: Oh yes, an awful lot of money. I don't know exactly how much
but I must have saved up about 75 billion dollars by now. I have it
sewed up in my jacket, and I never spend it. I'm saving it all up to
buy Australia.
Q: Do you like any of the protest singers who imitate you?
A: No. Have you heard me sing?
Q: No, I haven't.
A: Doesn't it feel strange to sit there asking questions about
something you don't know anything about?

When a reporter asked for an explanation of the title to his latest
single, Dylan riffed on all the different numbers 'Rainy Day Women'
had been assigned in the various territories—an idea absurd enough
to be taken at face value. For an informed fan like Murray, it was
depressing to find that 'everything that the journalists asked had
already appeared in all the papers'.
For Dylan—and his film crew, freshly arrived from the States—

it was a rare opportunity to capture on celluloid the great divide separating Hip from Square in the sixties. The forum he had in mind was *Stage '66*, an ABC TV documentary series scheduled for the fall. Dylan had been getting the measure of his adversaries for months. Now, he set about turning the tables for his own didactic purpose—one he discussed at length with John Cohen after showing him a rough cut of the resultant documentary in 1968:

> **John Cohen**: A feeling I got from watching the film ... is about this personal thing of put-ons, as a personal relationship. Like with the press, they ask such idiotic questions that they are answered by put-ons.
>
> **Bob Dylan**: The only thing there, is that [it] becomes a game in itself. The only way to not get involved in that is not to do it, because it'll happen every time. It even happens with the housewives who might be asked certain questions. ... It's this question and answer business. I can't see the importance of it. There's so many reporters now. That's an occupation in itself. You don't have to be any good at it at all. You get to go to fancy places. It's all on somebody else.
>
> **John Cohen**: Ridiculous questions get ridiculous answers, and the ridiculous response becomes the great moment.
>
> **Bob Dylan**: Yes, well you have to be able to do that now. I don't know who started that, but it happens to everybody ... [until] you end up wondering what you're doing.

All four European press conferences—Stockholm, Copenhagen, London and Paris—would be filmed and recorded by Pennebaker's rolling crew. They may well have been intended to form the centrepiece of the resulting film. But after his July 1966 motorcycle accident, Dylan and film editor Howard Alk would turn the footage they shot in Europe into an anti-documentary—the antithesis of *Dont Look Back*, hence its eventual title, *Eat The Document*. As a result, most of the press conference footage ended up on the cutting-room floor. Perhaps the auteur-in-Dylan felt Pennebaker had already cornered the market in those 'truth attacks' of his in the already-finished 1965 tour documentary.

But for now, both Dylan and Pennebaker seemed to view this film project as a logical extension of that previous film, and were content to capture the widening gulf separating artist from the media. In

Stockholm, the most innocuous request for biographical information was shut down by the Midwestern singer: 'You wanna hear my life story? Maybe we could meet some night in a dark alley and I'll tell it to you.'

A predictable question about protest songs brought an answer aimed more at Pennebaker's camera than its Swedish instigator: 'I'm not a protest singer. In the USA I haven't been called a protest singer since I was a little boy. I sing ordinary mathematical songs … the songs are a result of hunger and thirst.'

Nor did the cameras stop rolling after the official press conference came to a halt and Dylan turned his bayonet on the stooge sent by national radio. When asked almost exactly the same question about protest songs by radio presenter Klas Burling, he brusquely replied, 'I'm just not gonna sit here and talk about myself as a protest singer or anything like that.'

The longer the camera rolled, the more uncomfortable Burling grew, until, audibly flustered, he vainly attempted to place Dylan in a box, stamped and labelled, 'What would you call your style, then? The music you sing?' Pawn to rook four. 'I don't know. I've never heard anybody that plays or sings like me, so I don't know.' Check.

Burling stumbled blindly towards the cliff—seemingly unaware he was being set up to become this year's '*Time* reporter' for this year's *Dont Look Back*—asking for an explanation of 'Rainy Day Women's title. The singer was starting to enjoy himself: '"Rainy Day Women" happens to deal with a minority of cripples and Orientals and the world in which they live … It's another sort of a North Mexican kind of a thing. And one of the protestiest of all things I ever protested against in my protest years.'

'[But] why that title?' Burling pressed on. 'It's never mentioned in the song.'

Dylan moves his queen. 'Well, we never mention things that we love … it has to do with God.' Checkmate.

It had simply not occurred to Burling that Dylan might not be a cooperative subject. Sixties pop stars were meant to play by the rules of a generation of has-beens, not flagrantly ridicule the redundant rulebook. He made one last appeal to Dylan, invoking those Swedish fans who 'have read a lot of dumb things about you in the papers … I thought you could straighten them out yourself'. But he was headed off at the pass: 'I can't straighten them out. I don't think they have to be straightened out.' The only time Burling got a straight answer was when he asked Dylan why he had abandoned folk music:

Bob Dylan: All you heard [in America in the fifties] was rock'n'roll and country & western and rhythm & blues music. Now at a certain time the whole field got taken over into some milk ... Frankie Avalon, Fabian and this kind of thing ... so everybody got out of it ... but nobody really lost that whole thing. And then folk music came in and was some kind of substitute for a while. ... Now it's different again, because of the English thing. The English ... just proved that you could make money playing the same old kind of music that you used to play, and that's the truth. But the English people can't play rock'n'roll music.

The Swedish media seemed wholly unaware that Dylan's fans cared about his music, not his manners. They loved their English pop—and their 'rock'n'roll music'—leaving him cautiously optimistic they would 'dig' something that was now more than the sum of these parts. He now had two days in which to recover his equilibrium, get over his jet lag and make a start on the offstage component of the *Stage '66* film, having discussed his ideas with Howard Alk, who was sometimes wielding the camera and had his own ideas where it should be pointing.

What Alk had in mind failed to impress Pennebaker, who later suggested Dylan 'was very influenced by Howard's film ideas ... [which] tend to be intellectual ideas, but they're not visual ideas ... so personally, that film [they had in mind] was not that interesting. ... There would be strange women and guys and I would just film these little scenes and then [Dylan] would set up things—sometimes he wouldn't do anything—he was just totally into something else ... [but] making home movies well, it's simply that it doesn't interest me very much. ... In fact, I would never do a film like that again, under those conditions. It's just simply too hard. ... I think he felt ... he was going to be Ingmar Bergman or something, and make some new kind of film.'[42]

[42] For my own profile of the career of Howard Alk as director and editor, see *All Across The Telegraph*, ed. John Bauldie and Michael Gray (Sidgwick & Jackson 1988).

When Dylan finally got to examine the footage in the summer of 1966, he realised they had almost nothing suggestive of 'some new kind of film'.[43] Maybe next time.

While Pennebaker ran around filming press conferences and shooting incendiary live footage, it was left to Bobby Neuwirth—who had re-joined the happy band in Europe—and/or Alk to tag along when Dylan had a madcap idea he wanted captured. The first of these was shot the evening after the press conference at his hotel, as members of the local press temporarily joined the circus.

Carsten Grolin of *Ekstra Bladet* had been riding shotgun all afternoon. He even witnessed Dylan's delighted response when a familiar face—'a friend that travelled all the way up from Rome, an American that keeps on talking, a broke American'—made himself known to him. It was Geno Foreman, who once sat alongside Dylan at the infamous Emergency Civil Liberties Committee dinner in December 1963, on the occasion the protest singer first realised his relationship with the American Left was not destined to run along parallel lines. Grolin skilfully blended into the background as Dylan drove around the city centre taking in a gallery before finally reaching the refuge of the hotel lobby, where a few fans had been waiting so patiently:

> At Stureplan 6, in the gallery, a few people are standing waiting for us, for him. As he greets them he bows his head in the indifferent way he usually does after songs in response to applause. He immediately walks out again. Geno keeps talking in the background: 'I want you to dig that one, man.' … We arrive in the square next to the Royal Palace and park the car near by. Bob Dylan—strolling cautiously down Kakhusgrand, stops at Västerlånggatan, blinded by the stream of people. Not that way. Back the same way. We buy a cake in the milk shop and split it between us on the way back … he gulps large pieces with raisins in them.
>
> Only a few fans are waiting on the bench outside the hotel. A few schoolgirls have managed to slip into the lobby through the back

---

[43] '[*Eat The Document*] started as a television special. I wasn't the maker of that film, either. I was the—I was the victim … If I hadn't gotten into that motorcycle accident, they would have broadcast it, and that would have been that … [but] it was obvious from looking at the film that it was garbage. It was miles and miles of garbage. That was my introduction to film. My film concept was all formed in those early days when I was looking at that footage.'—Dylan to Ron Rosenbaum, *Playboy*, January 1978.

door. He waits at the desk for half a minute and Patricia sees her chance, rushes up and touches his shirt, gently, nervously rapping, almost stepping on his shoes in order to get close enough. He smiles at her, some kind of tenderness. 'What are you going to do?' she says in her best school-influenced English. 'How old are you?' he asks. 'Seventeen,' she says. 'I'm thirty-two,' he replies. 'What are you going to do?' she repeats. Just as she's leaving, he shouts, 'What's your name?' 'Patricia,' she says, and her eyes just beam. She jumps over a little fence out on the street and that's the last we see of her.

By now Dylan had been joined by Mike Rispoli and Pi Ann Murray, who had conveniently crossed paths in the hallway. Murray recalled, 'I was wearing pink stockings and he asked me why my legs were so pink. After he had asked a couple of times I understood that he was only joking, so I told him how my dad was a Red Indian but I had turned out pink instead of red. This answer was evidently appreciated and he asked me if I would like to be part of the film being made by a team which was following him during this whole tour. It was [to be] filmed in colour [which led me to] assume it was my pink stockings and sweater which made him ask me.' The blonde hair might also have echoed a former flame.

Murray, Rispoli, Dylan, Grossman and 'the local Stockholm record label secretary' adjourned to the hotel bar along with Grolin, 'some of the musicians, a sound engineer, another sound engineer [and] some groupies'. They promptly requisitioned a booth in the corner, where Dylan gave his usual drinks order:

> Bob and some others wanted tea (Bob drinks almost only tea!) After some fuss—as people are not used to being simply asked for ordinary tea in cocktail bars!—we all sat together sipping tea. By now some journalists had attached themselves to our group—but Bob didn't want them to follow us when we went up to his suite to do the filming which I would take part in, as he is quite sceptical about journalists.

Grolin, despite foregoing pink stockings, successfully attached himself to the select group invited up to Dylan's room. Once again, Dylan used the opportunity to gauge some critical reactions to his forthcoming long-player and Grolin took his chance to garner some insights into the group dynamic:

In an armchair, a pile of records in paper wrappings. He plays them one by one. We hear Bob Dylan sing. One hour, two hours. When he has played the last one, he turns off the record player. The room: filled with teacups, sugar bowls, ashtrays, rolls of film, fruit baskets, people, girls, managers. Dylan talks, short punchlines keep him going. Chunks of words flow out of his mouth. The stream of consciousness verbalized. We sit there listening to these drunken messages on film, people, New York, but mostly on film ... the fascination of free association. Everybody in the inner group has long since gotten used to not contradicting him, or coming up with any comments which are not in line. Way past midnight we sit still in the room at the Flamingo Hotel, hearing Dylan verbalizing his thoughts and impulses. The sky is turning grey. The light shall soon sneak in on us. The TV team, filming him for ABC, come in with their equipment. It's 3:30am. They shoot a scene in the bathroom. The water is turned on, we can hear it running as we head towards the elevator.

The time might have come for Grolin to leave, but pretty-in-pink Murray would stay on, preparing for her acting debut and soaking up the experience. Once again, the conversation flowed—mostly away from Dylan—as the folk-rocker asked for more tea and Murray offered to be Mommy:

Tea for fourteen people. ... We drank the tea, listened to Bob's records and I took my camera and placed it on the table but Bob didn't react. I breathed a deep sigh of relief—it would have been hugely embarrassing if he had asked me to leave! When he had played the records, he started to talk. What a storyteller! He stretched each story into a wilder and more bizarre one than the one before, he smoked constantly (Marlboro), holding a cup of tea which was growing ever more tepid. After a few hours he wanted to start the filming. We went to the bathroom, Bob and I, and there he wanted me to wash my hands while talking in Swedish while he spoke in English and sauntered around. The girl who held the microphone was squeezed in a corner so as to remain out of the frame and the cameraman filmed from the doorway. I washed my hands until they were almost wrinkly and spoke Swedish the whole time. After about a quarter of an hour Bob thought it was enough.

This was the running water Grolin heard heading for the elevator, imagining all sorts of water sports. Soon the sun started to peek above the buildings and even Dylan could see the morning light. Murray asked if he would mind her taking some informal photos. Having agreed, Dylan sat with Robertson and Neuwirth, like three wise monkeys who had just discovered wraparound shades.

After one more cup of tea for the road, Murray took her leave and Dylan took to his bed. Another dark teatime of the soul had passed, and Dylan had got to test the film equipment and the willingness of strangers to play along. As his last guest left, she turned to see 'him take out his typewriter'. When, oh when, did he intend to sleep? When he was dead?

The way he was going, that might be sooner than he thought. He certainly seemed to be maintaining a punishing personal schedule, prompting him to recall, some eight years later, 'We were going all the time, even when we weren't going. We were always doing something else, which is just as draining as performing. We were looking for Loch Ness monsters, staying up for four days running— and making all those eight o'clock curtains besides.'

Yet by the early afternoon, Dylan had risen from the dead and was raring to explore the city. Grolin again skilfully insinuated himself alongside Dylan as the hire car 'slowly makes its way through the city traffic'. Dylan was asking Grolin and the local record label rep. to translate 'every word the newspapers have written. We struggle through the reports from the press conference. Finally he just says: "They like me better today, don't they?"'

Their first and second stops were branches of Gulins, a chain of local clothes shops. At the second of these, Dylan found 'a blue suede jacket, two shirts. Payment in dollars. They helpfully calculate the rate. A Swedish fiver in change.' The next stop was the bookshop Sandbergs, where Dylan enquired whether they stocked 'Rimbaud in English … not a chance. We must be getting back to the hotel. The unrest spreads all over the bookshop. The vibrations. The assistant looking desperately through the catalogues.' Dylan now took the discernible 'unrest' as his cue to leave, without illumination.

Back at the hotel, he prepared for his first-ever paying concert to a non-English-speaking audience—albeit one that had been through the Swedish school system, where English was commonly taught as a second language.

The language barrier—real or imagined—still conquered at least one reviewer, *Svenska Dagbladet*'s Ludvig Rasmusson, who found it 'just about impossible to understand his American accent, and that's a pity, because the lyrics are always so important in his songs'. *Expressen*'s Peter Himmelstrand also struggled with Dylan's idiomatic lyrics, when not complaining about the inordinate amount of time Dylan seemed 'to spend ... with the guitar [trying] to get it reasonably in tune. He sang long songs. His voice is nasal, his articulation difficult ... but even what you can hear isn't readily understood. Mostly the songs give glimpses of desperation and hopelessness.'

Hans Fridlund, writing in *Aftonbladet*, confirmed how Dylan's guitar 'caused him some trouble', adding that 'Dylan excused his repeated—and, on the whole, futile—attempts to tune it by explaining that it, like himself, had been to Australia: "And you can't be sure what happens to things that go over there."' It was his first informal rebuke of the former British colony.

But the difficulties reviewers had understanding the acoustic Dylan was as nothing to what they faced in the second half. The author of a feature on Dylan's trip to Sweden, appositely called 'The Mystery', was so troubled by Dylan's diction that night, he imagined he heard 'Positively 4th Street' and 'I Want You'. He still left feeling that the singer had something to say, and that the audience was with him all the way:

> He hasn't the world's best singing voice, his phrasing is against all rules, his guitar playing mediocre and he is no harmonica virtuoso. But the total effect is exactly right. ... He creates a 'feeling' and an atmosphere no one else can mimic. He stands on the dark stage and the spotlight captures his pale form. He forces the words out as if it was a physical effort. Even if one doesn't always understand the words one is compelled to listen.

The locals, fans and critics alike, had come to listen, as the annoyingly incomplete audience tape suggests in those rare moments when the taper allows a song to live and breathe.[44] In what was a

---

[44] Though the acoustic songs are mostly intact, only snatches of the electric set were recorded by the taper.

welcome change, the majority seemed enraptured by all they heard. One person who knew just how tired Dylan must feel, and how much he was pushing himself to communicate, revelled in the communal rapture. For Pi Ann Murray, it was a near-religious experience:

> The first note is out of tune, hesitating. Then he braces himself, looking down at the guitar as if to get support. He closes his eyes, becomes a medium for the song which presses itself out of his throat, painfully, relentlessly. One second he looks like a Belsen prisoner, the other his cheeks are round like those of a choirboy. His hair makes a halo, further accentuated by the blinding light from the spotlights that seem able to burn to shreds the spindly little form on the stage.
>
> And we do recognise his songs. We've heard them ever so many times when playing his records, or on the radio [when] we had the possibility of switching him off if we didn't feel like listening. But here he can't be switched off. Nobody would want to, anyway. The text has become alive; it isn't just a string of well-chosen words any longer, meandering around the melody.
>
> Everybody in the concert hall holds their breath, frowning in concentration, eyes glued to this tiny human being down there in the floodlights, singing of the injustices and meanness in our world. Deafening applause. It feels wrong, somehow. There ought to be silence so that all of us might get the time to think, to digest the words, incorporate them with their own selves. And then comes the interval. People go out to have a Coke ...
>
> Bob's band has [now] invaded the stage with their electric guitars, organ and drums. But this must surely be wrong. How on earth could Bob Dylan's message get to us through the din of loudspeakers, the throbbing of drums? They start at once, and you realise that you were wrong again. The only way is just to let yourself go, to listen, absorb, follow Bob when he sings ... the microphone cable trailing after him. So at last the concert's over. A lonely spotlight shines on the curtain where they just disappeared.

Hans Fridlund was almost as bowled over by the symbiotic connection between Dylan and what was, after all, a foreign audience: 'A completely filled concert hall listened attentively to ... Dylan with a roaring electric band. It was a demanding task for the listeners—but rewarding. And, above all, a brilliant sounding concert—[thanks to] the huge sound equipment which they had brought.' Even *Expressen*'s reporter, who thought The Hawks were 'one of the roughest ever to play in the concert hall', had to admit to hearing no audible dissent. The first European show had passed off without a hitch. But it was a close run thing. Alderson had left the original PA in Australia on Grossman's instructions, and been obliged to construct an entirely new PA setup for Europe:

Richard Alderson: In Stockholm I was still putting the equipment together on the stage fifteen minutes before the concert. John Court [had] bought all the equipment [in New York]—it was Mac amplifiers, a couple of stage monitors, a five-channel Altech mixer and some microphones. ... I didn't go to sleep for five days. But that sound system never worked as well as the first one. ... I was so crazed getting it together and it wasn't quite right. ... There wasn't enough time to get it right. I was also getting burnt out.

★ ★ ★

Across the sea in Denmark, ticket sales had not been so brisk, having been pitched at a population with far less of a reputation for embracing Anglo-American pop than Sweden. Its press was also less inclined to give Dylan the benefit of the doubt, his performance in front of another battery of reporters and cameras being scheduled before he had even got the gist of the place. He was now determined to make the film the thing, and at least one reporter realised the true purpose of the movie camera Alk (or Pennebaker) was wielding—to produce an authentic document of another Danish play within a play:

A few believers sit down at his feet and are cross-examined by Bob Dylan. They are unknowing participants in the TV film—maybe a way of getting variation at the press conferences, to let the victim ask the questions himself. Tea. Dylan drinks tea. Dylan refuses to answer. Mumbles through his fingers. The air is filled with the journalists' attempts to explain Dylan to the man himself: I understand you, it must be awful ... but why do you give press conferences when it's such a pain for you? Other journalists stand behind his back, trying to say mean things and frequently using the word 'fuck'. All is doomed to fail. It's going to end soon, he says to one of the tour managers. Once in a while he repeats his standard line: I'm so bad I cannot be insulted. The press—a bunch of people arriving at a precise time, an opportunity for him to test his resistance, his ability to strike back. A load of questions that don't concern him—a collection of subjects to improvise on. The fear of the journalists turns into spite: if he can be mean, so can we. A mirrored image of reality.

The Danish media presumably knew all about the previous conflagration with their Swedish kinfolk and were determined they would not be hoist by their own petty petards. But no matter how they worded their condescending enquiries, Dylan kept lobbing their verbal volleys back. When one impertinent Dane asked Dylan if there were times when he couldn't stand himself, the singer rejoined, 'How could that be possible? ... I don't know who I am. There's a mirror on the inside of my dark glasses.'

When the singer was asked a perfectly reasonable question, about when and how he wrote his songs, he was more conciliatory, but no less obtuse: 'I write when I'm alone. When I'm with a lot of people I'm so alone that I have to sing my songs to find out if it's reality.'

In the end, it turned predictably fractious. When another reporter wanted to know how much money meant to him, Dylan spat back, 'I don't care about money. Nothing has changed me. I'm not a prophet. I don't care how much money I make; only you do. I don't spend my money on cars and boats and castles like an idiot, but people look at me like a poor fool. Well so I am, a man of the people.'

As in Sydney, he felt he had been left little alternative but to parody the whole charade. This time, though, he did not wait until the room was cleared before he began playing the wise fool. Pi Ann Murray, having already witnessed Dylan's capacity for shape-shifting in Stockholm, knew enough to stand back as he again turned the conventions of press vs. pop personality upside down:

Having held many press conferences, Bob Dylan has learned that most of the journalists who turn up don't know the slightest thing about his music, his art, and that consequently meaningful dialogue with them is impossible. The questions that are directed toward him are usually pointless. 'What do you think of Danish girls? Where are you going after this concert? Where have you just come from, and how was it there?' When these and similar questions came raining in on Bob Dylan in the first ten minutes of the press conference, it all got too much for him. He took out a notebook and pencil himself and asked the nearest reporter: 'Incidentally, when does the sun rise in this country?' The reporter replied, somewhat taken aback. Dylan nodded. 'Very interesting—I see—yes,' and eagerly wrote it all down. Then he turned to another reporter and asked him when the sun sets, again carefully jotting down his answer. Then he asked a third question:

'And this castle, where Hamlet lived, Kronborg, how long will it take to get there on horseback? You don't know? What do you know?' 'And your favourite music,' he asked a woman reporter. 'What's your favourite music?' 'Beethoven,' she replied in a cultured voice, 'I'm very fond of Beethoven's symphonies.' 'Yes, but I was thinking more of your favourite music,' Dylan continued. 'But it is Beethoven,' the woman repeated rather brusquely. 'Oh come on,' said Dylan, 'what's your favourite *music*?' Dylan's parody of a press conference was perfect, but the journalists were furious at the end of it all. 'Who does he think he is?' some of them muttered.

His enquiry about Kronborg's castle was not entirely specious. Dylan planned to visit the famous site, just not on horseback. He may well have seen it as an opportunity to bone up on Shakespeare and a play he referenced nightly in 'Desolation Row'. A crash-course in the bard seems to have been something he felt he required. Carsten Grolin, who remained on his tail—and in shot—throughout the visit to Helsingør, later reported, 'He wanted to know everything about the history of Kronborg—if Shakespeare had ever been there, where it was that Hamlet had met his father's ghost. All the time the film crew were shooting ... for the TV film, which will be called *The Twentieth Century Hamlet*.' Or not.

A journalist from *Idun/VJ* watched from afar as a pensive Dylan imagined himself taking up arms against a mixed metaphor; wandering the grounds of the castle in silence, undisturbed and undaunted. But then he took a wrong turn:

A Danish soldier stops him. Even the old castle of Kronborg has forbidden areas. It's Saturday afternoon and the soldier's eyes start to roll, he seems to tremble inside his baggy uniform. Bob Dylan turns around and walks to the castle square. His silhouette, far away

on a hill. Like Phoenix against the clear blue sky of April. Close,
watching over the sea and flying behind the camera. Flying over
the hillsides, tripping in the gravel, crowing in the air, and finally,
dragging his legs heading toward the exit.

The two-hour visit yielded very little footage that made the final
cut of Dylan's film, but it confirmed he was in a play of his own
making. Surrounded by his own princely entourage, he would soon
be heading for England just as things were hotting up in Denmark.

Having returned to his city-centre hotel—hoping to get a good
night's rest before giving the Danes what for—he was fleetingly
distracted over dinner by 'a couple of school girls who have been
permitted to come in and say hello. "How about a game of table
tennis, Bob?" He removes his sunglasses and shuts his eyelids …
He says he's too tired to play, that he's going to take a sauna, a bath,
massage, but maybe later. He puts on his glasses and heads toward the
exit … swaying and strutting … not rhythmical nor unrhythmical.'
Aye, to sleep, to dream.

The following night he arrived at the KB-Hallen to discover the
Danish press were more concerned with his failure to sell out the
show than whether he had personally sold out. Asked to proffer an
explanation for such disinterest, Grossman delivered his own Dylanesque retort: 'There simply aren't very many Danes who want to hear
Bob. That's the way it is.'

Carsten Grolin, one of the few in attendance who could compare
performances, considered the 'Sunday concert at KB-Hallen, … an
even stranger experience than the show in Stockholm … because of
[the] bad acoustics'. More worryingly, one thing the two gigs shared
was the difficulty Dylan had tuning his acoustic guitar 'while the
people patiently waited … [twice, for] over five minutes'.

He continued to blame his problems on the Aussies, insisting he had
bought the guitar there some twenty years earlier (i.e. at the age of four).
His electric guitar was waiting in the wings, and he couldn't wait—and
nor could the Danes. Bjarne Jensens's review verged on hagiography:

> What a show! Never have we experienced something so intense, so
> beautiful and so universal on KB-Hallen's stage. Here was a true
> genius revealing himself … [When] he plugs in his electric guitar

... the hall is rolling, as if washed over by an enormous wave. This wave grows as the music becomes more and more intense. One of the older numbers, 'One Too Many Mornings' ... [has] the restlessness of its lyrics ... now sharply underlined by the music.

Ole John, writing for *Politiken*, was similarly swept up by the music, and delighted to see Dylan himself become progressively more animated until, during the final two numbers, 'a complete transformation takes place. Dylan becomes intense, the hall comes alive, and everything is important ... a chill runs down one's spine. He doesn't sell any alibis but keeps moving towards a constantly stronger calling. His music finally becomes more real and true as he reaches and surpasses his best recordings ... I think many people left the concert completely stunned.'

For the first time in a year, Pennebaker had set up cameras either side of the stage, hoping to capture elements of a magical night. He was in luck. By the time Dylan got to 'Ballad Of A Thin Man', an increasingly animated frontman could barely contain himself. This appears to be the performance later used as a promotional film for Dylan's 1988 induction into the Rock and Roll Hall of Fame, edited together by Dylan's son Jesse. The power of this performance blew everyone away that night. Two decades earlier, it had pretty much the same effect, while also convincing Pennebaker he was making the wrong goddamn film:

D.A. Pennebaker: It was Bob's film. And he wasn't really interested in making a concert film. He was interested in making a film for television ... he basically was interested primarily in directing material off the stage. Stage material did not interest him and in fact I shot a lot of it kinda on my own. ... The music was so fantastic and they were all so into it and Dylan's role in it—I mean, Dylan was so happy, he was jumping around like a cricket in the middle of the thing. ... It was the first time I had ever seen him really happy in the middle of the music. And the music was incredible. People would listen to that stuff and it would actually blow the life out of them.

To his eternal credit, Pennebaker decided then and there to film as much of this onstage drama as he could and leave Dylan to make of it what he would. Only with the 2005 release of Martin Scorsese's *No Direction Home* did it become clear just how much footage this prime exponent of cinéma-vérité *had* filmed. Yet even this four-hour documentary—and its complementary two-CD 'soundtrack'—gave only the barest hint of the size of the audio iceberg, the tip of which has been steadily dripping into the public domain since the early seventies.

Fortunately for Jensens, John, and posterity, the last five songs of the electric set that night in Copenhagen were recorded from the desk in pulsating mono on a Nagra reel-to-reel recorder, to sync-up sound with the film Pennebaker was shooting.[45] Recorded by Richard Alderson, they are clearly marked reels one and two, though they comprise only the last half of the electric set, evidently all that was recorded on this occasion.

However, from this point forward, Alderson would tape as much of each show as he could manage, technical difficulties notwithstanding, providing an almost complete record of the British, Irish and French shows that would change the world of song in the month of May. He missed some of the action, but not a lot. As he says, 'While the audience was reacting, I had plenty of time to change the reels. I didn't get every reel change right every night, but I got most of them right. … The tape recorder sat right next to me. I had a good sensibility of how people were gonna react after the first couple of concerts.'

For now, Dylan was in no mood to listen back to the night's show in his hotel suite. Instead, as the still-attendant Grolin later noted, 'The tables in the living room [of Dylan's suite] are filled with tea cups, ashtrays, sugar bowls and pieces of a sandwich. The hours after the concert will pass during extensive preaching. The believers are here. Dylan sits in a black leather armchair and starts tonight's happenings.'

It was a now-familiar nightly ritual, designed to wile away the wee hours. No one in that lofty suite was inclined to remind Dylan, a big Stanley Brothers fan, that the darkest hour was just before the dawn. Or that in Denmark ghosts of the undead appeared at midnight to remind the living that acts of revenge were sometimes necessary to correct a world out of joint.

---

[45] According to Alderson, 'The Nagra was supposed to be hooked up with sync. [But] I plugged the sync [head] in and it never worked.' The same Nagra would be put to service recording the songs Dylan and The Hawks would record in the Big Pink 'basement' the following year.

8. THE UNFORGIVEN
[May 3–11 1966]

ANNOUNCING A LIMITED SEASON OF CONCERTS

BOB DYLAN

BY ARRANGEMENT WITH TITO BURNS

DUBLIN ADELPHI THEATRE **THURS., MAY 5**	8 p.m. 25/-, 20/-, 15/-, 10/-, Box Office open 26 March	**SHEFFIELD** GAUMONT THEATRE **MON., MAY 16**	8.15 p.m. 20/-, 15/-, 12/-, 10/-, 8/6. Box Office open 21 March	
BELFAST A.B.C. THEATRE **FRI., MAY 6**	8 p.m. 25/-, 20/-, 15/-, 10/-. Box Office open 26 March	**MANCHESTER** FREE TRADES HALL **TUES., MAY 17** 7.30 p.m.	**SOLD OUT**	
BRISTOL COLSTON HALL **TUES., MAY 10** in association with Charles H. Lockier Ltd.	7.45 p.m. 20/-, 17/6, 15/-, 13/6, 10/6, 8/6. Box Office now open.	**GLASGOW** ODEON THEATRE Renfield Street **THURS., MAY 19**	8 p.m. 20/-, 15/-, 12/-, 10/-, 8/6. Box Office open 21 March	
CARDIFF CAPITOL THEATRE **WED., MAY 11**	7.30 p.m. 20/-, 15/-, 12/6, 10/-, 8/6. Box Office open 21 March	**EDINBURGH** A.B.C. THEATRE **FRI., MAY 20**	7.45 p.m. 20/-, 17/6, 15/-, 12/6, 10/-. Box Office now open	
BIRMINGHAM ODEON THEATRE NEW STREET **THURS., MAY 12**	8.15 p.m. 20/-, 16/-, 13/-, 10/6, 8/6. Box Office open 27 March	**NEWCASTLE** ODEON THEATRE **SAT., MAY 21**	8.30 p.m. 20/-, 17/6, 15/-, 12/-, 10/-, 8/6. Box Office open 21 March	
LIVERPOOL ODEON THEATRE **SAT., MAY 14**	7.45 p.m. 20/-, 18/-, 13/-, 10/6, 7/6. Box Office open 21 March	**LONDON** ROYAL ALBERT HALL **THURS., MAY 26** 7.30 p.m.	**SOLD OUT**	
LEICESTER DE MONTFORT HALL **SUN., MAY 15** in association with Arthur Kimbrell	7.45 p.m. 20/-, 17/6, 15/-, 12/6, 10/6, 8/6, 7/6, 3/6. Box Office now open	EXTRA PERFORMANCE **LONDON** ROYAL ALBERT HALL Kensington Gore **FRI., MAY 27**	7.30 p.m. 20/-, 15/-, 10/6, 7/6, 3/6. Box Office now open	

PERSONAL & POSTAL BOOKING ONLY.
PLEASE ENCLOSE S.A.E.

Bob Dylan arrives in Britain for his second British tour on Monday (May 2)—
and is bringing his American backing group with him. The group—just called
The Group—will play all Dylan's British dates with him. They will accompany
the singer for half of each concert and he will do the other half alone.
—'DYLAN BRINGS OWN GROUP', *MELODY MAKER*, APRIL 30 1966

This brief news story, in the music paper most British Dylan fans liked to read, served as an all-important backdrop to his May 1966 UK tour, scheduled to run from the fifth to the twenty-seventh. To those of a folk-minded disposition, for whom two electric albums and five electric singles were not enough of a clue as to Dylan's 'current bag', it confirmed their worst fears. It also suggested they should look to scalp any tickets already purchased—especially in London and Manchester, where shows were already sold out.

Whereas in 1965 articles announcing how 'The Beatles Dig Dylan' and whether an acoustic troubadour could be a poet had lit the way for Dylan's arrival, by 1966 he was a bona fide pop star with a #1 album (*Bringing It All Back Home*), a #4 album (*Highway 61 Revisited*) and three Top 10 singles ('Subterranean Homesick Blues', 'Like A Rolling Stone' and 'Positively 4th Street') to his name, all in the twelve months since last he played the City Halls of Albion.

This time, he needed no advance hype to sell out a full tour of the British Isles. Nor did he need the press to follow him around firing questions. So, instead of multiple formal and informal press conferences, backstage interviews with student reporters, one-on-one interviews with all the important music weeklies and the odd impertinent questionnaire, he agreed to exactly one press conference at the Mayfair Hotel—having relocated from the Savoy (perhaps still unhappy about the previous year's 'who threw the fucking glass' incident, captured in *Dont Look Back*). At the press conference scheduled for the day after he flew in, he would again use the film crew as personal foils in another grand charade.

Not surprisingly, members of the English music press were a little put out to find themselves sitting cheek to jowl with 'the establishment press … [who] didn't understand what was going on in the musical arena'. As to what they could expect, they might have seen one of the questionnaires he had filled in the previous May, for *Jackie*, which listed the 'loves and hates of Bob Dylan'. In the former category he had included 'originality in anybody—makes such a big difference when they've got their own ideas to give out'. Personal bugbears included, 'Rules. Why should we have them? … the importance that money has in our society …[and] that strange feeling when you come into a room that something's gone wrong.'

There was certainly a 'strange feeling' in the Mayfair Hotel suite on the May day Dylan deigned to lock horns with another querulous quorum. Even familiar faces were given short shrift, Dylan 'blanking' Max Jones before making him the butt of one of his best one-liners. When Jones suggested he had heard he didn't write protest songs any more, Dylan fired back, 'All my songs are protest songs. You name something, I'll protest about it. All I do is protest.'[46]

Jones had been the first person Dylan called on when he visited London in December 1962 (Jones having been recommended by Ramblin' Jack Elliott), and had been someone Dylan opened up to on both previous May visits, in 1964 and 1965. So he was bemused to find Dylan being wholly uncooperative but relieved to find he was not singled out for the treatment, prompting the headline to his resultant feature, 'Will The Real Bob Dylan Please Stand Up?':

Chatting up Bob Dylan … used to be easier, but as he gets older he seems to grow more and more fed-up with questions. Very difficult it is getting him alone. When you've failed in that, the next hindrance is his reluctance to impart information. It's not that he won't answer. But his replies, sometimes oblique and often designed to send-up, carry vagueness to the borders of evasion. Asked if the label folk-rock, sometimes applied to his current music making, meant anything to him, he queried back at me: 'Folk-rot?'

To raise the level of the conversation a bit, I injected the names of Bukka White, Son House and Big Joe Williams. Did Dylan listen to such blues singers?

[46] This memorable exchange appears in both *Eat The Document* and *No Direction Home*.

THE UNFORGIVEN 210

'I know Big Joe, of course. But I never listen to these men on records too much. Lately I've been listening to Bartok and Vivaldi and that sort of thing. So I wouldn't know what's happening.'

Before we parted, another journalist was questioned by Dylan. He mentioned his paper. Dylan looked blank. 'It's the leading musical paper in the country,' said the reporter firmly.

'The only paper I know is the *Melody Maker*,' was Dylan's reply. One way or another he makes it clear he's not out to win friends and influence newspaper men.

The reporter from the 'leading musical paper in the country' was Keith Altham, *NME*'s hippest reporter. But even this well-known face made very little headway with the man behind the shades when trying to raise the tone:

For posterity's sake, I framed a question which might have been construed as 'being aware' ... why is it that the titles of his recent singles, like 'Rainy Day Women #12 + 35' apparently bore no connections with the lyric? 'It has every significance,' returned Dylan. 'Have you ever been down in North Mexico?' 'Not recently ...'

A nonplussed Altham turned his attention to 'a large gentleman with a grey top hat and movie camera permanently affixed to his shoulder, lurch[ing] about the room like Quasimodo, alternately scratching his ear and his nose, with the occasional break to "whirr" the machine in the face of perplexed reporters'. It was Pennebaker, of course.

Altham also observed 'a lady in grey denims wav[ing] what appeared to be huge grey frankfurters about ... [which] proved to be microphones attached to tape recorders'. The lady was Jones Alk.

Mrs Alk—whose husband Howard was hovering somewhere in the background—found herself an unwitting bit-part actor in another of Dylan's games for May on the one occasion the 'establishment press' managed to ruffle Dylan's feathers. He found himself ducking a series of questions regarding his recently reported marriage, a touchy subject at the best of times, until the mirror behind the glasses almost cracked:

Q: Are you married?
A: I'd be a liar if I answered that, and I don't lie.
Q: Well, tell the truth then.

A: I might be married. I might not. It's hard to explain really.

Q: Is she your wife? [*points to Jones Alk*].

A: Her? Oh yeah, you can say she's my wife.

Jones Alk: No, my husband wouldn't like it.

Q: Are you married to Joan Baez?

A: Joan Baez was an accident … I brought my wife over last time and nobody took any notice of her.

Q: So you are married then?

A: It would be very misleading if I said yes, I was married; and I would be a fool if I said no.

Q: But you just said you had a wife.

A: That depends on what you mean by married.

The four music press reps in attendance—Jones and Altham, plus *Record Mirror*'s Richard Green and an unnamed correspondent from *Disc & Music Echo*—valiantly tried to stem the tide of inanity, but it was a losing battle. Time to just sit back and enjoy the ride:

Q: What do you own?

A: Oh, thirty Cadillacs, three yachts, an airport at San Diego, a railroad station in Miami. I was planning to bus all the Mormons.

Q: What are your medical problems?

A: Well, there's glass in the back of my head. I'm a very sick person. I can't see too well on Tuesdays. These dark glasses are prescribed. I'm not trying to be a beatnik. I have very mercury-esque eyes. And another thing—my toenails don't fit.

Q: Tell us about the book you've just completed!

A: It's about spiders, called *Tarantula*. It's an insect book. Took about a week to write, off and on … my next book is a collection of epitaphs.

Q: Who's the guy with the top hat?

A: I don't know. I thought he was with you. I sometimes wear a top hat in the bathroom.

Eventually, as in Copenhagen, 'Mr Dylan started to interview the journalists', as things again turned sour. After he told the *Daily Sketch*'s Dermot Purgavie they were boring, 'the stroppier ones among us indicated that they weren't too enchanted by him, either'. At the end of proceedings, the *Sun*'s Christopher Reed spoke for his fellow

Fleet Streeters when he observed how Dylan had 'managed to answer questions for an hour without really answering any of them at all'.

As the press filed out, a CBS publicist suggested, 'Cliff Richard was never like this.' Mr Reed now had his headline. Purgavie was equally sniffy about the uncooperative artist in his *Sketch* headline, 'At least in his songs Mr Dylan has something to say.' On the other hand, England's thriving mid-sixties music press, to a man, sided with the star. Appropriately, *Disc & Music Echo*, the weekly that had run his notorious 'Mr Send-Up' interview the previous May, seemed particularly amused:

> Bob Dylan arrived preceded by an almost violent reputation for being rude and uncooperative. He is rude—to people whom he considers ask stupid questions. He is uncooperative—he doesn't like giving up his precious free time for individual interviews. But Bob Dylan is also a very sympathetic man with a vast sense of humour. He explained why he was wearing dark glasses. 'I have glasses at the back of my head too. Look. I'm not trying to come on like a beatnik. I have to wear them under prescription because my eyes are so bad.' ... He played with a huge ashtray and then, this man who has said more with his songs than many say in ten thousand words, was asked some of the most ridiculous questions in the world. Things like a barrage of question[s] about whether he was married as though it was the most important thing since the nuclear bomb. No wonder he lost his patience.

Record Mirror's Richard Green took equal delight in quoting ill-advised questions from the straight press, juxtaposed with the non-sequiturs Dylan provided for answers. Like Altham, he had realised immediately that 'the farce ... was obviously being staged' for the cameras' benefit and played dumb:

> Until then, I'd always thought that *Juke Box Jury* was the funniest thing ever. But Dylan's handling of the press left that standing. Asked if he had any children, he said, 'Every man with medical problems has children.' Asked what his medical problems were, he said, 'Well, there's glass in the back of my head and my toenails don't fit properly.' Dylan's bunch of assorted film cameramen and sound recordists were happily enjoying the farce which was obviously

being staged for their benefit. They continually trained cameras on
the reporters and pushed weird microphones at people who spoke.
Then somebody mentioned folk singer Dana Gillespie and at once
Dylan brightened up. He laughed out loud, smiled broadly and
asked, 'Yeah, where is Dana. Come on out, Dana. I've got some
baskets for her. Put your clothes on.'

As the penultimate press conference of the world tour wound to
its predictable conclusion, Keith Altham went looking for one last
usable quote, not from Dylan but from one of his sidekicks: taking
'one of Dylan's undercover agents to one side (I knew he was a Dylan
man as he had dark glasses on) I enquired why a man with Dylan's
obvious intelligence bothered to arrange this farce of a meeting'. It
was Bobby Neuwirth, whom he recognised from the previous year.
He wasn't about to sugar-coat it; 'Dylan just wanted us to come along
and record a press reception so we could hear how ridiculous and
infantile all reporters are.'

For the remainder of his time in the British Isles, Dylan kept the
press at arm's length—clearly a conscious decision. The one time he
decided to rebut accusations fired his way by reviewers of the shows,
it would be from the Royal Albert Hall stage to a captive audience.

Unlike in Australia, Sweden, Denmark and, later, France, no
figure from the English press would be invited into his hotel suite
or backstage. The one reporter who enjoyed this rare privilege on
the British mainland worked for the French paper *Salut Les Copains*.
And yet Dylan was sociability itself where British musicians were
concerned, hanging out with current and/or former members of The
Beatles, the Stones, The Who, The Spencer Davis Group, Manfred
Mann and The Animals, soaking up every element of that 'English
thing' by proxy.

He also reacquainted himself with the buxom Ms Gillespie,
with whom he had enjoyed a few lowland flings the previous May.
Indeed, the night after the press conference he was seen at the Blaises
nightclub, in the company of Dana, a confirmed blues fan in her
own right. Both were there to see John Lee Hooker. When a music
journalist summoned up the nerve to approach the pair, he singularly
failed to comprehend the conversation: 'Dylan was talking a language
of his own. English words but used in a sequence of phrases that could

be understood only by his close friends. And there were plenty of them.'

While Dylan refrained from explaining his idiosyncratic use of the mother tongue, Dana did eventually offer one—to *NME*'s Norrie Drummond. But it was only after the tour had ended, and her friend had returned to the bosom of his family. Only then did she agree to answer the burning question: why had he been so difficult with the many reporters who wanted to interview him?

Dana Gillespie: Bobby is only interested in the international, glossy magazines like *Time*, *Paris Match* and the like. He's really very concerned about publicity, but then he only reads the glossies. He's very choosy about his friends as well. He likes Paul McCartney, John Lennon, Keith Moon and Marianne Faithfull and her husband. But he has very few close friends. Paul Simon told me recently that when Bobby went back to see some of his old friends in Greenwich Village last year they were very offhand. They were jealous of his success. Now he only has one or two real friends who go round to his place.

If he had been largely friendless on his international travels to date, Bobby Neuwirth and Victor Maymudes were now there for him. Also part of the close-knit group which now provided a physical and psychological buffer was Tom Keylock, the chauffeur-cum-bodyguard loaned to Dylan for the duration by The Rolling Stones. However, Keylock would not be required for the first two shows, which were in Ireland's twin capitals, Dublin and Belfast, on May 5 and 6. The British tour proper would not start until the tenth. By then the reviews of the Irish shows would be in, setting the media agenda for most shows to come. Perhaps opening in Dublin, with its long-standing tradition of judgemental critics and *faux* folklorists, might not have been such a wise move—even for someone never known to make a foolish one.

★ ★ ★

Dublin was unfamiliar territory for Dylan—as were Belfast, Bristol and Cardiff, the next three shows, all places he'd bypassed the previous year. Each represented a different country and a distinct folk tradition. If Dylan was trying to gauge the likely reaction to his new music prior to playing the places he already knew—Sheffield, Liverpool, Manchester, Birmingham, Leicester, Newcastle and London—the Irish capital would serve as a worrying barometer. Fifty years after the Easter Rising, it retained its gift for rewriting history and critical misrepresentation.

The Dublin acoustic set—minus 'She Belongs To Me', only partially captured by Alderson—has been familiar to Dylan fans since 1970, when it formed part of a famous double-album bootleg of the so-called Royal Albert Hall, *Looking Back*, and later the TMQ single album, *While The Establishment Burns*.

What is clear from the mono soundboard tape is that Dylan had not been burning the candle at both ends the night before. The performance is controlled, sensual, gripping, which may be why a dub ended up in the Columbia archives—from where the bootleg would be sourced. Released just four years after the concert, it contradicted almost every misguided judgement made by the reviewer for the *Dublin Evening Press* who wondered why the place was so full and why the *acoustic* set had to be so loud!

> If the poets of former years were content to wile away their winter years in poverty for lack of financial appreciation of their works, not so the youthful, long-haired Bob Dylan. ... Plenty of crinkly notes changed hands in the process of filling the Adelphi Cinema last night for his long-awaited concert. Some members of that large audience, obviously very familiar with his recordings, got value for money. But the remainder? From where I sat, the raspy voice of Dylan, backed by his guitar and harmonica, was ear-piercing, but few of the actual words were distinguishable.

The ever-contrary Irish press had really got their britches in a twist about the very notion that a poet might be paid well or command a large audience. Some still preferred their 'poets' to spout revolutionary rhetoric and incite rebellion rather than display a grasp of syntax, alliteration or metaphor. The *Irish Times*' George D. Hodnett, who had adopted the Yeatsian middle initial, was one of those who spent most of his next-day review trying to come up with some explanation for the words 'sold out' at the entrance to the Adelphi:

> Bob Dylan is a phenomenon … [whose] long-awaited concert at the Adelphi Cinema, Dublin, was revealing. Audience reaction, though very enthusiastic, of itself meant little, for most of those present were patently pre-conditioned, like a Beatle audience; one had to like Dylan so one obediently did; this social conformity might or might not coincide with what one would have liked had one's tastes been left to themselves, and the odd genuine rebel who said he didn't would have narrowly escaped lynching. … One cannot apply the ordinary criteria of musical criticism to this type of performance, for one would have to be musically unsophisticated indeed to imagine that Mr Dylan exploits the possibilities of the harmonica, guitar, or voice adequately.

Having dutifully stayed around for the electric half, Hodnett found 'most of the group numbers were rather a blur. Also there was some over-amplification. But I forgot; this isn't music, but something else: something sociologically interesting even after allowing for the ad-men.'

A frustrated Trinity man, it never occurred to Hodnett that he was unqualified to pass judgement on Dylan's poetic credentials. He was even impertinent enough to suggest Dylan would have been 'a minor one were he to publish in slim volumes without the assistance of guitar, harmonica and publicity machine'.

But Mr Hodnett was hardly the least informed reviewer sent along to the Adelphi. He faced serious competition in this department from both the *Sunday Independent*'s Norman Barry and the *Dublin Evening Herald*'s 'J.K.'. The former's review, which ran beneath the headline 'Oh What A Shock For Dylan Fans!', he wrote after turning a deaf ear to the entire second half:

> For the second half of the programme he forsook the folk material the now-restless audience had paid, and paid heavily, to see. There were shouts of 'traitor', 'stuffed golliwog' and 'positively BORE street', plus slow-handclapping and boos. The barrage of amplification equipment completely drowned Dylan's nasal voice, which requires the utmost concentration at the best of times. His beat arrangements were monotonous and painful, as folk useless and as beat, inferior. 'Like A Rolling Stone' had some merit. There were a few diehards who clapped until the end. They'll never learn.

Meanwhile, 'J.K.' decided his press-pass gave him a license to exaggerate, a permit to misrepresent and an excuse to display profound ignorance of the roots of R&B:

> Oh what a storm blew up when Dylan came to town! They booed. They said things (mostly unprintable). They whistled. They jeered. Someone groaned 'pos-it-ively MOORE street' ... and he shot back, quick as a flash: 'Would you be so positive on 4th Street?' ... Dylan [now] assumed the role of a slightly down-at-heel paperback edition of Mick Jagger, and with the exception of the powerful 'Like A Rolling Stone' and 'One Too Many Mornings', what came out of the amplifiers was nothing more than watered-down R&B. ... It was unbelievable to see Dylan trying to look and sound like Jagger, and to realise after a stunning first few minutes that it wasn't a 'take-off'. Someone shouted 'Traitor!', someone else, 'Leave it to The Beatles!' ... The 2,000-odd who came to hear him will remember it as the Night of the Great Let-Down. It was just brutal, as they say ... in Dublin.

Evidently, all copies of last week's *Melody Maker* earmarked for the Emerald Isle had been lost at sea. Phrases like 'slightly down-at-heel paperback edition of Mick Jagger' suggested ongoing lessons in grammatical English were not going particularly well, either. But what annoyed Dublin's Dylan fans the most were the bald-faced lies. If one had just these reviews to go on, one might imagine the sound of his 'watered-down R&B' was drowned out by the dissent. Nothing was further from the truth, as fans made plain, raining the scorn of the Irish down on Eire's fourth estate.

The enraged of Erin directed their ire not at Dylan but at the *Sunday Independent* and the *Herald*, presaging similar epistolean fury from British brethren. Mary Morrissey of Dublin 6 actually challenged the *Sunday Independent* to prove its reviewer bothered to attend the show:

> Having read Norman Barry's review of the Bob Dylan concert at the Adelphi on May 5th, I wondered if Mr Barry was present. He describes Dylan during the first half of the concert as 'slightly more incoherent than on record'. Every word he sang was perfectly lucid. Mr Barry says 'there were a few diehards who clapped until the end'.

At the concert that I attended, at least 90 percent of the audience applauded enthusiastically.

But it was mainly J.K.'s review that drew fans' fury as moths to a flame. Among the various letter-writers who took up their pens to question the accuracy of J.K.'s piece (and even his journalistic integrity), 'The Ghost' went to some pains to correct J.K. on the scale of dissent:

> For [J.K.]'s information, the lack of appreciation was shown by a small ignorant group of people who knew no better anyway. Secondly, he apparently thought that Dylan's guitar kept going out of tune when, in fact, he was only altering the keys for different songs. ... He also misquoted Dylan as having said, 'Would you be so positive on 4th Street?' when in actual fact he said, 'Would you like to take a walk down positively 4th street?' ... In closing, I would like to say I was disgusted at the reception he got, and it only goes to show that some of the public do not recognise a genius when they see one.

'Disgusted of Foxrock' was a fellow insurrectionist, incensed by the Irish media and enthused by the experience of seeing Dylan skip the light electric:

> My blood is boiling. I am fuming, astounded and positively disgusted that anyone could write such a load of rubbish! ... He ends up [claiming], 'the 2,000-odd who came to hear him will remember it as the night of the Great Let-Down.' Well, I can assure you that I, a member of the audience, will do no such thing ... Admittedly there was some booing and even jeering, but Mr J.K. would lead us to believe that practically the whole audience was participating in this, whereas I doubt if there were forty people responsible. I see that he omitted to mention the enthusiastic applause at the end of each number ... [Dylan] belted out the ingenious lyrics with an overpowering, driving, dynamic voice which shook the whole building ... the whole effect was unbelievable, weird and wild.

Dermote Meleady, of Finglas Bridge, questioned why J.K. 'seemed to take such [a] fiendish delight in exaggerating the [so-called] incidents', while taking issue with

the misrepresentation of the facts … concerning the reception given
to Bob Dylan at his concert on May 5th. J.K.'s review seemed …
a deliberate accentuation of a small amount of unpleasantness. The
'whistling', the 'unprintable' things said were childishly exaggerated.
… In fact, the only remarks shouted were during the amplified
second half when somebody called for the microphone to be turned
down, this being followed by the shouts of 'stuffed golliwog' &c.,
which, it must be emphasised, were completely isolated. The only
mob action was an outburst of slow-handclapping which could be
traced to one or two rows.

Yet Mr Meleady was not one of those for whom Dylan could do
no wrong, He was 'extremely disappointed at the second half of the
concert'. Another 'extremely disappointed' reader, who agreed that
'the booing and slow-handclapping were the work of an ignorant
minority' also convinced himself that 'the rest of the audience (myself
included) were too polite to register their disappointment vociferously'.
Brian Fry of Donnybrook, far from rebuking his fellow former fans,
felt that 'the Irish audience … acted admirably. They were extremely
polite and gave [Dylan] plenty of opportunity to prove himself.' Mr
Fry seemed to feel he never did manage to 'communicate with the
audience in any way … [or] show any emotion whatsoever'.

Yet on the full Dublin tape there is plenty of emotion on display—
from artist *and* audience—the electric Dylan being met with stony
silence from some, vocal vituperation by others and audible acclaim
from the majority at the Adelphi. But even this scale of dissent took
Dylan by surprise. Yes, it was just another minority shouting rude
things, but they were awfully persistent, and it was not a reaction the
musicians and film crew had expected here, of all places. Later that
month, Robertson claimed, 'They were [actually] holding up "Stop
The War" signs.'

For the first time on a world tour tape, one hears clear dissent
throughout. Dylan is also subjected to a brief 'slow handclap' before
'Ballad Of A Thin Man', and there are audible taunts at the end of 'I
Don't Believe You' and 'Baby Let Me Follow You Down', and before
'Ballad Of A Thin Man' and 'Like A Rolling Stone'. On the first of
these, someone shouts something that sounds like 'lower the mic',
as *Disc* reported, though they could just as easily have meant *lower*

the mic, in the sense that it's too close and he's popping his words (a common occurrence at a number of shows— particularly Paris).

The not-so-Wildean wit who shouted something about 'Moore Street' or, more likely 'Bore Street', before the finale is promptly shouted down, proving that the majority approve of the band, before Dylan delivers his one verbal retort of the evening: 'Have you ever been on Positively 4th Street?' Playing the ubiquitous 'Like A Rolling Stone' he spits out the line 'How does it feel?' with something close to triumph.

The Irish press, though, was determined to have its jaundiced way. The truth was not going to be allowed to get in the way of a good story. And, as Dylan was about to discover, in the days when English music journalists rarely ventured west of Reading, the pop weeklies garnered their own reports from the Irish reviews, even when it was Dylan's first return gig in the British Isles. In *Melody Maker*, Vincent Doyle's primary (and possibly only) source was J.K.'s wayward account, from which he even purloined the title, 'Dublin: Night Of The Big Let-Down':

> After an hour of the opening Dublin concert on Thursday, Bob Dylan, the folk-poet genius who is credited with re-routing the entire cause of contemporary folk music, suffered the humiliation of a slow handclap. It was the climax of growing mutual contempt— Dylan for the audience and the audience for Dylan's new big sound. … Like Newport last year where he was booed off stage with his new sound, it proved a disaster … dozens walked out. … For most, it was the night of the big let-down.

Disc & Music Echo's reviewer preferred anonymity, but if he wasn't Norman Barry in disguise, he mirrored large chunks of Barry's *Independent* review—even the insults supposedly fired in Dylan's direction—while condemning Dylan for 'his attempts at beat arrangements of "Like A Rolling Stone" and "Tell Me My Love" [sic] [which] were painful and remote from the folk material they had paid to hear'.

But they hadn't 'paid to hear' anything of the sort, a point made most forcefully by Dublin resident Mary Morrissey: 'At the concert that I attended, at least 90 percent of the audience applauded enthusiastically.' Her recollection is borne out by Alderson's board recording, which suggests the electric set was generally well received, especially the more familiar songs, like 'Just Like Tom Thumb's Blues', 'One Too Many Mornings' and 'Like A Rolling Stone'. It mattered not. Dylan could not fight his own Irish rebellion with only a motley crew of disaffected letter-writers.

One reviewer seriously complained about the fact that 'after only ninety-five minutes performing, Dylan and his electric men left with the audience remaining seated'. As Dylan later observed, 'We were doing a whole show, no other acts. It's pretty straining to do a show like that.' (This was an era when the two biggest bands in the world, The Beatles and The Rolling Stones, played on average twenty-five to thirty minutes.) The strain was starting to tell.

★ ★ ★

Because the majority of Dublin reviews ran the following day, they did the damage long before country folk invoked their right to reply. And the reviews certainly got to Dylan, who complained about 'the lousy reception he'd been given in Dublin' to a reporter 'invited' backstage for an informal chat the following evening, confirming that his practice of reading all the reviews, good and bad, endured even unto Eire.

In the same informal conversation Dylan also revealed real feelings of 'homesickness' that would grow more acute as the tour wore on. But none of these comments were 'on the record'. Dylan's blanket ban on talking to the British press remained firmly in place. What the *Ulsterweek* journalist got instead was 'a lil' talkie' with the latest *enfant terrible*:

> The door of the drab dressing room was ajar. A fuzzy golliwog in a tight diamond pattern suit stood staring at me with wild wide-open eyes. 'What'd'ya want?' asked Bob Dylan. ... Dylan was on the second day of his second European tour. So far he had spoken to nobody except his sound recordist, his managers and Victor—his cowboy general factotum. ... He won't accept the fact that fame like his makes him a public spectacle ...
> This wasn't an interview, he emphasised, 'We're just gonna have a lil' talkie!' Name singers who do ABC concerts usually talk

about sex, drink, parties and the girls they've known. Dylan talked guitars and homesickness. He claimed to have no feelings about the tour. All he wanted to do was go home. He told me of the lousy reception he'd been given in Dublin. The southern press had slayed him because of his non-cooperation. … He asked about the border. About Irish folk music and about Belfast in general. Bob poured a cup of black tea and shovelled in a few spoonfuls of honey. He lit a king-size cigarette. 'Do you ever do any real writing?' he asked. … The tour manager came in again. 'Come on!' he urged Dylan. 'Come on!' Bob Dylan's hand was very limp as he shook goodbye. His eyes were looking at the blank wall.

The reporter's intriguing account confirms the return of Maymudes, while chiming with a similar experience enjoyed by Paul Williams three months earlier. With no tape recorder in sight, Dylan could relax, discussing the affairs of the day with a fellow traveller and sharing an abiding interest in 'Irish folk music' dating back to his youthful friendship with Liam Clancy. But he soon had to go. He had a show to do, a performance the *Belfast Telegraph* had previewed a week earlier, expressing the fervent hope Dylan would deliver where many had not:

Next Friday a young American who has been called 'the most influential poet of his generation' will give his first concert in Belfast. … I hope that he transmits all the pathos, power and feeling of his songs to the Belfast audiences next week. … Too many highly talented entertainers tend to give Belfast audiences neatly packaged but uninspired performances.

If Belfast turned into as much of a battleground for Bobby D as for the British troops soon stationed there, it went unreported. Dublin having done its worst, there was little left to say. Even the splenetic 'I Don't Believe You' released on *Biograph* in 1985, attributed to Belfast, came from a mislabelled Columbia reel of 'the night of the big let-down'. No reviewer bothered to file a contemporary account of any Ulster showdown.

Dylan was still looking for feedback, though, and after the show he was joined by Roger Daltrey, of all people, fresh from a nearby gig with The Who. With a local gossip columnist in tow, Daltrey had 'caught Dylan singing "Tambourine Man" and charged backstage. Rog [Daltrey] and Dylan drank tea and talked. They compared Belfast, London and New York. Belfast was a non-runner in Dylan's popularity charts.'

Neither night in Ireland had endeared Dylan to the quiet land of Erin. He left the belle isle if not under a cloud then certainly in a hurry—returning to London on the first flight out the following morning, allowing himself three whole days to film more mind games and prepare for a two-week assault on Anglo-Saxon sensibilities.

It would prove his greatest challenge to date. The Colston Hall, where he ventured forth first, remains one of the few 1966 venues still standing and regularly used as a rock venue. The acoustics of the Avon arena are notoriously bad (its omission from the 1965 schedule may reflect this very concern), but such was the demand in 1966 that the Bristol show sold out almost immediately. The event also had sufficient local interest to enjoin the *Western Daily Press* and the *Bristol Evening Post* to dispatch reporters, neither of whom proved able to name a single Dylan song or hear any difference between The Hawks' sound and that of British beat bands. All that Peter Gibbs of the *Daily Press* knew for sure was that fame had spoilt this 'folksinger prophet of the modern generation':

> Bob Dylan ... parted company with many of his fans at the Colston Hall, Bristol, this week. His long-awaited second appearance [sic] in the city turned out to be a noisy, blaring, ear-splitting disaster. When he first appeared on stage, the full house greeted him with the type of applause reserved by fans for their idols. By the time he left the stage at the end of the concert, the hand-clapping had diminished to the level of politeness. And some of the audience had already walked out—presumably in disgust. The fans were lulled into a false sense of security during the first half, with Dylan accompanying himself on the acoustic guitar and harmonica that have become his trademark. But in the second half, he was joined by a pianist, organist, drummer and two guitarists, who proceeded to bombard the audience with wave upon wave of amplified notes. Even Dylan joined in the punishment of his audience, gyrating with an electric guitar like a second-hand Rolling Stone. ... Perhaps this exaggerated Top 10 sound has been forced upon him by others who want him to cash in on what they suppose to be a commercial sound.

The *Bristol Evening Post* used up part of its review taking issue with the Colston Hall acoustics, complaining at length that one 'could not hear him clearly', a view seemingly borne out by the reporter's description of Dylan as 'the bard of Nihilism, hope, Anti-Convention and protest'. The volume had again played havoc with the delicate sensibilities of a reporter for whom the times were ever remainin':

> The second half of the evening was spent listening to beat music 'à la Bob Dylan' with volume turned on full. Two guitarists, a drummer and an organist accompanied Mr Dylan. The resulting rivalry was wearying and not very enjoyable. At rare intervals the pianist could be heard fighting his battle against the rest of the noise … but he was drowned.

Our deaf-as-a-*Post* man was not alone in finding the volume at Colston Hall a tad high. Nicholas Williams, dispatched by the *NME*, reported that 'performance[s] of "Like A Rolling Stone" and "I See You've Got A Brand New Leopard-Skin Pill-Box Hat" [were] deafening and brought shouts of "Turn the volume down" from the auditorium!' Actually, it was 'I Don't Believe You' that prompted the *solitary* shout to turn it down—one of two songs Williams identified as bearing 'only very vague resemblances to the originals'. (The other was 'Baby Let Me Follow You Down', which was so different to the 1961 original that Dylan re-copyrighted it.)

For the only time on the world tour, local letter-writers came out on the side of these ignorant scribes. Marilyn Johnson expressed profound feelings of betrayal and loathing to the Bristol evening paper. Too busy on the local ostrich farm to renew her *Melody Maker* subscription, she had attended the show wholly unaware that Dylan had released two albums and four non-album singles of electric rock, or that his (semi-)electric shows had been creating a media storm for nine months now:

> Dylan's performance until the interval did him great credit; his words were sung from his heart and together with his acoustic guitar playing he revealed his outstanding gift of poetry. After the interval we waited for the second half of the concert to commence.

At last the stage door opened but unexpectedly a group with electric instruments walked on stage followed by Mr Dylan, who also carried an electric guitar. My heart sank as they proceeded to produce the most dreadful din I have ever experienced. ... A few people shouted objections and I found it especially encouraging to see some of his old admirers simply stand up and walk out on him. Just as I decided to do the same, the concert abruptly ended. Nobody realised it had finished until suddenly the National Anthem played.

Marilyn even had epistolean allies. Jenny Leigh from Bristol and Miss L. Cutler from Upper Gornal, felt similarly jilted, but could hardly claim a similar ignorance of *Melody Maker*'s pre-tour announcement as both complained about the very same show to the esteemed weekly, Miss Cutler telling a tale of two halves: 'The first half was superb with Dylan singing and playing in his natural way. Then came the Group, making Dylan's singing inaudible and the songs absolutely meaningless.'

Leigh delivered her own outlined epitaph: 'I have just attended a funeral at Bristol's Colston Hall. They buried Bob Dylan, the folksinger, in a grave of electric guitars, enormous loudspeakers and deafening drums. It was a sad end to one of the most phenomenal influences in music. My only consolation is that Woody Guthrie wasn't there to witness it.'

One suspects that a John Cage fan like Guthrie would have seen Dylan's mid-sixties work as a natural progression, but this wasn't the only occasion at a British show where his hallowed name would be invoked.[47]

Again, the irrefutable audio evidence—this time from the audience, where some commotion was apparently going on—reveals it was only those with great expectations and albums one to four who really thought this could be the end. Not only does the tumultuous applause frequently overload the cassette player's condenser mic, but when someone does shout, very audibly, 'Can you turn the volume down please?' after 'I Don't Believe You', the audience ignores him.

Throughout the set, the vast majority of the audience are clearly on Dylan's (and The Hawks') side. After the band stutters their way

[47] One of the occasions features in *No Direction Home* with helpful subtitles, the shout being all but inaudible on the film itself.

through 'Tell Me, Momma' and 'I Don't Believe You', the Bristol audience are pinned to their seats for the remainder of the set. After Mickey Jones whips 'Baby Let Me Follow You Down' senseless, the applause is resounding. If anything, the band get louder. Yet out in the auditorium a condenser mic is picking up a high melodic content and Dylan's vocals, crisp and clean, and in no sense buried in the mix. The problem was not the soundman but the sound, man; more rock than folk, just not folk-rock.

In Cardiff the following night, at an ideal-size venue, the sound was spot on. Despite this, as attendee Erica Davies observed, people were actually 'walk[ing] out because he appeared with an electric guitar'. The *South Wales Echo*'s Jon Holliday stuck it out reluctantly. He had sat enraptured through the first half as Dylan held 'last night's audience of about 1,500 in Cardiff's Capitol Theatre in rapt silence for … fifty-five minutes completely without assistance or showbiz gimmickry'. But after the interval, *quelle horreur*, it all sounded to Mr Holliday like 'just another beat group singer, hollering, gyrating, gesticulating, mouthing, indistinguishable from the countless grains of sand on that beach called Merseyside'.

Those who left missed out on one of the best shows of the tour. The Hawks, with Jones now fully integrated into the setup, hit their marks from the off. Dylan introduces 'Just Like Tom Thumb's Blues' with his now familiar dedication to 'a very notorious painter called Tom Thumb. He's a very old painter. He's been around a long time. He lives in Del Rio, Texas, he goes from Del Rio to Juarez', but what he delivers keeps blazing like a forest fire while the equally inspired band burns as bright as any sun.

The board tape cuts at various crucial points—at the conclusions to 'I Don't Believe You', 'Leopard-Skin Pill-Box Hat' and 'Ballad Of A Thin Man'—so there may have been more name-calling than appears to be the case. But the only audible dissent precedes 'Like A Rolling Stone'. The tape starts rolling as people are shouting (inaudibly) and trying to inaugurate a slow handclap.

They do not succeed. Indeed, it sounds like most of the audible shouts are directed at the slow-hand-clappers. Dylan just plays the waiting game. He even laughs at something someone has said, while tuning, tuning, tuning up. When calm is restored, he promptly shatters it with a 'Like A Rolling Stone' that could crack Plexiglas. And then he is gone, gone, gone, heading for the Black Country and a second visit to Birmingham's newly opened Bull Ring.

9. ENGLISH CIVIL WAR
[May 12–17 1966]

We've said it before and we say it again...

Nobody sings Dylan like Dylan!

The original 'Just Like a Woman'
—written by Bob Dylan

From his sensational new a

On COLUMBIA RECORDS

Letter

Repartee

SO the knockers are all stations go again! I am referring to the fantastic performance given by Bob Dylan at the Manchester Free Trade Hall last Tuesday night. Everyone enjoyed the first performance, as no doubt every Dylan fan would. He sang folk songs accompanied with his guitar and harmonica for the first half of the show, which went just great; but when he decided to change his style of music for the second half, the knockers and so-called Dylan fans began calling him a traitor.

If they really liked him and his music as much as they pretended, then they wouldn't mind him changing his style every so often.

And even if the group's equipment was over-amplified, there was no need to take it out on the gearest folk singer of our generation.

I think Bob put his feelings over to the knockers just great. When someone shouted out to him "Judas," he just calmly went to the microphone and quietly drawled "Ya liar."

He is no Judas, and he should know. We don't see and hear enough of the one and only Dylan in person as it is, so why don't the knockers leave him alone? Let Dylan change his type of music any time he wants to, 'cos no matter what kind of backing sound he uses, the message of his songs still comes over to his real fans.

DYLAN FAN

Someone had primed the audience [in some of these places] into an anti-folk hero thing. They were all ready for Bob when he arrived [onstage]. There must have been something in the press. The audience couldn't have reacted that way unprompted.

—RICHARD ALDERSON TO THE AUTHOR, 2016

With The Band [in 1966] … it seemed a lot of it was a media thing, where they were telling the audience ahead of the show what to expect. It would cause the audience to react a certain way, instead of deciding for themselves. It was one of those things that [struck me as] very corrosive.

—DYLAN TO GREG KOT, AUGUST 1993

Though it is unlikely that Dylan laid his hands immediately on a copy of the following day's *South Wales Echo*, he would surely have picked up copies of the week's music papers on the road to Birmingham. It was Thursday, after all, the day when *Melody Maker*, *NME*, *Disc & Music Echo* and *Record Mirror* vied for the pennies of a music-obsessed teenage nation.

The first three all ran reviews of the shows, *MM* and *Disc* carrying reports of Dublin that must have seemed like déjà vu to Dylan who had already poured over the Irish originals. Photographer Barry Feinstein, husband of Mary Travers of Peter Paul &, had joined Dylan in Ireland to provide a visual record of the tour, and later wrote, 'Bob was interested in what the music press had to say about him. It didn't really affect him, but he would get pissed off once in a while.'[48] This was doubtless just such an occasion.

NME had elected to include Nicholas Williams's nominally informed report of Tuesday's Bristol show, but it was the reviews from Dublin that did the damage, serving as an antagonistic undercurrent to all that was to come. These music paper reviews prompted one furious fan from the valleys of South Wales to point out something rather

---

[48] Feinstein's 1966 photos of Dylan were published in 2008 by Omnibus Press, under the title *Real Moments*, with commentary by the photographer himself.

obvious. Erica Davies of Merthyr Tydfil gave her direct response to the *Melody Maker* review, fresh from a similar experience at Cardiff:

> I would like to protest against the attitude of some of Dylan's audiences. To shout 'traitor' and walk out because he appeared with an electric guitar was puerile. These people must have been walking round with their cars plugged as Dylan's last two LPs and seven singles have all featured electric guitars, and it was well-known in advance he was bringing a backing group with him.

But the damage had been done. The first paragraph of *Melody Maker*'s own review of the Birmingham show, the following week, began: 'Just like the Irish in Dublin a week earlier, Thursday's audience at the Odeon, Birmingham, flatly rejected Bob Dylan's all-electric folk.' They didn't—but neither had the Dubliners. Once again, the majority of Brummies were happy to hear whatever Dylan wanted to play. Nonetheless such national media reports seemed to play their part in emboldening a miffed minority into letting their feelings be known—as Dylan had insisted they should, the night of the Forest Hills furore.

Back then, the controversy seemed to help put bums on seats, but by May 1966 the effect on the audiences—and on Dylan himself—had become 'very corrosive'. From Birmingham on, there would be no real letup in the shouting and slow handclapping. Perhaps it was a northern thing. Certainly those audibly declaiming which side they are on in Birmingham, Liverpool, Leicester, Sheffield and Manchester seem as proud of their regional accents as 'their' folk music. If another hostile reviewer can be believed, those at the Birmingham show had decided that, rather than mourn, they would organise:

> The audience showed no signs of irritation during his first-half solo session. [But] his return with an electric guitar and a backing group after the interval was the signal for the protests to begin. There was slow-handclapping, shouts of 'Folk Phoney' and some simply made for the exit. Dylan seemed unconcerned. Between numbers, he turned his back to the audience for long periods while apparently deciding with his group what numbers to play next, giving the hecklers plenty of opportunity to express their dislike of his Mick-Jagger-like antics.

With no hiatus from the hecklers in sight, Dylan had decided to fight ire with fire, turning up the volume another notch and between songs stoking the flames of indignation by deliberately 'turn[ing] his back to the audience for long periods while apparently deciding with his group what numbers to play next'.

The set list had been fixed in stone for three months now, so that certainly wasn't the nub of any inter-band banter. Maybe he was deciding what retort to make, because Dylan also started talking back. In Birmingham, he wound up all the folkies—and a student reporter from the university paper, *Redbrick*—with a song introduction that suggested he positively enjoyed dancing on the grave of traditional music. *Redbrick* recoiled to report:

> The man in the second half was not the Bob Dylan the audience had come for. He was the shell of a man who had gained the whole world but had lost his soul. From behind an electric guitar and backed by a five-piece band, he endured heckling from the audience: 'Now I'll sing you a folk song,' said the shell, 'that ma granddaddy sang to ma mother when she was a little girl.' If his mother had heard what followed, the chances are that Bob would never have been born ... The crowning atrocity was yet to come in the form of 'One Too Many Mornings', which most of his followers remember as the real 'Dylan'. I was contemplating the Exit as the electric guitar and organ took it and strangled the soul from it. ... The evening ended abruptly to the dying chords of 'Like A Rolling Stone', without an encore.

And yet our *Redbrick* reporter failed to fully dramatize the moment when Dylan snapped back, failing to note *which* song Dylan prefaced by offering to 'sing you a folk song'. It was the most apposite choice imaginable. Yes, 'Baby Let Me Follow You Down' had begun life as a folk song but it had been repeatedly bastardised by commercial recording artists from Memphis Minnie in 1930 and Blind Boy Fuller in 1936 to The Mustangs and The Animals in 1964, both of whom made it into a pop song (courtesy of Bert Berns's conscious adaptation of Dylan's original acoustic reinterpretation).

According to Graham Ashton—an eyewitness for whom the events of May 12 1966 were still seared in the memory two decades later—Dylan was responding directly to shouts from an audience incensed

by an almost apocalyptic 'I Don't Believe You' (with Garth's organ,
for once, to the fore in the mix):

> Some were catcalling to turn the sound down and others were
> shouting, 'Play some folk music' and 'Stop trying to be a pop star'.
> Dylan scowled and spoke, 'Aaah, folk music. If you want *folk* music,
> I'll play you some folk music ... this is a *folk* song that my granddaddy
> used to sing to me. ... He used to take me on his knees and he used
> to sing this song to me. It goes like this ...'

Frustratingly, although the Birmingham performance of 'Baby
Let Me Follow You Down' has been preserved by Alderson, the pre-
song rap is missing. (He was changing reels, as he often was at this
juncture.) The front part of another 'crowning atrocity', 'One Too
Many Mornings', is also missing. But the sorority of female folkies
can be heard in full voice between 'Tom Thumb' and 'Leopard-Skin
Pill-Box Hat'; nor do they let up, shouting down others before both
'Thin Man' and 'Rolling Stone' and trying to start a slow handclap
before the former. But despite their best endeavours, even *Redbrick's*
reactionary reporter was forced to admit, 'Applause still drowned the
spasmodic groans of [true] Dylan fans.'

At the end of the show, Dylan did another of his disappearing
acts. He later informed Jann Wenner he had headed off to suburban
Solihull, in the company of the Winwood brothers, Steve and Muff:
'We went out to see a haunted house, where a man and his dog was to
have burned up in the thirteenth century. Boy, that place was spooky.'

With Dylan long gone, *Melody Maker's* Bob Dawson, the one
intrepid reporter from the music papers to review this provincial show,
grabbed hold of Dylan's favourite musical foil, Robbie Robertson,
and asked him how it felt to be touring Britain. The Canadian's
answer was surprisingly matter of fact: 'Well, it's kind of like eating
a pumpkin pie. It's sweet—but it gets very sticky sometimes. ... At
every concert, out of all the younger people present, there are bound
to be some who insist on saying something.'

Asked directly whether Dylan was 'trying to look and sound like
Mick Jagger', the Barnacle Man—as Mickey Jones cruelly christened
him—insisted, 'It's the furthest thing from his mind. He doesn't even
come into contact with any of that kind of stuff.' Pushed to define the

music they were playing, in true Dylan fashion Robertson defined it not by what it is but by what it's not, 'It's not rhythm and blues and I certainly wouldn't call it folk-rock. It's street music. Everybody in the organization comes from the street. It's not folk music, either ... I can't class Bob Dylan as a folk musician or a protest singer. And most of the people who know anything about it don't.'

★ ★ ★

Unfortunately, those 'who know anything about it' were not being dispatched to review the shows. In fact, after Birmingham, reviews of the remaining provincial English shows all but dried up. It was as if the media had decided the story now wrote itself. As such, Britain's scandal-hungry media stayed away from gigs in Liverpool, Sheffield and Manchester, thus missing the decisive battles in this war of words. As for Dylan, he had really started to hit it:

Mickey Jones: Bob was bored with the first half of the show. All that acoustical folk music was now boring to Bob. At the intermission, he started to get pumped up. He was walking around backstage with his [guitar. He] could not wait to get out there and rock'n'roll. ... Sometimes we all got off in a rather unusual way. ... Our attitude was FUCK the audience. ... As the tour went on, Bob seemed to have more fun every day. As soon as he strapped on that black Telecaster, he was ready to rock. He would jump around in the dressing room. He could not wait to get on that stage. It's true, sometimes Bob would hardly face the audience in the electric set. He played to the band. That was where his focus was, on us.

Richard Alderson: It was like he changed personalities from one half of the concert to the next. He came out a different guy. He acted different. He carried himself different. It was amazing. Really animated—jumping around and carrying on, obviously trying to incite the crowd to [display] the very thing he's annoyed by.

D.A. Pennebaker: In general he was having so much a better time with the band than he was by himself that you could see right away that the difference was night and day in terms of his performance ... I've never heard a concert like that since. Never.

Liverpool, with its two daily papers and the population's heartfelt conviction that it lay at the centre of sixties pop culture, was certainly one place where he might have expected critics a-plenty to spend their Saturday night at the Odeon. But that Saturday afternoon, the entire city had been glued to its television sets watching one of the most extraordinary comebacks in the FA Cup Final's 94-year history: Everton recovering from a two-goal deficit versus Sheffield Wednesday to win 3-2 in the last twenty-five minutes. The city's eponymous football club had just won the First Division, seeming confirmation that the famous port now dominated the only two fields of human endeavour that really mattered to Merseyside: pop music and soccer.

While the rest of the city tore it up in the clubs and bars, those with tickets made their way to the Odeon. For one future playwright of real note, the temptation to leave after the first half of the show proved almost too great:

Willy Russell: I reluctantly stayed after the interval in 1966. I had been there the year before when he played an acoustic set and *Bringing It All Back Home* had just come out. He had such commitment to those songs in 1965 and I was hearing 'Mr Tambourine Man' for the first time. In 1966 I wasn't angry with him for bringing the band on, but what I hated was the obligatory first half which was acoustic and performed with no commitment. Clearly a commercial decision had been taken to appease the fans who were objecting to his electric band and his heart wasn't in it. He was mangling his own songs. I stayed for the second half and it was so much better. I think he had become more and more angry and he was funnelling and controlling that anger towards the audience. I did stay until the end. And I'm glad I did.

It was a smart move on Russell's part. Not only was the Odeon electric set a notch above Birmingham and Bristol—and on a par with Cardiff—but Alderson was getting the hang of how to record the band. Where he remained hamstrung was capturing the audience reaction, which seemed to be getting more vehement with every passing gig despite Dylan's directional mic pointing away from all the angry audience members.

Paul Cable may have fondly imagined, in his 1978 book, that, 'true to tradition, Liverpool welcomes electric Dylan with open arms. There is not a negative noise to be heard from the audience throughout and I would imagine that Dylan … must have been well pleased.' But his mislabelled four-song 'Liverpool '66' tape actually comprised one song from Sheffield ('Tell Me, Momma'), two from Edinburgh ('One Too Many Mornings' and 'Like A Rolling Stone'), plus the infamous 'I Want You' B-side. He still should have realised that the vitriol with which Dylan delivered 'Just Like Tom Thumb's Blues'—which *was* from Liverpool—was directed at members of the audience shouting through their sound holes.

On the *genuine* Liverpool soundboard tape, there are at least two occasions during the electric set when Dylan has to bide his time and let the ranters draw breath. The first of these comes before 'Leopard-Skin Pill-Box Hat' as Dylan figures out how to make them shut up and let him sing.

After a prolonged bout of taunts and catcalls, Dylan slurs, 'I just want to talk to you'—a request that just fans the flames—so he begins to burble into the mic. Eventually, curiosity gets the better of rudeness, at which point he states, 'I just want to say the name of the next song is "Yes, I See You Got Your Brand New Leopard-Skin Pill-Box Hat",' before The Hawks hammer the point home. (The title, at this point, meant nothing to the audience, but it sure didn't sound like a Child ballad.)

The barracking resumes at song's end, but Dylan won't quit, either, announcing that the next song 'is dedicated to all the people who read *Time* magazine'—the ultimate putdown in his little black book. If the resultant performance has more balls than Strawberry Fields on a Sunday afternoon, the tape cuts on the final note, curtailing any further rejoinders.

The Nagra reel-to-reel is up and running again through 'One Too Many Mornings' and 'Thin Man'. This time the shouting preceding the latter is sustained. But Dylan's mic picks up very little of what is being shouted, save for an audible 'we want Dylan' (presumably as a follow-up to an earlier, 'Where's Bob Dylan?'). Through the deluge of taunts, one appears to hit its mark, 'Woody Guthrie would turn in his grave'—an odd comment given that Guthrie was still very much alive. Dylan settles himself at the piano stool, warms his hands and then delivers a droll riposte, 'There's a fellow up there looking for the Saviour. [Well,] the Saviour's backstage ...'

Once again, Dylan displays remarkable composure throughout the verbal onslaught. He is confident he has allies a-plenty out in the auditorium. In fact, as T. Hardern from Nantwich wrote later in *Disc* (which retained a strong Liverpool connection, having recently amalgamated with *Music Echo*, formerly the *Mersey Beat*), 'Dylan can certainly keep his temper with an audience. At his Liverpool concert the audience appreciated the quiet sense of humour he showed to hecklers. No trace of the arrogance they try to pin on him. Incidentally, all the kids round us were digging the new Dylan very much.'

A fortnight later, Hardern's view was reaffirmed in the same pages by a lady from Sheffield, Barbara Ellis, who had evidently attended *both* Liverpool and Sheffield shows. (Such devotion was highly unusual in 1966.) She too was firmly on Dylan's side, but was worried that the sensitive artist onstage might take the whole thing personal:

At Liverpool and Sheffield, this ... little man, looking quite defenceless in spite of his backing group, faced a barrage of insults from a large section of the audience with a tolerance and humour the press could well take an example from. Dylan has not appointed himself an idol, but has been made into one; largely it seems by people who treat artists as toys, to be smashed when they do not come up to their expectations.

Any such voices of reason were wielding pens because the British press was either ignoring the battle between folk and rock or siding with those who shouted loudest. They were now providing a much-needed static charge to a tour that was already being mythologised by those who swore they were there—whichever side they were on.

But Dylan needed to know what was happening out there in the auditoriums now! Which is why he and Neuwirth cooked up the idea that the latter venture out into the theatres with a boom mic and record the crowd reaction from the bear pit.

If Pennebaker had become convinced that the drama was all onstage, he had taken a temporary leave of absence to secure distribution for *Dont Look Back* at the Cannes film festival, leaving Neuwirth to pick up the thread of the current film project. While D.A. was away, the two Bobbies decided to play, as Neuwirth hit on the idea of interviewing attendees as they were leaving the auditoriums, offering a vox pop of viewpoints.

Willy Russell was one of those asked for his thoughts on leaving the Liverpool Odeon. Alan Bleasdale was another. Both future playwrights were as yet mere students of pop culture, but came out firmly on Bob's side. Others expressed themselves in a way ABC TV was unlikely to air: 'It was CRAP!!!' But the experiment in Liverpool was such a resounding success that Neuwirth decided to repeat it at another show where the reaction was at its most polarised: Manchester.

Meanwhile, Dylan, Neuwirth and the band retired to Dylan's suite at the Liverpool Adelphi and, having decided to listen again to the night's show, set about hooking up the trusty Nagra Richard Alderson deployed nightly to a crude mono sound system. Maybe they could figure out what all the fuss was about. Robertson would later claim that 'the only reason tapes of those shows exist today is because we wanted to know: are we crazy? We'd go back to the hotel room, listen to a tape of the show and … [wonder,] why is everybody so upset?'

The new drummer instinctively realised the tapes were not being made because Dylan doubted his direction. Just the opposite. They were a form of aural vindication:

Mickey Jones: I do remember listening to recordings of some of the concerts after the shows. We would all get together to listen and we were pretty happy with the results … [even after] listening to the audiences' boos. It didn't bother us at all … We talked about the music every night after the show … about how good the electric set sounded and how much fun it was.

In Britain, this 'nightly ritual' began to replace the playing of *Blonde On Blonde* acetates, reaffirming that he wasn't crazy—as yet— even as he continued sailing toward the rapids in his drunken boat. He certainly dug what he heard. In fact, at some point a tape of that night's 'Just Like Tom Thumb's Blues' was dispatched to New York at Dylan's behest, the first indication he thought these recordings were good enough to release. Of course, releasing this raucous rendition as his next single (B-side) also twisted the blade on those who barracked him in Liverpool that night—and the night after, and the night after that …

★ ★ ★

The dissent the following night at Leicester's De Montfort Hall was captured by both Alderson and an audience taper, whose investment in a sixty-minute cassette proved unwise, curtailing his taping activities after 'Just Like Tom Thumb's Blues', just as things were getting out of hand.

What he captured, though, was enough to give a flavour, starting with the usual half-hearted shouts prefacing 'I Don't Believe You'. But at song's end the applause is plentiful and enthusiastic. By the conclusion of 'Baby Let Me Follow You Down', though, boos have become mixed with the applause. Sensing the now-familiar rising tide of protest, Dylan smashes into 'Just Like Tom Thumb's Blues' with nary a pause, using a voice that is spitting tacks. Just as The Hawks seem about to transcend even Liverpool, the tape cuts. The taper had caught enough of the concert to suggest it was contentious, if not enough to confirm the outcome.

That there was another showdown was confirmed by two letters to the *Leicester Mercury*. Christine Kynaston wrote to express her absolute disgust 'at the narrow-mindedness displayed by some of the audience at Bob Dylan's Sunday visit to Leicester. Never before have I seen such an exhibition of childish mentality; they booed and slow-handclapped a man who was merely proving how amazingly versatile he is'; and Jane from Shakespeare Street concurred: 'When they very childishly booed … this great genuine star was man enough to take it without retaliating or stooping to their level.'

Thankfully, the local Leicester papers were on the ball—unlike at the press-free Liverpool gig—dispatching two entirely different reporters: one, a local journalist who wanted a story; the other, a sympathetic writer-fan on his way to A&R glory. The former filed his fanciful account with the local *Mercury*, who came up with the catchy headline, 'Pop Goes Bob Dylan—And Boo Go Fans'. Hoping for something dramatic in the second half, the anonymous reporter imagined far greater dissent than there was:

After a highly successful first half, in which he performed as one would have expected and hoped—just a guitar and himself—he spent the second half of the show with an electric guitar and an instrumental group thumping his way through a number of fast numbers with a strong rhythm and blues flavour. The transformation brought much dissatisfaction among his thousands of followers who crammed into the De Montfort Hall. They booed, slow-handclapped, chanted 'Off! Off!' and 'We want Dylan!' These were not, I hasten to add, the majority of the audience, but certainly a large minority. Many walked out in disgust.

The Leicester *Illustrated Chronicle*'s David Sandison never even considered walking out in disgust. This young tyke was surely the same man who, in a later life, was A&R man at Island Records and EMI, discovering and/or cultivating the likes of Sandy Denny, Nick Drake, Julie Covington and The Only Ones' Peter Perrett. Even on May 15 1966, this lifelong music fan was in no doubt as to the more interesting segment of the Leicester performance, even mistaking a particularly majestic 'Tambourine Man' harp solo for a moment of levity.[49]

I was a bit bored with the first half of Dylan's show, with its subdued, hushed quality and the church-like reverence afforded the poet. Dylan looked slightly fed up with the whole affair and got so hung up on one phrase during his '[Mr] Tambourine Man' harp solo that I'm sure he was mocking the audience. I know I laughed at it. But what a contrast when Bob Dylan, the shouting electric poet with his all-steam rave band, jumped on the stage for the second half! ...

After months of waiting to see whether The Group were as good as recent Dylan albums suggest, those who did stay to listen heard the good news: Dylan has a great band to support him and help him develop as he obviously wants to. ... He has grown up and out of the missionary zeal that was so much a feature of his early career. Perhaps those who spoiled the De Montfort Hall concert will also mature in time and realise that their prejudice is almost as great as the prejudices Dylan used to campaign against. Dylan, as usual, has words for it all ... 'You know something is happening, but you don't know what it is—Do you Mr Jones?'

---

[49] It may well be the harmonica coda from this performance that features in *Eat The Document*, as Dylan's mercury mouth slides effortlessly across the mouth harp.

For all that its folk harpies threw at Dylan, Leicester had been a relative breeze compared with Liverpool, reflected in a more controlled but equally powerful performance. The hostility that had rolled in off the Mersey was a sustained howl of hatred that had made Dylan scale the heights of antipathy in search of his Olympian muse. The shows would stay at this sonic summit for the next ten days.

'The shouting electric poet with his all-steam rave band' was now feeding off all this negative energy. Listening back after the Liverpool show/s had convinced Dylan he should enlist Columbia's help to get a studio-quality recording of this electrical storm. His contract with Columbia was almost up and a live record might be one way to sign off in style, maintaining the commercial momentum without recourse to another studio record better and brighter than *Blonde On Blonde*.

As such, when Dylan arrived in Sheffield, twenty-four hours after Leicester, he was happy to find a Columbia sound engineer painstakingly running the leads needed to make a professional three-track record of the evening's performance across the stage.

Thankfully, the decision to capture this concert—and, indeed, the following night's concert—on Columbia's dime did not dissuade Richard Alderson from continuing to make his mono board tapes. And it is lucky he did because, as Alderson recalls, '[Columbia] brought all this gear, and all these microphones, and a whole crew, and I'm just by myself, taping off the PA feed [but] I listened to [their] tapes and they [didn't] have the ambience of the tapes I got, the depth of everything, [which was] the sound mix of the hall—that's all it was.' Not only that, but when the levels on the three-track tape of Sheffield were examined, all the needles were on red.

This could have been a crying shame. Dylan had again raised his game in the teeth of fierce aesthetic resistance at Sheffield's Gaumont Theatre. If it wasn't for Columbia's pin-drop recording of the acoustic set and the industrious Alderson's of the electric, all that would be left would be faded memories and a single passing comment from letter-writer Barbara Ellis suggesting Dylan again faced an almost Liverpudlian 'barrage of insults from a large section of the audience'.

The one reporter who was supposed to be there reporting on the show, French journalist Jean-Marc Pascal, arrived 'at the Grand Hotel in Sheffield just as a black Rolls roars away, pursued by a crowd of screaming fans'. He would have to wait three hours to rendezvous with Dylan's party, and until Manchester for his first taste of this very uncivil war.

The Gaumont Theatre cloakroom attendant, meanwhile, had settled in for a quiet evening of poetry and warm applause. After all, that is what Dylan had delivered the year before, when he had debuted his first English tour at another venerable Sheffield theatre. Once again, the first half was plain sailing. Dylan even opened the show with one of the highlights of last year's set, 'She Belongs To Me'. However, if the attendant's memory served him well, it never sounded like this. The only similarity, in fact, was 'the church-like reverence afforded the poet'.

Dylan was not fooled for a minute—even when the two elliptical excerpts from his forthcoming album, 'Fourth Time Around' and 'Visions Of Johanna', were received with near-universal equanimity (and much amusement when he sang, 'I never asked for your crutch, now don't ask for mine').

The Columbia engineer was delighted. Recording a man with a guitar and a harmonica was child's play. The seven-song acoustic set, as rapturously received as ever, concluded with a 'Mr Tambourine Man' for the ages. It had been almost exactly two years since he had debuted the song at the Royal Festival Hall in front of his first-ever Anglo-Saxon audience, and it had never sounded more ethereal.

And still he was not fooled. The electric set—as always—would be the acid test. Both Sheffield's folkies and the sound engineer would be found wanting. The sound on tape was already up the creek, cutting in and out, distorting at both ends, when Dylan introduced 'Just Like Tom Thumb's Blues' with his longest 'Mexican painter' rap to date. Having got to the bit where he informed the audience the painter's name was Tom Thumb, he elected to embellish the story some:

> He's a very underrated painter. He's a kinda hermit. The newspapers neglect him. This is about his Blue period. I want to explain this in case you think you're not in on anything. This is called 'Just Like Tom Thumb's Blues'. Now you can understand it, too. If you [do] understand it, tell me.

On tape, the reaction to another top-notch performance—packing much the same punch as Liverpool—seems muted by comparison. The standard introduction to 'Leopard-Skin Pill-Box Hat' passes off without a hitch. However, before 'One Too Many Mornings' a mini-War of the Roses breaks out as the audience divides itself into contradistinct factions: those who have had enough, and those who want more, more, more; those who think 'Dylan's crap' and those who plead, 'C'mon Bob, sing!'

Even though the Yorkist ticket holders seem to be shouting at each other more than at the stage, eventually a slow handclap gains enough momentum for Dylan to resume burbling into the mic. The nonsensical sounds again make the catcallers curious enough to cease their clapping, at which point Dylan admits to childish proclivities, 'Remember, I was a baby once.' The roar of affirmation from an audience largely composed of allies merges into the electric roar of a 'One Too Many Mornings' conceived in another lifetime from its recorded kith and kin.

But the heavily outnumbered phalanx of Pennine folkies refuses to be silenced, and when Dylan moves to the piano for his nightly tickle on the ivories, the hallowed hall rings to yet more calls of complaint. Again, Dylan tries waiting for Godot. When that doesn't work, he pleads, 'Come on, come on.' Finally the vocal chords of the disaffected give out—or are silenced by the baleful stares of the many—at which point Dylan informs them, 'All right, I'm playing this on a Blüthner piano. So you can't say anything after the song— no boos.'

Remarkably, it works. The passage into 'Like A Rolling Stone' is almost seamless, the only audible sound being Dylan scratching on his Fender, searching for a rhythm that suits the band until—to co-opt Cable's description of the opening song in Sheffield—'you hear a few vague footstomps and a just audible one–two–three and then suddenly they are all in together. It is a pinpoint in time, yet they are all on it simultaneously.' At the end of 'Rolling Stone', Dylan graciously thanks the crowd and heads for the green Exit sign as the national anthem plays. A few minutes later, he is in the foyer of the Grand Hotel, where Monsieur Pascal, there to write an article for *Salut Les Copains*, has been waiting patiently, biding his time:

The totally British calm of the luxury hotel was suddenly disturbed by an enormous crowd of people, Bob flanked by two well-built beatnik types. This was the main part of the company. … Amongst these people I fortunately recognised two of my friends: Bob Neuwirth … and Al Grossman, his manager. … Al is an easy-going giant of a man, who appreciates pretty girls, good wine and French cooking. With his silvery hair hanging over his shoulders, he looks like a beatnik who has aged gracefully. Without waiting any longer, I hand him the bottle of Beaujolais wine that I owed him, selected from my personal collection. Neuwirth rushes towards me and claps me on the shoulder. … They invite me to come and sit at their table in the hotel restaurant. A few minutes later Bob Dylan comes and joins us. He's wearing a very tight pair of trousers with violet and white stripes and a blue velvet jacket. His hair flows all around his skull in straight and wiry locks which are strangely curly at their ends. But we are in England—not one of the customers present allows himself to show any surprise or to turn round. A proper gentleman isn't offended by any eccentric behaviour.

It had been a while since Dylan last allowed himself to relax in the company of a journalist, but Pascal had already been vetted by Grossman *and* Neuwirth, and was deemed friend, not foe. He would in fact tag along for the next couple of days, given an all-access press pass denied to his English music paper peers, before boarding a flight to Paris with the singer. Pascal was even allowed to break bread with Bob after the Sheffield show, where he witnessed his first Dylanesque mind game:

Bob sits down, grabs a menu and chooses his meal: some sticks of celery and a variety of appetizers. His eating habits deserve to be mentioned. He eats very little, only some raw vegetables and fruit, some pate or some cheese (which he puts on the same plate, making a horrible mixture of food), or sandwiches, hastily swallowed. I've never seen him eat a hot meal. As the waiter leans over, taking the order away … he turns towards me: 'What'll they think of me in Paris? How is it that French people who don't understand English are interested in my songs?' And, without waiting for my reply, he turns towards somebody else to talk about this evening's concert. Then, turning back towards me once more, he exclaims … 'People

who speak English don't understand me. I wonder why so many
people claim to like me when they don't understand anything of
what I'm doing ... But why do all these people come to hear me?
Humanity is truly made up of too many people with non-artistic
temperaments.' At that moment a very young waiter passes by and
he stares at our table. 'Oh, you!' Bob calls towards him, 'Tell me,
this Cheshire cheese—it isn't very good Cheshire, is it?' 'Yes it is,
Sir. It's an excellent Cheshire cheese.' 'Ah, but there's someone here
from Cheshire who tells us that this cheese wasn't really made in
Cheshire. Do you come from Cheshire yourself?' ... The former
moves away with a vague idea of having taken part in a joke, but
without having really understood Bob's very unusual humour.

The well-respected reporter suspected that this was going to be
another long evening as Dylan expressed an interest in a late-night
listening session, and what he really wanted to hear was that night's
show, such was the charge he was getting from all those electric cables
and power chords. It was Alderson's mono board tape that provided
the evening's entertainment while, back at the Gaumont Theatre,
Columbia's sound engineer was mortified to see that needle go off
the dial whenever the band turned it up.

The overloaded three-track tape was simply not up to scratch. They
would have to try again. Dylan, oblivious to the problems, thought
Alderson's mono soundtrack tape sounded just dandy, especially when
played loud, fucking loud. Pascal, having missed the real-life drama,
felt obliged to help Dylan make it through the night:

> After the meal all the clan met up again in Bob's room: five
> musicians, four cameramen and soundmen, with a sound-dubbing
> machine, Tom (the driver of the Rolls, who acts at the same time as
> a bodyguard), Henry (whose job it is to look after the star's guitars),
> Al Grossman, Bob Neuwirth, Mr Perry (from CBS London and
> the tour director), Bob Dylan and myself, plus a few girls who have
> been picked up at the end of the concert. In all about twenty people.
> We have to judge and select the tapes which have been recorded
> during the concert.
>
>   This is a small daily ceremony. Lying on the floor, sitting on
> cushions or on chairs, the members of the tour listen in silence.
> Whether they have long or short hair, whether they are well-

dressed or slovenly dressed, they all have a beatnik appearance which immediately makes them different from the other guests in the hotel. The sound system plays so loud that it could burst your eardrums, and confused waiters come in and out carrying trays loaded with cups of tea or bottles of beer. Indeed, the evening will go on late into the night.

Bob is taking advantage of this trip to make a film for American television, and these recordings must be synchronised with the pictures. Gradually the clan thins out. One after another, the wisest of them go to bed. So we find ourselves, at about six o'clock in the morning, with just three or four people left. Bob and I amongst them, in the bedroom of one of the members of the band, discussing the respective merits of John Lennon, Mick Jagger and the present day trends in world cinema.

★ ★ ★

Determined not to miss the next curtain call, a bleary-eyed Pascal rose just in time for a noon departure—destination Manchester; an hour's drive away down the winding roads crisscrossing the Pennines. Experienced getaway driver Keylock was at the wheel of the Rolls-Royce that housed Dylan, Grossman, Neuwirth and Alk, which invariably meant the others had to go some to keep up.[50] After the troupe arrive in one piece at the imposing Midland Hotel, a stone's throw from the Free Trade Hall, Pascal, left to his own devices, found his way to the Free Trade Hall:

Immediately after we arrive, Dylan goes up to his room to sleep until concert time. The others make their way to the concert hall to set up the sound equipment that Bob has brought over from America: an Ampex set—('The best there is,' he says). Three-quarters of an hour before the show, Dylan appears. He has given up his gaudy clothes for a severe suit in black corduroy and a black cotton shirt, with no tie. While he is doing a short soundcheck with his band, the two cameramen and two soundmen film around him.

---

[50] A scene in *Eat The Document* shows Dylan's car driving at speed down country roads, the tyres skidding on the surface of the road. It may well have been filmed when they were crossing the Pennines.

It was going to be a remarkably well-documented evening. Every form of archivist seemed to have shown up. The cameras this time would be rolling both at the soundcheck and the show. For the latter, Pennebaker positioned himself at the stage-left promontory that jutted out toward the stage, which gave him the best vantage point with minimal imposition on paying punters.

The Columbia engineer displayed no such consideration. He knew he was under the gun. The soundcheck had been organised partly to allay his fears; a snippet of it ('Just Like Tom Thumb's Blues') even found its way onto the first Free Trade Hall reel.

Evidently, the deficiencies on the Sheffield tapes had already been discerned and a decision made to try catching audio lightning again on ferric tape. The difficulties recording a rock'n'roll band in 1966 were manifold, starting with the lack of stage monitors. Dylan himself was under no illusion as to the challenge. As he told *NME*'s Neil Spencer in 1981, 'It's a little hard to reproduce that [sound]. ... The only thing we were really able to do was [what we did] with The Band ... in the sixties. Because the sound back then was so raw and primitive, the sound systems wouldn't give us anything else.'

If it had taken Dylan and The Hawks eight months of hard road-time to figure things out, Columbia's engineer had been given two days. For which, praise be to the gods of happenstance. Had the Sheffield Gaumont Theatre gone smoothly, the most famous audience/artist confrontation in rock's recorded history may never have been captured, let alone heard around the world.

The last-minute nature of the decision to record Manchester 'officially' was only confirmed some years later, after the Free Trade Hall's written archives were lodged at Manchester's Central Reference Library. They duly revealed a letter sent by concert hall manager, 'A.S.', to the promoter Tito Burns, the day after the show. In it, the jobsworth complained at length about the way the recording project had been sprung on him:

> You will be aware that the conditions of letting permit[ted] recordings to be taken [required] that the written consent of the Manager (myself) is given and that the hirer must inform me in writing no less than 21 days beforehand. ... The patrons attending paid to hear and see a concert, not a recording session. ... The public

[should] not [be] misled into paying good money for a concert, only to be annoyed by all the extraneous ritual of recording. ... I was extremely annoyed myself by the arrogant and overbearing manner adopted by the persons employed on the recording. We were practically held to ransom—if recording was not permitted, then no concert, practically sums up the situation.

In no way had 'A.S.' exaggerated the brinkmanship Grossman brought to bear, nor the belligerence of his adversary. Grossman gave him an ultimatum: let the recording go ahead or we cancel the show, which had been sold out for weeks. A.S. had no choice but to accede to Dylan's demands. He agreed to reseat the poor sods who woke up that morning thinking they had seats in the front three rows of the Free Trade Hall for the most eagerly-awaited pop concert of the season.

Fortunately, the Free Trade Hall had a long tradition of selling seats (actually a series of hard wooden steps) on the stage itself, behind the band—and photos from Barry Feinstein confirm this arrangement applied in 1966, as it had in 1965. This was where the choir sat when the Hallé Orchestra was in town doing choral work. Though it has gone unrecorded where they relocated those who bought those front-row seats, behind the band—usually the worst of places—would turn out to be the best seats in the house when the real drama unfolded that evening.

The scale of the equipment the engineer had brought in—'the best there is'—took everyone by surprise. In 1985, hardcore Dylan fan John Kappes recalled, 'The stage was completely covered with equipment which was even spread out in front of the stage on the floor of the stalls.' Kappes had 'arrived at the hall ... ready for anything— we had read and heard what had happened in America', but he had not expected this. Nor would there be any precedent for the volume of what he was about to hear.

Thankfully, the Free Trade Hall had acoustics to die for, and the louder a band played, the better they got. So when, in the words of attendee Stewart Tray, 'They struck into "Tell Me, Momma" ... it was loud for '66. Very loud. A huge noise, but very clear.'

Another eyewitness conveyed the impact to pop historian C.P. Lee, thirty years later, 'The level of sound was something that I'd never heard before, especially being so close up to it. I was just blasted out of my skin. It was physical, rather than just listening to music.'

Before Dylan drained all the power from Manchester's mains, though, there was an acoustic set to negotiate. It was Jean-Marc Pascal's first opportunity to hear aural evidence of the speed at which Dylan was moving, artistically. He even had time to note the names of songs:

> The first half of the concert passes without incident. Bob is alone on stage with his acoustic guitar. Of his old songs, he has kept only 'She Belongs To Me', 'Desolation Row', 'It's All Over Now Baby Blue' and 'Mr Tambourine Man', deliberately moving away from songs protesting about social and racial unrest and moving toward more personal, introspective problems. Nevertheless he is given rapturous applause.

It seems the daytime sleeping regime Dylan allowed himself on the road had its upside. Once again sharply focused, the acoustic set tonight was delivered with real vocal precision, and with none of the tuning issues that had blighted some shows to date (and would return with a vengeance in Paris). Only a particularly churlish critic could take issue with Dylan's commitment to his material in Manchester that May. And yet, as the one complete acoustic set to have been released officially to date, the set comes across now as ever so slightly 'by rote'; not mechanical but not mercurial either. It certainly provides no hint of the melodrama to come—the end of the musical world as we know it.

The controversy about what really happened during the second half on May 17 1966 continues to rage on half a century later, even after an official release of the full concert, from that precious three-track; a whole book on the subject from attendee C.P. Lee; at least two radio documentaries; the tracking down of at least two people who claimed they shouted 'Judas'; and even, unexpectedly, the emergence in 2005 of footage shot by Pennebaker from the overhanging balcony, capturing the moment Dylan was accused of crucifying Christ (by proxy).

Even before this historic confrontation, there were more than enough signs this was going to be a battleground like no other and this time Dylan was taking no prisoners. The evening's events proved dramatic enough to imprint themselves on John Kappes's memory for the next two decades:

> The start of the second half ... Bob appeared onstage and the band very quickly followed him. ... The drummer seemed to be the odd one out ... Bob appeared to be enjoying himself, smiling quite frequently and during guitar riffs etc. was dancing around in front of the drums, extraordinary for a folkie! The slow handclapping gradually spreads and at the start of 'Baby Let Me Follow You Down', the band seemed not to take Bob's lead. He looked to his right and then to his left to Robbie Robertson, I thought he was going to walk off! The song then took off. I can also remember quite vividly the incoherent talking into the microphone [before 'One Too Many Mornings']. Everyone was shushing, [thinking] he's trying to say something. The noise grew louder and louder, people were walking out and one fellow walked by the stage with his hands over his ears, within a few feet of Bob who, I am sure, saw him. People around me were arguing amongst themselves. ... People were shouting, 'Ignore them Bobby!', 'You're still great!' and similar things. At the end of each song Bob would make deep bows and blow kisses with both hands to the audience as if acknowledging tremendous acclaim. While this was all going on the band continued as if nothing was happening. Robbie Robertson always seemed to have that half-smile. There was also a long pause before 'Ballad Of A Thin Man'—someone was leaning onto the front of the stage waving a piece of paper at Bob. ... Someone said it was a petition.

Though the 'petition' turned out to have a single signature, the petitioner felt she was speaking for her whole sorority. The lady in question had somehow convinced herself Dylan simply did not realise what he was doing, as she finally admitted to C.P. Lee in 1995. And so, as another heckler cried out, 'Where's your silver?'—the first reference of the evening to Judas, it would appear—ballad-fan Barbara 'walked up the central aisle to the front of the stage. Dylan stopped tuning up and bent down towards her. She reached up and passed him a note ... [She says,] "He came forward. I thought he was actually going to give me a kiss. Instead of that he blew me a kiss and I went, 'No, no, read the note.' ... He did take the note ...

I saw him look at it." ... [He] put it in his pocket and turned back to the band. The woman went back to her seat. The tuning and slow hand-clapping resumed. On the tape of the gig you can make out ... Robertson ask[ing] Dylan, "What's it say?" Dylan replies, "I dunno, pick it up man."'

Dylan knew only too well what it said: 'Tell the band to go home.' But if Barbara thought Dylan was oblivious to the effect he was having, a fair few people there, including at least one person working the hall, Rick Sanders, had already realised 'the long tune-ups were [an act of] defiance. Very calculated. ... Whatever he was on had him operating on a very different velocity to anyone else, even the band, and they were his cohorts.'

Barbara and her soured sisters had no excuse for not knowing at this late date what they were about to receive. Kevin Fletcher remembers thinking, beforehand, that 'there might be trouble, because we'd read about it in the press. Even in the *Daily Mirror* or the *News Chronicle*, there'd been an article about booing at other concerts.'

In fact, it is quite remarkable that this did not become the night of the big punch-up. Steve Currie, another person C.P. Lee tracked down, admitted he 'wasn't too impressed by [Dylan's] velvet suits, but I was even less impressed by the dickhead sat next to me who decided to start booing and shouting along with the others who were scattered around the hall. I told him to fuck off home if he didn't like it.'

Similar scenarios played out throughout the hallowed home of the Hallé; as indeed it would across the entire British Isles—which is why for the next two decades no one could definitively prove that the most bootlegged concert in rock history came from Manchester—as opposed to the Royal Albert Hall, as the bootleg claimed, or Glasgow (where almost identical confrontations took place before 'Baby Let Me Follow You Down' and 'Leopard-Skin Pill-Box Hat'). Matters weren't greatly helped by the person who marked up that night's Columbia reels, crediting them to the 'Royal Albert Hall, Manchester'.

Much of this confusion could have been settled long ago had someone, anyone, from a thriving local press or national music press bothered to report on the show to end all shows, or followed the tour as it headed north. But the only reporter who paid witness to this Mancunian soap opera was French, and his own report of time spent 'with the uncompromising Bob Dylan'—as he called his article—was published in French magazine *Salut Les Copains*. And at no point does Monsieur Pascal specifically mention any exchange before the night's finale, though he had plenty to say about the reaction Dylan's electric set generated:

> The second half firmly divides the audience. Bob has chosen to surround himself with a rock group; all excellent musicians, however, who play remarkable music. Unfortunately this music doesn't please everyone. I hear shouts of 'Traitor', 'Play some folk songs', 'Go and join the Rolling Stones', 'We don't need you— we've already got The Animals'. However, other spectators applaud warmly. Unruffled, Bob continues his show, which closes with 'Like A Rolling Stone'.

Surely, Pascal remembered more than this. He did, and this was not his only account of the Manchester show. An alternate gospel appeared five months later in a most unlikely place: the American pop monthly *Hullabaloo*. 'A Plea For A Better Dylan' contained the kernel of Pascal's previous account of that dramatic evening now spun out to greater effect:

> From the audience, a restless one, come several epithets that can be heard above the huge sound of the rock'n'roll group; words like 'Play some folk songs ...' and 'Go get some work with the Rolling Stones ...' and 'Traitor ...' and 'We don't need you! We already have The Animals, and The Beatles', while the rest of the audience which doesn't participate in the rout, applauds, clasping hands and feet, shouting approvingly. Undaunted by the noise, protected by some cops who have lined out in front of the stage[!], the object of both animosity and marks of allegiance keeps singing, soberly dressed in an all-black outfit, strumming his guitar, occasionally blowing his harmonica, his long, crazy hair looking like a halo in the stage lights. Bob Dylan has long ago accepted his fate. He looks imperturbable, and song after song, goes on his own way, whether accepted or not. I look at the frightening sight of this tempestuous crowd agitated by different feelings, while on stage, surrounded by a jazz-rock combo, Dylan seems to play more for himself than for those who try to catch the meaning of his songs over the noise made by those who deny the singer the right to have changed his style.

However, the US music paper failed to identify the concert in question—or the article's author. In fact, the article as printed gave the general impression that the described show was in America, even reporting a supposed post-gig conversation between Dylan and his 'agent': 'What's next?' 'You have an interview tomorrow with an editor from the *New York Times*.' 'What does he want from me?' 'I guess the usual round of questions about the war in Vietnam, LSD and the other questions of the moment.' 'Fine ... I'll tell him anything ... Stupid questions deserve stupid answers.'

This 'revealing' discussion was actually about a forthcoming press conference in Paris, and Dylan was conversing with Mr Pascal, not his agent. In fact, the whole *Hullabaloo* feature appears to have been bastardised by the magazine to make it 'relevant' to the American teen—which, given Dylan's recent motorcycle accident, it never could be. Through this unnecessary fog of confusion, Pascal's account of the Manchester performance—fuller and more colourful than the *Salut Les Copains* version—survived relatively unscathed. But he still failed to mention the now-infamous 'Judas' shout.

Nor was there any direct reference to the incident in a pair of letters published the week after in the *Manchester Evening News*—belatedly responding to its own failure to report directly—one from each side of the great folk/rock divide. Representing the anti-Dylan camp was J.M. Whittaker, who just wanted to know, 'What has happened to the Dylan who visited Britain in 1965 and sang with such feeling and sincerity?' (This being the very tour Dylan had said some months earlier he would not have bothered to attend.) R.A. McCann had more to say, mustering a greater eloquence. But his one reference to the 'Judas' incident was so cryptic no one noticed its relevance:

> Apparently I was under a wrong impression in believing that Manchester people make fair audiences! On Tuesday, at the Bob Dylan concert, I witnessed a childish display of audience participation. This was most distasteful because the second half of Bob Dylan's concert was a new type of presentation for him, with a backing group, and as with all new ventures a certain amount of technical difficulty is bound to arise. But certain members of the audience would not give him a chance to overcome these difficulties.

They jeered and slow-clapped him so much, even after he had
apologised for playing too loud, that the show was cut short.

Like many a '66 attendee, Mr McCann misinterpreted the lack of
an encore as Dylan's way of rebuking the audience. His suggestion
that Dylan 'apologised for playing too loud' shortly before 'the show
was cut short' probably refers to the partly unintelligible off-mic
comment Dylan (or Danko) made after he drawled, 'I don't believe
you, you're a liar'. That semi-audible remark was reported for many
years as 'You're a fucking liar', until someone (myself) suggested in
a long *Telegraph* article on 1966 line recordings that he might actually
be saying, 'Play fucking loud.' Mr McCann, it would seem, thought
he growled, 'It's too fucking loud.'

If so, he misheard what was said—and probably who said it—but
the fact that he was close enough to hear this aside suggests he was
probably seated behind the band, because Dylan was not only off-
mike but had his back to the microphone when someone uttered the
infamous expletive.[51]

A close analysis of the three isolated tracks recorded by Columbia
confirms it was the overhanging onstage mic that picked up that
line—and captured the 'Judas' shout so clearly. What is no longer
in doubt—even though a surprising number of attendees didn't hear
or remember it—is that the 'Judas' incident occurred in Manchester,
and only there.

That affirmation only came about because—unbeknownst to the
galvanised generation who cherished the 1970 bootleg album called
variously *Looking Back*, *In 1966 There Was* or *The Royal Albert Hall
Concert*—Dylan had instructed his British publicist, Ken Pitt, to
employ a press-cuttings service to collect all the write-ups of the shows
and forward them to Pitt's office. This meticulous organisation even
collated the various letter-pages from local papers. But no one bothered
to go through the full file until a Wanted Man chanced upon it. Lo
and behold, there in the file collecting dust was a letter to the *Oldham
Evening Chronicle* by an anonymous 'Dylan fan' who complained:

---

[51] Martin Scorsese dubbed in the Sony line recording for the 2005 *No Direction Home* DVD,
and unhelpfully added subtitles, as if there was no doubt whether Dylan declaimed, 'Play
[it] fucking loud.'

The knockers are all stations go again! I am referring to the fantastic performance given by Bob Dylan at the Manchester Free Trade Hall last Tuesday night. Everyone enjoyed the first [set], as no doubt every Dylan fan would. He sang folk songs accompanied with his guitar and harmonica for the first half of the show, which went just great; but when he decided to change his style of music for the second half, the knockers and so-called Dylan fans began calling him a traitor. If they really liked him and his music as much as they pretended, then they wouldn't mind him changing his style every so often. And even if the group's equipment was over-amplified, there was no need to take it out on the gearest folk singer of our generation. I think Bob put his feelings over to the knockers just great. When someone shouted out to him 'Judas!', he just calmly went to the microphone and quietly drawled, 'Ya liar!'

Even this anonymous soul could not confirm whether it was really the 'Judas' shout to which Dylan drawled his reply or one of the other epithets hurled his way in its immediate aftermath. One of these certainly includes a name check for Dylan Thomas; another, according to Mr Kappes, came from 'a fellow behind me [who] was shouting something about Bob being finished. This was to what Bob replied: "I don't believe you. You're a liar!"'

Whatever the truth, such had become the hold the 'Judas' shout had on the popular imagination that by the time Sony gave the full concert an official release as volume four of *The Bootleg Series* in 1998, the one burning question that remained unanswered was the identity of the angry young man who shouted the loaded word. The matter was seemingly settled a few months later when Keith Butler, a twenty year-old Keele student in 1966, came forward.

He was certainly at the show. Indeed, as far back as 1991, I suggested in *Behind The Shades* that if there was ever a candidate for the man who shouted 'Judas', it was an individual ranting at Dylan's camera crew in the foyer of the Free Trade Hall afterward. Halfway through *Eat The Document*, an as-yet-unidentified Butler almost grabs the microphone out of Bobby Neuwirth's hands as he splutters, 'Any pop group could produce better rubbish than that. It was a bloody disgrace. He wants shooting. He's a traitor.'

So Butler was certainly there, and he was certainly angry. In January 1999, Mr Butler tried to explain his reasoning: 'I was very disappointed about what I was hearing. But I think what really sent me over the top was when he did those lovely songs … "Baby Let Me Follow You Down", and the other one was "One Too Many Mornings". I was emotional, and I think my anger just welled up inside of me. It was "One Too Many Mornings" that really sent me over the top.'

But like a scene from *Spartacus*, another attendee came forward claiming to be this person with a penchant for biblical analogies. John Cordwell's account was less believable. For starters, he claimed he 'stood up on the second balcony of the Free Trade Hall all those years ago and felt betrayed enough to give voice to my feelings'.

From the Free Trade Hall balcony—the level *above* the circle—it would need to be a superhuman shout to be picked up with such clarity on what is an onstage microphone. Butler, on the other hand, was at the front of the circle, on the stage-right horseshoe, perfectly situated to make his feelings known to that onstage mic.

Cordwell was asked how he felt about Dylan's reaction. He responded, 'I don't recall that bit at all. I don't recall hearing Dylan say anything back.' This also rather beggars belief. Dylan certainly remembered the shout, and how it made him feel, as late as 2012. Promoting possibly his last-ever album of all-original material, *Tempest*, he gave vent to those feelings to Mikal Gilmore:

> Judas, the most hated name in human history! If you think you've been called a bad name, try to work your way out from under that. Yeah, and for what? For playing an electric guitar? As if that is in some kind of way equitable to betraying our Lord and delivering him up to be crucified.

Even at the time, Dylan couldn't quite believe what had just happened. This is perhaps why someone was dispatched to London's IBC Studios to get a mono acetate cut from the Columbia reels. They proudly returned with the electric set on acetate, intended for the musicians' ears only. But, unbeknownst to Dylan and/or the label, the studio engineer at IBC was enough of a fan to simultaneously take his own reel-to-reel dub from the recording. He even decided to have a little fun with the tapes, mixing stereo versions of the last two songs, 'Ballad Of A Thin Man' and 'Like A Rolling Stone'.

He would sometimes play these reels for friends, who would shake their heads in wonder. Finally, one of them with a music industry connection prevailed on him to make a dub of his dub, which he took with him to California, by then home to a new form of vinyl product—the bootleg album. While there, he decided to make the monumental maelstrom available 'under the counter'. Imagine the engineer's surprise when one day a single album turned up in London's independent record stores, and all it said was: 'In 1966 There Was … Live In Concert … Not Reissued or Reshuffled Material.' Nor was it.

10. AT THE STILL POINT
OF THE TURNING WORLD

[May 18–27 1966]

It's hard to do a tour, and in the after hours make a movie. What we were doing was to try to fulfil this contract, to make a television show, and the only time I had to do it was when I was on tour, because I was on tour all the time.

—DYLAN TO JOHN COHEN, JUNE 1968

In the ten days after Manchester, Dylan was due to play three capital cities— Edinburgh, Paris and London—where he perhaps hoped to discover more cosmopolitan audiences. But he also had to negotiate the madding crowds of Glasgow and Newcastle. Only the music he and The Hawks were collectively making sustained him now, even as his nerves were becoming decidedly frayed by the relentless negativity.

His drug regime was also starting to wear him down. Part of the problem was that he no longer had a reliable drug supply. At some point Maymudes departed the tour (according to Victor, after telling Dylan the extent of the financial liberties Grossman was taking with *his* money), and so Dylan's East End minder, on loan from the Stones, was tasked with finding the right cocktail. It was a task for which he was ill-equipped:

Richard Alderson: Dylan hated LSD [but] he drank a lot of red wine and he took these little amphetamine pills. But we had this guy in Britain called Tom Keylock and we would always send him out for drugs in Britain and he would never come back with what we sent him for. We'd send him for hash and he'd come back with kif, and we'd send him for kif and he'd come back with heroin. He always came back with something, but he never came back with the right thing.

And then there was the tiresome film, the reality of its demands beginning to try Dylan's patience. Because it wasn't just in the wee small hours that his thoughts perforce turned to the movie he was

now obligated to complete. On rare days off he shot rolls of film
to keep ABC happy and himself amused and/or sane, on occasions
venturing out in public to see what the man on the street thought.
Even in May, though, the British weather could make a hermit of
one. (At least it didn't drive him to chop up a piano to stay warm, as
it had on his first visit in 1963.)

Arriving at Glasgow's North British Station Hotel on the afternoon
of the eighteenth, he found the weather as inclement as tradition
suggested it could be. A folkloric expedition across the country that
had been the very font of Anglo-American folk song for centuries
was out of the question. Rather than a trip to the Mitchell Library,
or a visit to a local record store to find some rare Jeannie Robertson
recordings, Dylan summoned Robbie Robertson—and the camera
crew—to his hotel room, where he composed four outlined epitaphs
in song as Robertson picked his way through the musical maze this
inspired singer-songwriter weaved for the cameras' benefit.

Two of the four songs recorded would be excerpted in *Eat The
Document*, hinting at some lost greatness in the afterglow of the fabled
accident. But the entire (re-sequenced) session would not be released
until 2015's *Cutting Edge*. When it was, it contained a song that could
have been smelted in the Scotch forge of folksong ('If I Was A King')
and another that tipped its hat to the blues ('What Kind Of Friend Is
This?'), while the exquisite pair, 'I Can't Leave Her Behind' and 'On
A Rainy Afternoon', evoked a yearning for home and Her. Although
Pennebaker insists, 'He wrote a lot of music on that trip,' these four
snatches would be the last hints recorded in reel time before Dylan's
career skidded to a halt on a New York State back road. Hence their
resonance.

If only the 'trad' fans could hear him now—but they could not.
When he emerged from the hotel twenty-four hours later, heading
for the Odeon, he had again metamorphosed into a demon man child
born of the holy ghost of electricity.

It had been two days since Manchester, but the word had failed to
seep across the northern marches or over the border about which so
many ballads had been written. As a result, according to the *Daily
Record*, "The capacity audience clapped, stamped and cheered but only
between numbers. During the first half ... there was utter silence.
Clad in black the twenty-four-year-old legend seemed to sing exactly

what took his fancy. [But] the second half brought a different face of Dylan. He let fly with some up-tempo numbers, almost verging on rock.'

Fortunately, a more reliable national reporter kept better notes that night. Even *Daily Mail* man Andrew Young, though, was taken aback by the tenor of a crowd fuelled by Tennent's beer and 'trad' folk music:

> Dozens of fans walked out on American folk-singer Bob Dylan last night. There was a shouting battle between the folk-song purists … and the beat fans. All had gone smoothly in the first half. … Dressed in checked suit, he stood alone on stage and gasped out the protest songs which have made him a millionaire. It was when he came on in the second half dressed in black and accompanied by a five-man beat group that the trouble started. There were shouts of 'rubbish' from the purists and 'shut up' from the beat fans. He got the slow handclap when he launched into a number called 'I See You've Still Got Your Leopard-Skin Pill-Box Hat On'. To shouts of 'We want Dylan' he replied: 'Dylan got sick backstage and I'm here to take his place.'

For once, a reporter—and a *Daily Mail* one at that—was not exaggerating. In many ways, the Glasgow show made Manchester seem like a love-fest. According to Barry Feinstein, who took some evocative photos of Dylan in Glasgow, 'A girl fan even punched him', though he does not say whether this was during the show. Pennebaker, who had clambered on stage to catch the wind of change, missed any such incident.

What is clear from another exemplary Alderson recording is that tempers soon become so frayed an affray seems inevitable. At one point—just before 'Ballad Of A Thin Man'—even Dylan seems to have lost his famous cool. As another slow handclap emerges out of the darkness, he semi-whispers, 'Yes, yes, we know all about it. C'mon now. Shush.' He duly delivers a 'Thin Man' that drips disdain from every sibilant syllable. He even starts riffing on its burden like a true ballad-singer, at one point berating the barrackers, 'Something is happening and you better find out what it is/ You Know That, *Don't* You, Mr Jones.'

The shouting between songs—when not lost to the reel changes—

comes across as long and sustained, Young's account of the two verbal confrontations proving surprisingly accurate. The one before 'Leopard-Skin Pill-Box Hat' sounds from his description so similar to Manchester, it could suggest someone mixed up the reels.

This time Dylan really is fighting to get a word in edgewise. A first attempt only gets as far as, 'This is called … .' A pause allows the more belligerent Scots to shout themselves hoarse, before take two, 'This is called, da-da-da, da-da-da … .' Eventually curiosity kills the catcalls again. Finally, third time lucky, Dylan gets to complete the introduction: 'This is called, "Yes I See You Got Your Brand New Leopard-Skin Pill-Box … Hat".' Even then, another shout pierces the night, dismissed by Dylan with a 'Yes, I know' just as The Hawks tip a kitchen sink of cutlery into the sound mix.

Even a 'Thin Man' that has drilled every word in their askew direction fails to shut the Scottish dissidents up. As Dylan begins to cue up the band for a 'Like A Rolling Stone' cut from the same rock face as Manchester and Liverpool, another slow handclap and inaudible shouts (presumably along the lines of 'We want Dylan' or 'Where is Dylan?') prompts Dylan to deliver his most pointed rejoinder yet: 'He couldn't make it through the second half. Bob Dylan got very sick backstage and I'm here to take his place.'

Cut to the quick, he bleeds pure bile, which he uses to fuel 'Like A Rolling Stone'—and fire up a crowd of Glaswegians. He would not play the city again for another twenty-three years, but when he did, he debuted a new song with the opening couplet: 'Congratulations for breaking my heart / Congratulations for tearing it all apart.'

Evidently, this all-electric music was making the lowland Scots as angry as the other Celts Dylan had ticked off on the tour. Perhaps Edinburgh, as a former English garrison, would be different. Not according to another *Daily Mail* reporter, whose article was titled, 'Dylan Faces Second Night of Cat Calls'. This reviewer even went so far as to suggest 'American folk-singer Bob Dylan was booed off the stage again last night when he appeared with a beat group', though it was actually one of the longer shows that month. This reviewer—unable to name even 'Like A Rolling Stone'—seemed more bothered about the fact that Dylan had decided to document a capital performance on film:

Playing to an audience of nearly 3,000 in the ABC cinema, Edinburgh, he was continually catcalled and many of his fans ... walked out. ... Throughout his performance Dylan repeatedly turned his back on the audience and posed for his personal cine photographers. After every number he stopped to tune his guitar. ... The catcalls and shouts grew louder when Dylan played the piano with the beat group and eventually the singer walked off the stage still posing for his photographers [sic].

The 'catcalls and shouts' that apparently grew ever louder did so in a way that failed to register on a complete audience tape of the show. They also washed over an impervious Dylan, who unleashed a 'Thin Man' which, were it not for the two performances either side of it, might qualify as definitive.[52]

But such was the very nature of performances on this one-off tour—a near-definitive rendition relegated to rubble the following night as Dylan raised his game again and again. As Feinstein observed, 'He was a believer in ... going forward, not doing the same show every time.' As was the case with another landmark tour fourteen years later—when audiences were baying for lamb's blood—playing the same set each night made for a different experience each and every time.

And for some, it was a life-affirming experience, as it was for journalist and poet Barry MacSweeney, who later described the following night's electric half at Newcastle Odeon as pure 'vitriolic spite. And it was so loud, it was astounding. I remember thinking, "This is it." Some athletes talk of getting "zoned" when they hit their peak. It felt just like that. Dylan and Robbie Robertson had their guitars really close to each other, just getting off on the riffs ... Robertson grinning from ear to ear.'

Sadly, the local *Sunday Sun*, for whom MacSweeney was reviewing the show, expected something more prosaic, obliging him to economically extol the 'New-Look Bob Dylan' and enthuse about a 'second half [which] saw him backed by a five-piece beat group, and for my money this was the most exciting half with, for a finale, the immortal "Like A Rolling Stone"'.

[52] The Edinburgh 'Thin Man' is the penultimate track on *Bootleg Series Vol. 7*, which professes to be the soundtrack to *No Direction Home*. It rarely is.

The complete filmed performance of the Newcastle 'Like A Rolling Stone'—included as a bonus cut on the commercial *No Direction Home* DVD—confirms MacSweeney's acute appreciation. This is indeed an immortal performance, Dylan seemingly peaking with every chorus but finding yet more energy and venom on the next go around. By the end he can hardly contain himself so powerful is the music and so contagious the groove. It has been another hard day's night, but a rewarding one.

Playing to an audience positioned somewhere between Glasgow and Edinburgh in the antipathy stakes, the first half of the electric set had passed largely without incident. Only at the end of 'Just Like Tom Thumb's Blues' is there an attempted slow handclap, a 'Go home!' and at least four audible boos. When Dylan again struggles to introduce 'Leopard-Skin Pill-Box Hat', he finally tells his tormentors, 'You're talking to the wrong person.' It generates a huge cheer, explicating the allegiance of the many.

Once again, the break before 'Thin Man' provides the protesters with their optimum opportunity to make themselves heard, though by now others are shouting back. Dylan makes a further plea for understanding, 'C'mon now. You know I'm a sick man. Leave me alone. Shushh,' and begins to play the intro, to audible cheers. Starting to enjoy himself, he twists various lines to drive home the penknife of truth: 'Something is happening and you don't know what it is—isn't that right, Mr Jones?! ... And it's happening to you, *isn't it, Mr Jones*?!!'

Somehow, after this seven-minute catharsis he still summons the energy to repeatedly ask the audience, 'How does it feel? How does it feeeel? To be on your own ...' One can't help but wonder what Dylan made of the tweedy professor, pipe in hand, sitting mutely throughout the entire song, directly in his line of vision; or what said stoic squire made of the small but vociferous minority behind him who had been giving Dylan a piece of their made-up minds. The last provincial date thus passed by, not without incident. Paris beckoned and the Albert Hall, the real one ...

★ ★ ★

In the plane that takes us to Paris, Bob was keen to have Jean-Marie and myself sitting next to him. 'Can you tell me, boys, what I'm going to do in a country where no one understands what I'm saying? Do you think they'll boo me at the Olympia too?' As we assured him that they wouldn't, he continued, 'What sort of questions will they ask me at the press conference?' 'Nothing original, you can be assured. What do you think about the Vietnam war? Why you've changed your style of music, what do you think about long hair? That's about it.' On arrival at Le Bourget, there's a crowd of press photographers, Albert Raisner, the Olympia management and his fan club, all turned out in full force to welcome him, with streamers. … Surrounded by a few members of the clan, he charged into the crowd with his head down, muttering, 'Let me get through, you bunch of idiots. What do you all want with me?' He ducked into an enormous Cadillac and left at top speed to shut himself up in the George V Hotel. He only came out twice: once to visit Johnny Hallyday and secondly to give that famous concert at Olympia, for which people paid 60 [francs] a seat and about which no one has stopped talking to this day.

—JEAN-MARC PASCAL, *SALUT LES COPAINS*, JULY 1966

Photos of Dylan at Paris airport surrounded by fans, willingly conversing, rather call into question Pascal's account of the airport arrival. For now, Dylan seemed genuinely delighted to be back in Paris—for the first time since May 1964, a time when the complete unknown had hung out with French folksinger Hugues Aufray and met a particularly striking Nordic blonde called Nico.

As for not going out of the plush George Cinq, Dylan certainly ventured forth on the morning of the twenty-third—i.e. the day after his arrival—to visit a flea market in the company of Barry Feinstein. Looking for a visual prop, he settled on a ventriloquist's puppet. That afternoon he was due to conduct—or should one say orchestrate—his last press conference of the year (and his last for fifteen long years). Again the camera crew would be there, chronicling every ill-advised query. By now, everyone in the entourage knew what would happen, and how Dylan tended to respond to any questions he'd heard before. On this occasion, he had also brought a prop to help get the message across:

Barry Feinstein: If they asked him something sensible, he gave them a decent answer. If they asked a bullshit question, he gave them a bullshit answer. It just came with the territory as far as he was concerned. … Every time one of the [French] journalists asked him a [dumb] question, he put his ear to the puppet's mouth and pretended to listen to the answer. Then he would tell the press. It drove them nuts.

A year earlier, Dylan had delighted a previous entourage and camera crew, at his first London press conference, by holding a large industrial light bulb throughout proceedings. Only when he was asked for his main message did its purpose become clear: 'Keep a good head and always carry a light bulb.' He now resumed playing May games for the camera's benefit. Photos of the Paris press conference on the afternoon of May 23 confirm the American photographer's recollection. Someone even asked Dylan the puppet's name (Finian). It was all downhill from there:

Q: Why do you have a puppet by your side?
A: It's the puppet that follows me everywhere.
Q: What does it represent? A symbol? A fetish? A mascot?
A: It's a religion, of tears and mourning.
Q: What are your pleasures?
A: Smoking and eating.
Q: Smoking what?
A: Anything.
Q: Do you think that narcotics can inspire?
A: Do you yourself take drugs?
Q: Sometimes.
A: Then you ought to know!
Q: Do you have a special way of sleeping?
A: One hand under my leg, the other one on my ear. [*He demonstrates.*]
Q: What gave you the idea of singing folk songs?
A: In 1959, there were adverts everywhere—'sing folk songs'.
Q: Do you always live like a beatnik?
A: What do you mean by 'beatnik'?
Q: Someone who has no desire for money or honours, who travels when he wants to.
A: In that case, thanks for calling me a beatnik.
Q: Is there anything about which you are certain?
A: I'm certain of the existence of ashtrays, of doorknobs, of windowpanes.

This time the most heartfelt statements the American delivered to the French press were both made in response to 'bullshit questions'. When asked the meaning of certain songs, he bluntly requested, 'Would the gentlemen of the press who don't know my songs abstain from asking questions about those songs?' When they continued to enquire about his message, he made his feelings plain enough to transcend translation into a foreign tongue, 'I don't belong to any movement. I've only got some ideas in my head and I tell them. I don't support anybody's cause. No revolution ever came about because of songs.'

Two of the more astute attendees were a pair of French schoolgirls who had somehow blagged their way into the George V conference room, curious to know if he liked girls. He insisted, 'I like everybody.' They then asked if he was married ('I'd lie if I answered'), if he thought he was living in a foolish world ('No'), and if he knew what a comb was (he did not). At the end of proceedings, fifteen-year-old Elisabeth Jaury asked for his autograph, returning home 'pleased with my day, wondering if Bob Dylan was not making fun at us'.

Smart girl. The more worldly writer for *Paris Match* took a rather more cynical view of Dylan's verbal sparring: 'His sarcastic sense of humour shows itself all the time in his spontaneous replies, spoken in a subdued voice which is somewhat nasal. … He passes disconnectedly from one idea to another only to come back suddenly to the first. Sometimes he's obviously putting on an act. … But he can swing from one mood to the opposite and become totally earnest.'

If members of the (notoriously anti-American) French press found it hard to keep up with his hyperactive mind in the afternoon light of George V's conference room, they were at a complete loss the following evening. But a sell-out show at the legendary Olympia by the now-infamous anti-pop star also demanded the presence of *Le Monde*, *Le Figaro*, *Paris Match*, *Paris Soir*, et al, with or without prejudice. At least *Le Monde* sent their most astute pop critic, who was prepared to give Bob the benefit of the doubt:

> His appearance comes as a shock. … He looks like Sarah Bernhardt at the end of her life, frighteningly thin. Seeming tired, asleep even, hunchbacked and fragile as a china doll, Dylan staggers to the microphone and undergoes a transformation—the small,

insignificant man becomes the poet of the age. To fully appreciate Dylan you have to see him because this true poet has an incredible presence. On stage he lives the songs. It's there you discover the true person—a bohemian, crazy for freedom, hating having to be part of 'show-business' and deliberately breaking up the smooth running of his performance. But this poet and artist was above and beyond the comprehension of Tuesday night's crowd who were so unused to being in the presence of such a rich and diverse talent that they responded with a somewhat cold bewilderment.

However, such generosity of spirit was in short supply in Paris that evening. For those determined to depict Dylan's behaviour that night in the worst possible light, *Paris Jour* led the way, even directing its review—the headline of which read, *in English*, 'Bob Dylan Go Home!'—at the singer:

> Mr Dylan you've had us on. I heard that you are one of the highest-paid performers in the world. I'm told that you were paid fifteen million old francs for this one concert—more than a workingman gets in ten years! I'm told that you are acclaimed in America, that you represent revolt against injustice, that you have sold eighteen million records. Now I'm telling you that you should've stayed home. I don't presume to judge your songs. I'm told that you are a poet of genius. Alas, like 99 percent of the people who listened to you in absolute astonishment, I didn't understand a word of what you said. But I did understand your insults. After each song you spent ten minutes tuning your guitar. ... At the end of each song people applauded. In France we're taught to be polite. ... Each time you turned your back on us. You pretended to pick up your harmonica from a stool or to drink a glass of water or to adjust the amplifiers. You never acknowledged us or said thank you.

Nor was the *Paris Jour* the only European paper to suggest that tuning one's guitar was some covert way of insulting one's hosts. The German monthly magazine *Pop* had dispatched Mr Hirt to report—at length—on the concert. With typical Germanic efficiency, Hirt took painstaking notes but was still hopelessly wide of the mark in his analysis:

The performance—or rather the spectacle—began fifteen minutes late. The stage was sparsely illuminated and decorated with the American Star-Spangled Banner, when the heavy scarlet curtain rose. At the front of the stage was a high stool with a glass of water. A spotlight followed the star from the wings and guided him, as he staggered a little, to the front of the stage. ... Neglecting the applause, Bob inspected the glass of water and the microphones. Everything seemed to be all right, so Dylan began immediately with his first number. Obviously it was a new song. Nobody in the audience seemed to know it. It lasted ten minutes, was an 'original' Dylan, but it didn't fill the audience with enthusiasm as they understood the complex English lyrics only partially. After the song, Bob tuned his guitar. He did it so clumsily that you'd have thought he'd never done it before. He babbled some words in French ...

After the second song, which I also didn't know, he addressed himself to the English and the Americans in the hall. 'Anybody out there understand English?' Lots of yeses satisfied him. 'Well,' he said, 'sometimes I feel lonely.' Then he started the third song, again an obviously new, unknown song. After that he began again to tune up his guitar erratically. Two minutes, three minutes, five minutes went by. Someone in the audience had the effrontery to protest, and Dylan reacted sharply and sarcastically: 'I'm only doing this for you. I don't care. If you want to hear my songs on an out-of-tune guitar, OK.' ... Now it was 'Desolation Row' and about twenty verses of it. After that another drink of water and more guitar tuning. 'Don't you have anything you could be reading?' he asked the audience as he continued to tune, 'or maybe you could go to the bowling alley till I'm finished.' Some members of the audience heckled him, others told them to be quiet. Dylan carried on resolutely until the guitar was finally in tune. ... After one hour and five minutes, the curtain closed on the first half. Sum: seven songs. That makes nine minutes a song.

Although much of what Hirt reported really happened, the whole tenor of his account suggests an antipathy between artist and audience that is largely absent from the board recording. In fact, almost the entire audience display impressive patience and discernible sympathy for Dylan as he wrestles with his borrowed acoustic guitar and his seeming inability to get the damn thing in tune.

According to Tom Keylock, who went to Paris with him, Dylan

'was in a bit of a state with his pills. ... He wouldn't come out of the dressing room. Albert and Tito [Burns] couldn't get him out. ... It took me about fifteen minutes to get him onstage, [and then it] took him twenty minutes to tune his guitar ... [but] he was having a conversation as he was going along.' It is exactly that sense of 'having a conversation' with the audience that the press reports omit. This does come across on the tape, even as Dylan becomes progressively more freaked out by the genuine difficulties he is having tuning his Martin.

Initially, it is all very jolly, despite Dylan showing a minimal grasp of French by announcing, 'This is a request—requestez song,' before 'Fourth Time Around'. His language skills haven't discernibly improved five minutes later, when he prefaces 'Visions Of Johanna' by querying, 'Havez-vous de boeuf? Just what I thought.'

Already, the guitar is playing up, but after half a minute he has seemingly mastered the inanimate object well enough to deliver the usual word-perfect vision, leaning into each rhyme in the last verse with an air of resignation verging on finality: 'kerrrode / flowed / road / owed / load / ex-plode'.

Dylan has begun to realise that the guitar simply won't stay in tune. The minute he tunes it, it drifts. Knowing he is on borrowed time, he gamely tries to retune it in preparation for 'Baby Blue'—which requires two and a half minutes, obliging him to engage with the audience in more of that ongoing conversation.

Asking if 'anybody out there that understands English?' he is met in the affirmative. 'That's wonderful.' A cry of 'We love you' prompts Dylan to respond, 'It gets so lonesome sometimes.' But he says it with a smile, and the audience seem to sense he is sending himself up. At this point, he finally alludes to the problems he is having, 'I don't usually do this, but I don't want to waste any[body's] time.'

When he begins 'Baby Blue' there is a welcome burst of recognition. If 'Desolation Row' requires yet more tuning, it is measured in seconds not minutes, during which Dylan apologises for the fact that he has 'to keep drinking this water—it's such a long song'. Does he mean the one he has just done, or the one he is summoning the will to tackle? Either way, 'This is great water. I don't know if anybody's ever told you that.'

A pause, another manual tune, and then, 'This is the Olympia, huh. Great place.' By now, he is running out of things to say and resorts to his regular gag at such junctures, 'My electric guitar never goes out of tune.' Again, there is audible laughter and a complete absence of heckling. As Dylan weaves his way through 'Desolation Row' you can hear a centime drop.

It is between 'Desolation Row' and 'Just Like A Woman' that the mood changes. The guitar finally goes on strike, Robbie Robertson may or may not have now taken the guitar from Dylan to tune it (as he claims in his memoir) while Dylan has something of a mini-meltdown. What is certain is that Dylan begins to try the patience of the Parisians, taking some eight minutes to tune the guitar to his satisfaction, while his attempts at further conversation are interrupted, off-mic, by a couple of heckles.

But the majority of the audience stay resolutely on side. Only the local reviewers and a handful of fuming folkies down the front, who start to express their annoyance, seem to be in a hurry to get somewhere. Though their remarks are inaudible on the recording, Dylan responds in kind.

Describing the next song as 'another request song—I often do a lot of requests', Dylan takes twenty seconds to re-tune the guitar. When someone shouts something, he goes, 'I'm doing this for you. I don't care.' The retort draws huge applause, emboldening him to add, 'If you wanna hear it that way, I'll play it that way.' Further applause confirms that the majority of fans want the impatient few down front to go home, not their pop idol. He thanks them—in French—generating a further ripple of applause. However, by now, according to Alderson, 'There was an undercurrent of menace coming from the audience.'

It finally spills over into a war of words. Someone down front is not happy, and something they say prompts Dylan to lose his temper with an audience member for the first time on the tour. He lays into the heckler in no uncertain terms, 'You just can't wait, can ya? You have to go to work at ten o'clock? It's a drag for me, too. But that's folk music for ya! It does this all the time.' Placing the blame on folk music is a wonderful twist, proving that the absurdity of the situation—being heckled in the *first* half—is not entirely lost on him.

In despair, he asks, 'Does anybody have another guitar out there?' A burst of laughter suggests they are amused by the suggestion, but Dylan is deadly serious. Backstage, the search is on, while the singer is obliged to explain, 'My guitar's broken. It got broke on the way here. It's happened many times before. Nothing to worry about. Didn't you bring a magazine to read or something?'

By now, Dylan is desperately looking to the side of the stage for another guitar. Meanwhile, he continues to banter with the crowd, 'I can't play it out of tune. I gotta tune it. In the meantime you can go to the bowling alley. It don't matter.' As the evening threatens to go completely pear-shaped, Dylan wonders aloud, 'Is it true one French man is worth a thousand [other] lives?'

Just when it seems he might have lost the crowd, he finally launches into 'Just Like A Woman'. But barely has he started than he has to stop. He is growing extremely tetchy, and when another not-so-brave soul expresses displeasure, he goes, 'Oh come on, I wouldn't behave like this if I came to see you. I'm very sorry. Why must you … [at this point he is interrupted by somebody]. It's fun to just watch me tune it! Hey, I wanna get out of here as fast as you want to get out of here.'

Those in the audience who have sat patiently—despite the (apparently egregious) sixty-franc ticket price—are duly rewarded with a 'Just Like A Woman' worth the price of admission alone. An exquisite harmonica break completes the six-minute performance, bringing the house down in the process.

But he still has one more song to do, and when he tunes it to the right key for 'Tambourine Man', it immediately drifts. A despairing Dylan can be heard exclaiming, off-mic, 'No, no, no, no—not again.' He somehow wrestles it back into tune in under a minute and heads straight into an eight-minute-plus 'Tambourine Man' that summons the very ghost of Piaf, so warm is the vocal, so precise is his diction and heartbreaking the harp coda. The end of the set brings prolonged applause from an audience that had witnessed Dylan, on the brink of a near-breakdown, somehow pull it off at the last.

It had been a close run thing. Yet each of the seven songs in cold isolation—divorced from the endless tune-ups—would stand happily alongside any performance to date. And not all the critics were antagonistic, or unaware of the breadth of his achievement. The journalist from L'Humanité, for one, showed the requisite humanity and not a little critical awareness:

Dylan was himself on stage and thus incomprehensible to a public used to mediocre singers who in one way or another have to flatter their audiences. Dylan was totally indifferent to their responses. He was Bob Dylan—American poet, American singer, American artist—performing for French people. [But] the singer and his audiences were on different sides, and they never really met each other.

For once, the real drama had come during the first half of the evening. Thankfully, as Mr Pascal had been right to suggest, the Parisians were not inclined to boo the electric set. When Dylan came out for the second part of this Parisian passion play, he was determined to make amends, though only after he seemed inclined to provoke them further. When the curtain opened on a fifty-foot American flag, presumably another purchase at the flea market, those in the wings expected the worst.

And yet the audience sit and wait. There is a good minute between Dylan's appearance on stage and the start of 'Tell Me, Momma', for which the audience seems truly thankful. The hoots and hollers that accompany it in *Eat The Document* have been dubbed in. There is not a murmur of disapproval, before this or any other song.

Instead, warm applause (and one cry of 'Happy Birthday') greets 'Baby Let Me Follow You Down', 'Just Like Tom Thumb's Blues' and 'Ballad Of A Thin Man', while there is a sustained roar, the stomping of feet and cries for more after 'Like A Rolling Stone'. Even the *Pop* journalist seemed to enjoy the second half, despite suggesting, for the first time openly in print, that Dylan might be a drug fiend:

After the interval, Bob Dylan presented an orchestra. I say explicitly an orchestra because he neither introduced his musicians nor gave a statement whether they were his regular band. ... This orchestra produced beat. Or was it the thing normally called folk-rock. I would say it was a combination. Neither—nor. Besides which, Bob's singing got lost more or less in the roaring of the three guitars. The little orchestra played with remarkable precision and with swing. Bob on the other hand seemed to be a little out of control. The general presumption was that he performed on dope. [!] Without engagement and without any comments he pushed himself through ten songs [sic] in fifty minutes. Only when he played piano for one song did he seem to notice the event, and seem to be having fun playing and performing.

By 'Ballad Of A Thin Man', always the seventh of *eight* songs, the puppet-master has found his mojo. The little verbal interjections he has begun to introduce hit overdrive at the Olympia, where he interjects, 'Something is happening, and it's got nothing to do with it,' 'Something is happening, why don't they include you?' and, finally, 'Now you're *positive* something is happening and you *better* find out what it is, *shouldn't* you, Mr Jones?'

The Paris electric set is highly focused, the exact opposite of the first half, climaxing with a 'Like A Rolling Stone' that builds and builds until a slow-burn guitar/harmonica coda nudges the song past eight minutes. For the second time, Dylan dedicates the song 'to the Taj Mahal'. More unexpected is Dylan's impromptu addition to another 'Mexican painter' intro for 'Tom Thumb's Blues', 'We can make a stab at the truth—which is not the truth—but we can make a stab at it.' In the city of Rimbaud's wild illuminations, he duly finds the very heart of Tom Thumb's inner darkness.

Though one wouldn't know it from the sour headlines that greeted his Olympian performance, the Paris electric set had become a real triumph. Unfortunately, Dylan still vetoed a scheduled broadcast of the entire show on French radio, meaning we can only imagine how the legend might have developed if Olympia 1966 had been the earliest tape of the tour to circulate.

As such, jaundiced reports of the show filled the information void, while the more balanced and/or fulsome accounts only appeared after Dylan disappeared into the woods of Woodstock, such as Jean-Marc Pascal's feature in *Salut Les Copains*.

At the same time, *Variety* picked up on Bill Diehl's grossly distorted rewrite of the *Paris Jour* review, which suggested the Midwest's not-so-fortunate son 'was welcomed like a hero—[but] left town hooted like a carrier of the plague. On stage, during the show, he took as long as ten minutes between each number (tuning up, he said). He ignored the cheers of the audience, applause that grew skimpier as the show wore on.'

Whatever French reviews Dylan got (someone) to read (him) on the plane back to London rolled over him. He was still focused on the road ahead. Only after one final hurdle—two sold out shows in London—could he and The Hawks take that good long rest.

★ ★ ★

The two London shows would be Dylan's (and Columbia's) last chance to capture the sound and fury for possible commercial release. They decided, record and be damned. Both shows at the real Albert Hall would be taped to three-track, as the cameras rolled again and Alderson ran 'backup' mono reels. The challenges were huge. Unlike the Manchester and Sheffield venues, the Albert Hall was (and is) an acoustical nightmare, a circular barn more suited to ping-pong than rock music.

A lengthy soundcheck on the first night was again organised (and filmed), and was protracted enough for Dylan to fleetingly break into an acoustic 'Can You Please Crawl Out Your Window?'. But he wasn't about to tamper with the format at the death. He had just two more shots at the prize before he was homeward bound, having learnt there was no place like home. Sat in a car with John Lennon on the twenty-seventh, driving round Hyde Park on a break from the endless soundchecking, it all came out on camera just before a technicolor yawn:

Bob Dylan (*looking very ill*): I wanna go back home. I wanna go back home, man, see a baseball game, all-night TV. I come from a land of paradise, man.
John Lennon (*sarcastically*): Sounds great.
Bob Dylan: Well, I could make it sound so great that you wouldn't have the capacity to speak … I'll be glad when this is over, 'cause I'm getting very sick here.

Only sheer willpower was keeping him going—that, and some 'powerful medicine'. If the *Pop* reporter in Paris was the first to break some unspoken code of silence by suggesting Dylan was performing 'under the influence', such was immediately apparent to anyone who met him on those two nights in London. Irish poet Johnny Byrne—who 'happened to be staying in the flat where he came back' after one of the shows—remembered, 'Dylan was visibly vibrating. I should imagine it was the exhaustion and a good deal of substances. He was

totally away, there was a yawning chasm between him and any kind
of human activity.'

He was not the only one. When Johnny Cash turned up in London,
after his own UK tour, he was another walking medicine cabinet and
human wreck, so much so that he spent much of his time ducking
his former enabler, June Carter:

Richard Alderson: In London, I was alone in my hotel room and
Johnny [Cash] burst in and said, 'I'm hiding from my wife.' And I
had a vial of amphetamine pills sitting on my dresser, because I was
doing pure methedrine, so the pills did nothing for me. People would
always give them to me and John saw [the vial] and took the whole
thing and locked himself in my bathroom for a whole day. June was
trying to find him. [Bobby and Johnny] were so wasted—the two
of them—they never did anything. They were gonna record some
precious shit but nothing ever happened because they were so drunk
or stoned.

Everyone and everything connected with the tour seemed to be
unravelling. This was not perhaps surprising. Dylan himself was
coming apart at the seams. And it showed. In the papers the day after
the first London show, he was accused of 'beginning to show the
signs of a man who does not care whether he communicates or not',
a remark that came at the end of a typical review of the first London
concert, in the *Daily Telegraph*. 'R.F.D.G.' gleaned only a single line
from Dylan, spoken before 'Just Like Tom Thumb's Blues'. The rest
of the time he was too busy evaluating an audience response unlike
any he had ever seen:

Incredibly, although up to ten pounds was being offered for [a single
ticket] ... barracking broke out among a section of the audience.
It followed a series of noisy songs, most of whose words were
incomprehensible, in which Dylan was accompanied by a quite
ordinary rhythm group. He won over the main body of the audience
with a typical stroke, 'Oh come on,' he said with coaxing irony,
'these are all protest songs.' This apparent call to stand up and be
counted checked a dangerous situation, but after that whole rows
sat with scarcely a sign of applause at the end of numbers.

The *Times'* review bore the headline, 'The Better Half Of Dylan'. There were no prizes for guessing which half was meant: 'In the first and infinitely better half of the evening, Mr Dylan gave an agreeable solo rending of some of the songs for which he is best-known; in the second half he was accompanied by a thunderous quintet who made it virtually impossible to distinguish a single line of the lyrics.' The so-called 'quality' dailies neither knew, nor cared to know, why Dylan had become such a phenomenon while they were culturally sleeping. To the 'establishment press', the status quo was a desirable social state not a pop band.

Peter Willis of *Peace News* seems to have been the only reporter at the Albert Hall that first night who was aware enough to sense that 'the first—solo—half of Dylan's recent Albert Hall concert, although magnetic, seemed to be very slightly off-centre, a little dutiful almost, as if this was no longer quite where Dylan was at.' Willis was also the only fourth-estater paying sufficient attention in the second half:

> People will have to learn to appreciate Dylan for what he is, not for what they classified him as. ... All of which is to say that what Dylan is doing now, group and amplifiers and all, is real and as valid as anything he's ever done: and if you can't see it, might it not be your own inadequacy that's really to blame? ...
>
> When the group came on in the second half, it was soon evident that this was the part in which Dylan intended to have a ball. As far as I could judge, about half of the audience were with him on this. The remainder seemed to be in a state of sad, sometimes scabrous, non-comprehension. Dylan remained beatifically unaffected by this; during one of the few enfeebled outbursts of slow handclapping, he simply made faces, giggled and remarked: 'This isn't English music, this is American music.' ...
>
> Dylan has long since left the realms of mere protest (an impotent-sounding little word that never sat very easily on his shoulders, even in the days of 'Blowin' In The Wind'). His work is now much nearer home, expressing the need for one's whole life in both its intimate and social contacts, to be free of and therefore in revolt against all that is inhuman in society and people.

After two shows where dissenting voices had been largely becalmed, London town's hecklers—who according to the *Telegraph*, 'barracked after [multiple] songs'—had returned en masse. Dylan quickly evaluated the situation, prefacing the second song of the electric set by informing the audience, 'This is an old song. I like all my old songs. I don't know who said I don't,' before implausibly insisting, '"The Times They Are A-Changin'" influenced this song.'

Dylan seems to have maintained his good humour throughout. Even when he is about to break into 'Leopard-Skin Pill-Box Hat' and someone shouts something derogatory, to which he responds, 'Oh God! Are you talking to me? Come up here and say that,' there is precious little edge to his voice. Likewise, he prefaces 'Just Like Tom Thumb's Blues' by slurring, in the most stoned voice imaginable, 'These are *all* protest songs.' When someone audibly shouts, 'Rubbish,' he just pleads, 'Ah, c'mon now,' before reminding the detractor/s, 'This is not British music, this is American music.'

But if he was going to win the London audience over, they would have to meet him more than halfway. This was music made without compromise, particularly 'Like A Rolling Stone', which he again dedicated to the Taj Mahal. Thankfully, soundman Alderson outdid himself as the Albert Hall resounded to the sound of authentic American rock:

Dick Pountain: I saw Dylan at the Albert Hall ... I thought the second half was brilliant. It was the first time I'd ever heard heavy rock. It was probably the first time it had been played in this country, 'cause they just had all these amps that we didn't have. We were still using 25-watt amplifiers and they came on with a wall of amps ... and did 'Like A Rolling Stone' and shook the roof of the Albert Hall.

At the end of the show, Dylan gave his usual deep bow and a 'thank you', before adding, 'You were very nice.' Was he being disingenuous? Probably not. What barracking there had been was on a scale he knew well. The general reaction after each electric song fully vindicated his music. One down, one to go.

For the first time in a while, he had nowhere else he had to be. He could wait for the crowd to disperse and wend his way back to the Mayfair Hotel and a much-anticipated reunion with his favourite English blues aficionado, Dana Gillespie. Almost there. A single show and he'd be done. But of the many battlegrounds in Britain that May, the second Royal Albert Hall show would prove the bloodiest. He confided in Dana both his genuine surprise and a definite strategy:

Dana Gillespie: He was very surprised at the reaction of the English audiences. He thought England was far ahead of any other country in pop music and he just couldn't understand why he was booed and catcalled. The thing about Bobby is that he always wanted to be a rock'n'roll singer like Elvis Presley. When he achieved fame as a folk singer he thought he might be able to change and become accepted as a rock singer, too. When the audience booed and jeered his rock numbers in London, he just rocked more to annoy them. [1966]

★ ★ ★

Not only was Dylan determined to blast his electric sound into the dustiest crevices of this slightly shabby Victorian edifice, he had decided he would use this very public platform to talk back to the reviewers. Even before the final show, he was caught on camera joking with Richard Alderson, who had said he 'read in the paper that several people walked out of the concert', allowing Dylan to deliver the perfect punch line: 'Well, I read that the whole audience walked out.' He had long realised there were lies, damn lies and what one read in the papers.

If, as has been suggested, The Beatles really did shout at the ex-fans from their plush RAH eyrie on the twenty-seventh to leave him alone, they need not have bothered.[53] It was Dylan who wouldn't shut up, and he had the mic. It started, uncharacteristically, during the first half, as he prefaced 'Visions Of Johanna' with a jibe at 'your English newspapers':

I'm not gonna be playing any more concerts here in England and I just wanted to say, it's all wrong, [loses thread completely] ... This is a typical example of what your English newspapers here would call a drurg song. I don't write drurg songs. I never have. I wouldn't know how to. I'm not saying this for any defensive reason or anything like *that*. It's. Just. Not. A. Drurg. Song. It's just vulgar to think so.

[53] The suggestion that The Beatles shouted at the complaining fans to leave Dylan alone does not appear to derive from any contemporary report, but seems nonetheless to have become accepted as fact.

Unfortunately, he had chosen the wrong show to turn his verbal guns on the 'establishment press' who had all been there the night before—as the morning papers revealed. Tonight's show was for fans and the music press, those who had a weekly deadline and could take their time mulling over such an event. They at least came to review the music. To Norman Jopling, who had been championing Dylan in the pages of *Record Mirror* for the past eighteen months, the first half was everything he had hoped for:

A full half of his concert is given purely to his 'folk' image in which he accompanies himself on guitar and harmonica. He sang songs like 'She Belongs To Me' (nothing like the record), 'It's All Over Now Baby Blue', 'Desolation Row' and 'Mr Tambourine Man'. No songs of protest—of course. ... If any of The Beatles were in the audience they may have been embarrassed—or flattered—by Bob's version of 'Norwegian Wood' which enlarged and coloured upon the original theme by Lennon–McCartney. He also sang 'Visions Of Johanna' which he hasn't recorded, and another tune, beautiful and nameless, which proves his talent in this field is unblemished and unaffected by his rock exploits.

Jopling was the first critic in three months to notice that the still-unreleased 'Fourth Time Around' was 'Bob's version' of 'Norwegian Wood'. And Lennon was there that night to hear Dylan's rather obtuse homage. (It would take Lennon thirteen years to respond with the spiteful 'Serve Yourself'.) Apparently Dylan had already played him the song in private, in the hope that he would approve. For once, the mouthiest of the Fab Four had been lost for words.

But he loved the second half, even as he—and Dylan—were taken aback by the vehemence of the barrackers. Yet Lennon dismissed 'all that stuff about Dylan being booed [which] has been exaggerated. I saw the London concerts and about five or six people booed ... and everyone else in the audience were shutting them up.'

By the second half, Dylan sure wasn't shutting up. Even before his first recognisable song, 'I Don't Believe You', he was allowing feelings he'd previously bottled up to take the evening air, delivering his longest rap to date:

This is a song I wrote about three years ago. I like all my old songs. I never said they were 'rubbish' [*in a heavy northern accent*]. I don't use that word. It's not in my vocabulary. I wouldn't use it if it was there on the street to use for free—I would not use the word 'rubbish'. And I like all my old songs. It's just that things change all the time. Everybody knows that. [*ripple of applause*] And this music that you're gonna hear, no matter what it is, if anybody out there could offer any advice on how it could be played better or the words improved, we appreciate all suggestions. Other than that, we like these songs. I'm only saying this because this is the last night we're here and I luuurve England a lot; but we did this in the States from September on, and we've been playing this music since we were ten years old and folk music happens to be a thing which interrupted [*laughter*]—which was very useful y'know—because the rock'n'roll thing in the United States [*loses thread again*] ... . Anything I say now, please forgive me. I realise it's loud music but if you don't like it, well, that's fine. If you got improvements you could make on it, that's great. But the thing is, it's not English music you're listening to. It might sound like English music, if you've never heard American music before but the music is, er, is, er, is, er ... I would never venture to say what it is. What you're hearing now is the sound of the songs. You're not hearing anything else. You can take it or leave it. It doesn't matter to me, it really doesn't. I love you all. If you disagree, I'm not gonna fight you, discuss it with you. Anyway, this happens to be an old song, called 'I Don't Believe You'. It used to go like that and now it goes like this—and rightfully so!

Dylan sounds as tired as an Arctic husky, and more than a little stoned. Even the band sound a little out of control tonight, as if they were about to collectively down tools in sympathy with the homesick traveller. The band operating on radar at the Liverpool Odeon and Manchester Free Trade Hall performances has lost its way too, making tonight's electric set the live equivalent of take 11 of 'Like A Rolling Stone', the version recorded six takes after the incomparable released version—another electric experiment which pushed the envelope too far.

Appropriately, the most disjointed song tonight is 'Like A Rolling Stone' which turns into a near-nine minute jam-fest, as the sheer relief

of making it out alive consumes singer and band. Yet he still hurls the
words with the venom of a thousand furies. Ray Coleman, who had
championed Dylan since penning the famous 'The Beatles Dig Dylan'
feature back in January 1965, noted how 'he sang the words "You're
gonna have to get used to it" as if they had some hidden meaning'.

They did. This sung invective was being directed first and foremost
at the person/s Dylan targeted before the song, 'You promised me you
were gonna leave,' who may well be the same person that shouted,
before 'Ballad Of A Thin Man', 'Can we have the good stuff again?'
He picked on the wrong man tonight. Dylan again wields the rod
of home truths:

> The good stuff from the bad stuff? It's all the same stuff! You're not
> gonna see me anymore and I'm not gonna see you anyway. All you
> people are wonderful. You're the greatest. Why don't [you] people
> all say what you want to say for a minute. Say anything you wanna
> say for a whole minute. You got a watch? [Hey,] I'd trade places
> with you. Would you trade places with me?

For the first and only time, those who had lost their faith were
getting it back in shovels. As D.A. Pennebaker recalled, two decades
later, 'He was crazed on that last concert … Albert Hall was the
wildest. People were really shouting at him and he was screaming
back.' At one point he really does scream back. At the start of 'Just
Like Tom Thumb's Blues' he again prefaces the song with a variant of
the 'Mexican painter' rap. But when he starts to claim this is a valid
explanation of the song's inspiration, the barrackers cut loose. Dylan
is forced to return fire:

> He's a wonderful cosmic painter who's completely unknown to the
> universe, and he lives in Mexico City. He's an inspiration. I'm telling
> you this in case you think there's something you're missing. I don't
> want you to think you're Out Of It. I'm sick of people asking, what
> does it mean? It just means nothing. [*Applause, then shouting*] You're
> talking to the wrong person, man. I'm the last person to explain
> something but this is the last concert here. You don't want me to
> do it, I don't care. I couldn't care less. We'll just play the music and
> leave. And you and you and you can just go out and read some books.

As The Hawks launch into the song's frenetic intro, Dylan isn't done dispensing advice. Thinking of a good book to suggest, he shouts over the 'ear-splitting cacophony', 'Read J.D. SALINGER!!!'

Summoning up a vocal that could shred paper, Dylan drives the band to greater heights until the whole performance slashes at the edge of sound. No mistake, there is real rancour in Dylan's voice as he sings, 'I do believe I've had enough.' Those who had come with an open mind were appalled by the behaviour of the audience. Jopling, who had relayed the first British report of Forest Hills, was someone taken aback by what he saw and heard:

> After the interval he returned with his group and launched into an ear-splitting cacophony which he hadn't recorded. The sound, despite being electrical and groupy, was still so far removed from conventional group music as to be still strictly Dylan. Then the old guard started walking out. The people who had been secretly hoping that Dylan would reform and make a full confession of his musical sins realised that he was enjoying taunting them as much as ever. Before the end of the concert, about 25 percent of the total audience had walked out. Another 25 percent stayed under sufferance and didn't show overmuch enthusiasm. ... The hecklers were in full force ... and just about everything possible was hurled at Bob (verbally, no missiles were seen). He coped very well with them [as] he ploughed through 'I Don't Believe You', which was originally a folk tune and which he's now rocked up ... He then launched into 'Just Like Tom Thumb's Blues' amidst shouts of 'Rubbish' and 'Rock and Roll for ever'. The highlight came when Bob sat down to the piano and did 'Ballad Of A Thin Man', which silenced even the folksier elements.

Even Ray Coleman, who enjoyed the second half less than Jopling, thought the treatment doled out to Dylan was disgraceful:

> 'Go home', 'Get the group off', 'Drop dead, Dylan'. Bob suffered appalling treatment from some hecklers. But he battled on. And though the dreadful reception he got was unforgivable, the rowdies had some justification. We don't mind a wailing backing group, but MUST it be so LOUD? A lot of Dylan's talent lies in his words, and few could be heard above a caterwauling din, appallingly tasteless, thudding drumming, and electrification gone mad. The

electrified performance was a shambles of noise—a vivid contrast from the first half, which was the great Dylan-with-guitar at his best, singing with more clarity than ever, putting across beautiful songs like 'Desolation Row' with a sensitivity sadly lacking from his band-backed mess.

If, as seems to be the case, there was a problem with the sound out in the hall—not too surprising, given the Kensington venue's rap sheet—the between-song Dylan was coming through loud and clear even when what he was saying did not add up, or address the point. When in doubt Dylan just insisted he loved e-ver-y-one.

By the time he makes his extended spoken preface to 'Like A Rolling Stone', his own weariness amazes him. After introducing the whole band for the very first time (only to forget Richard Manuel's surname), he seems to lose the thread completely:

It doesn't mean a thing. But they're all poets. If it comes out that way. All poets. This song is dedicated to the Taj Mahal. And we're gonna leave after this song. You've been very, very nice people, very warm, here you are sitting in this huge place. And, believe me, we've enjoyed every minute of being here.

When he says he's 'enjoyed every minute', each word is stretched to breaking point. For the first time, heavy sarcasm creeps into Dylan's voice, a prelude to a 'Rolling Stone' that gathers no moss. Knowing just how this one goes, he throws himself into it. As Jopling wrote, Dylan was 'jumping and yelling all over the stage'. The regime of 'pills' seemed to have finally taken its toll. Even one of the hippest dudes present knew something was not right:

Mick Farren: There was this sort of phalanx of old fogies out to cause trouble, because they knew their days were numbered. ... Everybody knows the band are coming on after the interval. Then the band comes on and they all go crazy ... He was obviously exceedingly stoned and probably taking a lot of pills. ... We figured ... 'Hey, he's taking pills ... he's stoned.' Little did we know [it was] amphetamine and heroin.

The regime of self-medication that had kept Dylan going for the past nine months would remain a closely guarded secret for a few years yet. As late as June 1968, while fully admitting how close *he* had been to breaking point, he continued to still talk in code: 'I was touring for a couple of years … [at] a fast pace, plus we were doing a whole show, no other acts. It's pretty straining to do a show like that, plus a lot of really unhealthy situations rise up.'

Only when a return trip to the sceptred isle loomed, in the summer of 1969, did he admit that being 'on the road … wore me down. I was on drugs, a lot of things. A lot of things just to keep going, you know. … The last show, during the first half, of which there was about an hour, I only did maybe six songs.'

'The last show' had certainly been a long show—the longest electric set of the lot—but it was all over now. Dylan weaved his way off stage and the lights went up; the national anthem played; the fans, still dazed and confused, filed out into the Kensington night; the sound crew packed up their equipment; the film crew shut off their cameras for the last time.

For Dylan, there was a palpable sense this could really be the end. As he told Barbara Kerr in 1978, 'The audience no longer came to see me. They didn't even see me, and I was standing right in front of them. They came to see the myth of Bob Dylan, and that's all they saw. That myth could either please them or disappoint them. But whatever happened didn't have anything to do with me. Just with the myth.' He was also physically shattered. 'It took everything out of me. Everything was gone—I was drained.'

Ochs had been proven right. For the equally fearful filmmaker Pennebaker, this was exactly 'what happens if you don't look back … it took its toll on Dylan—I know [he] was really wrecked by that whole concert tour and he'd never do another one like that'. Nor would he. The myth had almost consumed the artist, and came dangerously close to consuming the man.

He would grow to resent anyone (with the initials A.G.) who had encouraged him to scale this electric Everest in the first place, 'It wasn't my own choice. I was more or less being pushed into it—pushed in and carried out.'

Somehow, he was still in one piece, physically if not mentally. Others were not so lucky. As Pennebaker observed, 'A lot of the people that just hung around, who were supposed to be helpers, got really into the process of knocking themselves out and became useless.' D.A. probably has in mind Alderson, who was in a bad way, as was Maymudes. Both duly dropped off the radar for a decade or more.

Dylan's survival instincts kicked in just in time. 'A lot of people didn't make it. They didn't live to tell about it, anyway ... I was straining pretty hard and couldn't have gone on living that way much longer. The fact that I made it through what I did is pretty miraculous.' Amen. Dylan made the above comment as he was about to embark on his next world tour. Twelve years had passed, and by now he knew just how close he had come to letting the poisons consume him, leaving him lost forever in the unknown region. He even allowed himself a couple of hours to reunite with Craig McGregor, the Australian journalist who had briefly befriended him at the start of the tightrope ride, to allow himself an uncharacteristic look back and acknowledge the saving grace in him:

Bob Dylan: When you see me on stage now, I mean, you don't get that feeling that I might die after the show. Whereas that's what happened the last time.

The average critic never recognizes an achievement when it happens. He explains it after it has become respectable.
— **RAYMOND CHANDLER, 1950**

OUTRO:
I DO BELIEVE I'VE HAD ENOUGH

In his concert in Albert Hall in London, Dylan met once again with the problem of a booing, dissatisfied audience. … However, he made a speech to the audience which seemed only to further alienate it. He informed them after only the first two or three numbers that he would never again perform in Great Britain. … He then went on to explain to the people, 'What you're hearing is just songs. You're not hearing anything else but words and sounds.' Once again he denied the great value, or 'genius' of his songs. Then he concluded, 'I'm sick of people asking what does it mean? It means nothing!' Despite this emphatic outburst, people will continue to search for a deeper meaning in Dylan. … Music critics have pinned the responsibility for the initiation of the current 'psychedelic' trend in pop music squarely on Dylan's shoulders.

—'DYLAN: IS HE WEIRD?', *KRLA BEAT*, AUGUST 27 1966

By the time the above story ran, American and European Dylan fans had all been given the opportunity to hear what the fuss had been about, and make up their own minds.

The release of the Liverpool 'Just Like Tom Thumb's Blues' was seemingly intended as just a taster, with rock's first double album, *Blonde On Blonde*, appearing the week after the 'I Want You' 45.[54] *Tarantula* was also due to go to press in August. Yet despite his best intentions, the proofs still lay untouched:

Bob Dylan: I [had] just looked at the first paragraph—and knew I just couldn't let that stand. So I took the whole thing with me on tour. I was going to rewrite it all. Carried a typewriter around … around the world. Trying to meet this deadline which they'd given me. [1969]

Try as he might, he could do nothing with it. His heart wasn't in it. The book was a relic of a time and a place he'd gone beyond. As was the film he was supposed to now finish. But he had learnt it

---

[54] After endless debates about the actual release date of *Blonde On Blonde*, and ludicrous suggestions it was during the tour itself, a Sony database of album release dates, for all titles in the vinyl era, confirms once and for all that it came out on June 20 1966, Radio 4, please note.

wasn't only Pennebaker who thought he had spent too much time making 'a home movie', not a document of the most explosive pop tour ever. The night after the Albert Hall, Dylan met up with a band of brothers, all four Beatles and their sidekick, Alf Bicknell, who recorded in his diary, 'Spent the evening in the company of the boys and Bob Dylan, watching some of his home movies that he is turning into a film. He and John get on very well, although John treats Bob almost like a God.'

The routine was replicated the following evening: 'Back to Bob's place again. This is getting a regular habit. It's funny how each of the boys gets on with him so differently. I mean … George [just] wanted to sit down and sing and play with Bob.'

So much for Dylan feeling desperately homesick. In fairness, he had a few loose ends to tie up, professionally *and* privately. Pennebaker also 'hung in there two or three more days 'cause we were getting film or getting equipment together'. Tom Keylock, meanwhile, was commandeered to clear Dylan's hotel room of all evidence of the man's self-medication. And at some point an instruction was issued to collect together all the acetates that had served as late-night entertainment, including that acetate of the second half of Manchester.

If the Albert Hall shows had yielded the wildest mercury music, after months of standing on the edge of the unknown on that final night, Dylan and The Hawks flung themselves headlong into the abyss. Manchester was the more musical peak. Provisional plans for some kind of official release were soon afoot. Dylan, for now, was as enthused as anyone. But this was before his world turned upside down on July 29 1966, after he failed to negotiate a curve he didn't see coming.

By the end of 1966, Dylan was holed up in upstate New York, not answering the phone, not talking to his manager (save through his wife, Sara); in seclusion after a 'near fatal' motorcycle accident. Columbia were looking around for product they could release, going out of their way to misrepresent the terms of Dylan's original 1961 contract in order to extort one more album out of the man before he became an MGM star.[55]

---

[55] Terms for a record deal with MGM were agreed early in 1967, but were apparently never ratified by the MGM board and, in the end, Dylan changed his mind.

Just when they began to look at the 1966 tapes afresh, lo and behold, in July 1967 Dylan re-signed to Columbia. All talk of everything owed under the previous contract went away. All Dylan was interested in was moving on. The last few months had been spent looking at those 'home movies' shot on the world tour. He had started to wonder what the hell had he been thinking.

The film he and Howard Alk compiled out of the footage Pennebaker discarded from his own edit would have its own telling title, *Eat The Document*. And it seemed that might just be its fate. After a weekend of screenings at the Academy of Music in February 1971, it was not to be seen again until 1979. The official word was that the 1966 world tour—'Just Like Tom Thumb's Blues' excepted[56]—was not something Dylan wished to revisit.

Meanwhile, the IBC engineer's own dub (and rough mix) of the Manchester set had flown the coop, all the way to LA, whose bootleggers—those unprincipled curators of rock archaeology—were not so squeamish. The so-called *Royal Albert Hall* appeared in 1970, in both an English edition and an American edition. Four songs from the Dublin acoustic set featured on the American edition, the double album *Looking Back*. Four years later, an immaculate copy of the Melbourne acoustic set appeared on (or under) counters of independent record retailers. In 1976, a pristine board tape of Dylan's Newport set provided another electrifying bookend.

The tour to end all tours became the gift that kept giving for the bootleg fraternity. In the mid-eighties, acetates from Manchester and both Albert Halls were sold to a cabal of Dylan tape-collectors and were promptly bootlegged in deluxe vinyl editions. They failed to confirm, once and for all, that the last Albert Hall show—represented on these acetates by the whole acoustic set—really was the 'wildest'. And still it continued raining soundboards.

The new millennium saw the second half of Liverpool, the first half of Sheffield and all of the first Sydney released on an eight-CD bootleg boxed-set of soundboard-only sources from the world tour

---

[56] Even that B-side seems to have been released in the face of label resistance. When the man responsible for the recording in question heard a test pressing, he remembers 'thinking they did a really bad job mastering … from the original tape. … They probably resented the fact they were putting out my mono tape in preference to theirs. [But I also] remember thinking, "Maybe I fucked up.".' He did not. The high-end distortion on the 45 was entirely of Columbia's making.

that shamed Sony's attempts to catalogue their most important artist's creative heyday. Scorpio's *Genuine Live '66* (2000) seemed like the final word. That is, until Dylan's manager Jeff Rosen asked Martin Scorsese to direct *No Direction Home*, a two-part documentary made possible by privileged access to Pennebaker's 1966 footage, culminating at the Free Trade Hall on May 17 1966, as Pennebaker looked through his viewfinder capturing the very moment Dylan responded to a shout from the horseshoe across the way.

Not surprisingly, the drama of the tour continues to capture the public imagination. One prescient filmmaker has offered an explanation—one that it would be hard to refute:

D.A. Pennebaker: That music was generating all music everywhere. People who didn't even see those concerts were getting something from it indirectly. ... [It had] the charismatic attraction that the centre of the storm will always hold.

CHAPTER NOTES AND SOURCES

The only previous book to deal with Dylan's '66 shows in their entirety is John Bauldie's *The Ghost Of Electricity*, but that volume is now a quarter of a century old. A pre-internet production, it was published privately in two extremely limited editions, and though it provides a generous overview of the published material from the spring 1966 world tour (a prefatory chapter excepted), it offers only the most perfunctory of commentaries on the material quoted (often verbatim) and no cross-referencing with the extant recordings.

As an active collaborator when it came to accumulating material for that project, I have drawn on much of that raw material for my own, more opinionated work, notably a private scrapbook compiled by Carl Harding of the Australian press in 1966, entitled *Dylan Down Under*, which somehow ended up in my possession.

Another essential (sub-)text for my own endeavours has been Craig McGregor's *Bob Dylan: A Retrospective* (Morrow 1971), which even after all these years remains the definitive anthology of sixties Dylan articles and interviews. His introduction also provides a valuable first-hand report as to Dylan's reception in Australia on that April 1966 visit.

The two other anthologies which provided invaluable primary resource material in an accessible form, including reviews and interviews from 1965–66, were both privately printed: Dave Percival's *This Wasn't Written In Tin Pan Alley* (1989) and the four-volume collection of Dylan interviews that was

a spin-off production from the *Dignity* fanzine, *The Fiddler Now Upspoke*. Otherwise, my various sources are as follows ...

Intro

The Dylan quotes are from interviews with Pete Oppel (*Dallas Morning News*, November 18–23 1978) and Kurt Loder (*Rolling Stone*, November 5 1987). The quote from Greil Marcus is from an overview of unreleased Dylan recordings in *Rolling Stone* (December 13 1969).

Chapter 1

The Dylan quotes are from interviews with Robert Shelton (*New York Times*, August 27 1965); Nora Ephron (*New York Post*, September 1965); Hubert Saal (*Newsweek*, February 26 1968); John Cohen and Happy Traum (*Sing Out!*, October 1968); Jann Wenner (*Rolling Stone*, November 29 1969); Ray Connolly (*London Evening Standard*, August 16 1969); Ron Rosenbaum (*Playboy*, January 1978); Jonathan Cott (*Rolling Stone*, November 16 1978); Robert Hilburn (*Los Angeles Times*, October 30 1983); Bill Flannagan (March 1985, as published in *Written In My Soul*, Contemporary, 1996); Scott Cohen (*Spin*, December 1985), and Robert Hilburn (*Los Angeles Times*, September 7 1987).

A transcript for the Beverly Hills Hotel press conference, September 4 1965, was derived from my own self-published 'rumourography', *More Rain Unravelled Tales* (1983), and the transcript for the San Francisco press conference,

December 3 1965, was culled from *The Rolling Stone Rock'n'Roll Reader* edited by Ben Fong-Torres (Bantam, 1974).

Other resources I have drawn on in this chapter include Jac Holzman's *Follow The Music* (First Media, 1998); the unpublished but no less fascinating 'Folk Scene Diary Summer 1965' by Richard Reuss, which resides at the Indiana University Libraries, Bloomington, Indiana; and draft lyrics from late July 1965 for the following songs: 'Ballad Of A Thin Man', 'Queen Jane Approximately' and 'Highway 61 Revisited'. Two resources were drawn on for Joe Boyd's ever-reliable recollections: a letter to *New York Observer*, November 5 1998, and his interview in *Telegraph* #31. Also of reference have been *Bob Dylan* by Daniel Kramer (Castle Books, 1967); and *Friends & Other Strangers* by Patrick Webster (private pamphlet).

The following contemporary reports provided further grist for the mill:

'Newport: It's All Right, Ma, I'm Only Playin' R & R', Arthur Kretchmer, *Village Voice*, August 5 1965
Letter from Phil Ochs, *Village Voice*, August 12 1965
Caryl Mirken, 'Newport: The Short Hot Summer', *Broadside* #61, August 15 1965
'Notes From A Variant Stanza Collector', Ed Freeman, *The Boston Broadside*, August 18 1965
'In Defence Of Dylan', Michael J. Carabetta, *The Boston Broadside*, August 18 1965
'What's Happening ...' pt. 1, Irwin Silber, *Sing Out!*, November 1965
'What's Happening ...' pt. 2, Paul Nelson, *Sing Out!*, November 1965
'Donovan Talks (guardedly) About Idol Dylan', *NME*, September 10 1965
'Dylan Conquers Unruly Audience', Robert Shelton, *New York Times*, August 30 1965

'Dylan Mixes Bag of Tricks at Music Fest', *Billboard*, September 11 1965
'Dylan Rocks The Joint', *Record Mirror*, September 18 1965
'Show Sold Out, But Did Dylan?', Joseph Gelmis, *Newsday*, August 30 1965
'Bob Dylan Moves Too Fast For Fans ...', Herm Schoenfeld, *Variety*, September 1 1965
'At Forest Hills—Mods, Rockers, Fight Over New Thing Called "Dylan"', Jack Newfield, *Village Voice*, September 2 1965
'Dylan As Dylan Part One', Paul Jay Robbins, *Los Angeles Free Press*, September 10 1965
'Folks Pay Homage To Dylan', Charles Champlin, *Los Angeles Times*, September 6 1965
'Dylan At The Bowl: We Had Known A Lion', Shirley Poston, *KRLA Beat*, October 2 1965

Chapter 2
The Dylan quotes are from interviews with Cameron Crowe (*Biograph*, 1985); Mary Merryfield (*Chicago Tribune*, November 21 1965); Paul Jay Robbins (*Los Angeles Free Press*, September 10 1965); Frances Taylor (*Long Island Press*, October 17 1965); Nora Ephron (*New York Post*, September 1965); Robert Fulford (*Toronto Star*, September 18 1965); Ann Carter (*Atlanta Journal*, October 10 1965); Margaret Steen (*Toronto Star Weekly*, January 29 1966); Joseph Haas (*Chicago Daily News*, November 27 1965); Jean-Marc Pascal (*Salut Les Copains*, July 1966); Jann Wenner (*Rolling Stone*, November 29 1969); Ben Fong-Torres, January 12 1974 (transcript reproduced in *Knockin' On Dylan's Door*, Straight Arrow, 1974), and Jeff Rosen (*No Direction Home* DVD, Sony 2005). A transcript for the San Francisco press conference, December 3 1965, was culled from *The Rolling Stone Rock'n'Roll Reader* edited by Ben Fong-Torres (Bantam, 1974).

Other resources I have drawn on in this chapter include *This Wheel's On Fire* by Levon Helm with Stephen Davis (William Morrow, 1993); *Backstage Passes: Rock'n'roll life In The Sixties* by Al Kooper (Stein & Day, 1977); *Bob Dylan* by Daniel Kramer (Castle Books, 1967) and an important, early article on The Band called 'Big Pink' by Tony Glover in *Eye* (October 1968).

The following contemporary reports have provided further grist for the mill:

'Message Music And Rock And Roll: Bob Dylan On The Concert Tour', Gilbert Shelton, *Texas Ranger*, November 1965
Judith Adams, *San Francisco Chronicle*, October 11 1965
'After Dark: Dylan Captures SMU Audience', Francis Raffetto, *Dallas Morning News*, September 27 1965
'Bob Dylan Scores Here In First Dallas Concert', Don Safran, *Dallas Times Herald*, September 27 1965
'What's Happening ...' pt. 1, Irwin Silber, *Sing Out!*, November 1965
'What's Happening ...' pt. 2, Paul Nelson, *Sing Out!*, November 1965
'Fan The Flames', Irwin Silber, *Sing Out!*, January 1966
Letter from Kathleen Ivans, Whitestone, NY, *Sing Out!*, January 1966
'Dylan In October', Jack Newfield, *Village Voice*, October 7 1965
'Bob Dylan Strikes A Chord of Empathy', William Bender, *New York Herald Tribune*, October 2 1965
'Dylan Would Rather Switch—And He Does', Herb Wood, *Billboard*, October 16 1965
Ann Carter, *Atlanta Journal*, October 10 1965
'Dylan: Renewal In Faith Of Rebellion', Andy Leader, *Burlington Free Press*, October 1965
'Dylan's BAND Angers Audience', Robin Blair, *NME*, November 12 1965

'Dylan's Return', Mann, *Twin City a Go Go*, November 1965 (reproduced in *Occasionally* #5)
'Bob Dylan Fires Vocal Guns Here', Glenn Pullen, *Cleveland Plain Dealer*, November 13 1965
'A Changed Bob Dylan Booed In Toronto', Bruce Lawson, *[Toronto] Globe and Mail*, November 15 1965
'Let's Face An Awful Truth: Dylan's Gone Commercial', Antony Ferry, *Toronto Daily Star*, November 15 1965
'Dylan: an explosion of poetry', Peter Gzowski, *MacLean's*, January 22 1966
'Dylan Pleases Audience', Charles G. Fenton, *Ohio State Lantern*, November 22 1965
'Bob Dylan Mixes Sentiment With Rock and Roll', Bruce Plowman, *Chicago Tribune*, November 27 1965
'The Gap', Studs Terkel, *Sing Out!*, February 1966
'Dylan Pleases Young Audience', Lawrence Sears, *Washington Evening Star*, November 29 1965
Bill Diehl, *St Paul Dispatch*, July 4 1966 (republished in part in 'Columnist Raps Bob Dylan's "Scorn" In Home State Performance', *Variety*, July 13 1966)

Chapter 3

The Dylan quotes are from an interview with Ben Fong-Torres, January 12 1974 (transcript reproduced in *Knockin' On Dylan's Door*, Straight Arrow, 1974). A transcript for the December 3 1965 San Francisco press conference was culled from *The Rolling Stone Rock'n'Roll Reader*, edited by Ben Fong-Torres (Bantam, 1974). The transcript for the Los Angeles press conference, December 16 1965, was compiled from *Dylan In His Own Words*, edited by Miles (Omnibus Press, 1979); *KRLA Beat*, January 22 1966; *TeenSet*, March 1966; and *NME*, February 11 1966.

Other resources I have drawn on in this chapter include the following pieces: 'Folk Rot' by Tom Paxton and 'Thunder Without Rain' by Josh Dunson, both from *Sing Out!*, January 1966; an interview with Larry Keenan in *On The Tracks* #14; an interview with Phil Ochs from *Broadside*, October 1965; Greil Marcus's overview of unreleased Dylan recordings in *Rolling Stone*, December 13 1969; and 'Dylan' by Eden, *KRLA Beat*, January 22 1966.

The following contemporary reports provided further grist for the mill:

'In Berkeley They Dig Bob Dylan', Ralph J. Gleason, *San Francisco Chronicle*, December 6 1965
'Bobby, Barbie and Ken', Patricia Oberhaus, *Berkeley Barb*, December 10 1965
'At The Civic Theatre—A One Man Show', Andrew Makarushka, *San Diego Tribune*, December 11 1965

Chapter 4
The Dylan quotes are from interviews with Nat Hentoff in October 1965 (privately published as the bookleg *Whaaaat!*) and January 1966 (*Playboy*, March 1966); Joseph Haas (*Chicago Daily News*, November 27 1965); and Robert Shelton from March 1966 (included in *No Direction Home*, NEL, 1986). A transcript for the WBAI Bob Fass phone-in, January 27 1966, came from *Hungry As A Raccoon* by John Way.

Other resources I have drawn on in this chapter include 'Dylan Goes Electric', the Christie's New York auction catalogue for the December 6 2013 sale, as well as draft lyrics for the following songs from late September 1965: 'Inside The Darkness Of Your Room' [x2], 'Jet Pilot', 'I Wanna Be Your Lover' and 'Medicine Sunday'; and the late November handwritten draft versions of the final verse to 'Freeze Out', aka 'Visions of Johanna'.

Published sources include the invaluable *The Crawdaddy Book* by Paul Williams, which includes a facsimile

of issue #1 (Hal Leonard, 2002). The following articles were also drawn on: 'The Charisma Kid', Robert Shelton, *Cavalier*, July 1965; 'The Big Beat of Folk-Rock-Protest', *Cavalier*, March 1966; 'A Night With Bob Dylan', Al Aronowitz (w/ Bob Dylan), *New York Herald Tribune*, December 12 1965; 'Public Writer Number One', Thomas Meehan, *New York Times*, December 12 1965; 'The Man In The Middle', Maurice Capel, *Jazz & Pop*, January 1966 (reprinted in *Occasionally* #1); 'The Children's Crusade', Ralph J. Gleason, *Ramparts*, March 1966; and 'Defence [of Dylan]', Henrietta Yurchenco, *Sound & Fury*, March 1966.

Chapter 5
The Dylan quotes are from interviews with Nat Hentoff in October 1965 (privately published as the bookleg *Whaaaat!*); Louise Sokol (*Datebook* September 1966); Robert Shelton in March 1966 (included in *No Direction Home*, NEL, 1986); Jules Siegel (*Saturday Evening Post*, July 30 1966); Hubert Saal (*Newsweek*, February 26 1968); John Cohen & Happy Traum (*Sing Out!*, October 1968); and Jann Wenner (*Rolling Stone*, November 29 1969).

A transcript for the San Francisco press conference, December 3 1965, was culled from *The Rolling Stone Rock'n'Roll Reader*, edited by Ben Fong-Torres (Bantam, 1974); the transcript for the London press conference at the Metropolitan Hotel, October 4 1997, from *The Fiddler Now Upspoke*; and the Rome Press Conference at InterContinental De la Ville Roma Hotel, July 23 2001, from *Isis* #99. Transcripts of the two WBAI Bob Fass phone-ins, on January 27 1966 and May 24 1986, come from *Hungry As A Raccoon* by John Way. The transcript of the Klas Burling interview for Radio Three, Sweden, April 28 1966, was sourced from *The Ghost Of Electricity*.

Other resources I have drawn on in this chapter include *Bob Dylan* by Anthony Scaduto (Grosset & Dunlap, 1971); *On The Road With Bob Dylan* by Larry Sloman (Bantam, 1978); *The Crawdaddy Book* by Paul Williams (Hal Leonard, 2002), as well as an original issue #3; and *Small Town Talk* by Barney Hoskyns (Faber & Faber, 2016). I have also referenced my own 1990 interview with Al Kooper and a copy of Simon Gee's contemporary notes to the March 1966 Vancouver concert.

The articles I have referenced include Norman Jopling's phone conversation with Johnny Cash from *Record Mirror*, June 16 1965; 'Bob Dylan: Man & Music', William Bender, *New York Herald Tribune*, December 12 1965; 'Dylan's Fortune', P.M. Clepper, *This Week*, March 27 1966; 'Talking To A Modern Myth', *Ulsterweek*, May 12 1966; Adam Sherwin's interview with Charlie McCoy in the *Independent*, June 24 2015; 'Don't Look Back ... Please!', by Martin Bronstein, *The Observatory*, June 15 1998; and the interview with Mickey Jones in *The Telegraph* #56.

The following contemporary reports provided further grist for the mill:

'"Old" Dylan Makes New Fans Wait—Then Makes Them Happy', Gerald Solomon, *Louisville Times*, February 5 1966
'Join The Dylan Rebellion—It's Pallid', Phillis Funke, *[Louisville] Courier-Journal*, February 5 1966
'Dylan Charms Big Audience At Center', El Kritzler, *Westchester Reporter-Dispatch*, February 7 1966
'Audience Is There And Not When Dylan "Communicates"', Larry Williams, *Memphis Commercial Appeal*, February 11 1966
'4,000 Fans Dig Dylan In Folk-Rock Concert', Dennis Foley, *Ottawa Citizen*, February 21 1966

'Dylan Thrills Auditorium Audience—Singing Crusader Casts Spell In Ottawa', Sandy Gardiner, *Ottawa Journal*, February 21 1966
'Bob Dylan Makes His Montreal Debut', Zelda Heller, *Montreal Gazette*, February 21 1966
'Bob Dylan Sings Folk, Pop, Poetry', Wouter de Wet, *Montreal Star*, February 21 1966
'Electric Dylan Turns To Banality', William Littler, *Vancouver Sun*, March 28 1966

Chapter 6

A transcript for the Sydney Airport press conference, April 12 1966, was sourced from *The Fiddler Now Upspoke*, as well as Adrian Rawlins' piece in *Music Maker*, November 1966. The Sydney Hotel press conferences, April 12 1966, were reported on by Ron Saw in the Sydney *Daily Mirror*, April 13 1966, and by Uli Schmetzer, in the Sydney *Sun*, April 13 1966. The transcript for the Melbourne press conference, April 17 1966, came from *The Ghost Of Electricity*; the Adelaide press conference, April 21 1966, from *The Fiddler Now Upspoke*; and the Perth press conference, April 23 1966, from Murray Jennings' extensive transcript in the June 1966 issue of *Music Maker* and Val and Brian Lawlan's *Steppin' Out* pamphlet, a reprint of an article in the Perth *Daily News*. Other Dylan quotes are from interviews with Randy Anderson (*The Minnesota Daily*, February 17 1978) and Craig McGregor (*Sydney Morning Herald*, March 18 1978).

Other resources I have drawn on in this chapter include John Lattanzio's interview with Adrian Rawlins from April 25 1994, provided to me in transcript, along with the 1994 collection of Adrian's writings on Dylan, *Dylan Through The Looking Glass: A Collection Of Writings On Bob Dylan*, which included 'What's Happening, Mr Jones', *Farrago*, April

29 1966; his four-part feature in *Music Maker*, October 1966 to January 1967 inclusive; and his 1981 essay 'Through The Looking Glass'. Also referenced were *Bob Dylan: A Retrospective* by Craig McGregor (William Morrow, 1972); *Bob Dylan* by Anthony Scaduto (Grosset & Dunlap, 1971); and *Bob Dylan: The Unreleased Recordings*—Paul Cable (Dark Star Books, 1978).

The first two parts of Zac Dadic's authoritative overview of the Australian leg, 'Australia 1966 Approximately', in *Isis* issues 185 and 186 have been invaluable, and I thank Zac for letting me see the latter in draft form.

The following contemporary reports provided further grist for the mill:

Datebook, November 1966
'Bob Dylan's Anti-Interview', Craig McGregor, *Sydney Morning Herald*, April 13 1966
'Message Singer Hits A Few Sour Notes', Roy Castle, *[Sydney] Daily Telegraph*, April 13 1966
'Dylan Evening A Big Let-Down', Bruce Cook, *Honolulu Advertiser*, April 11 1966
'Dylan, Very Much In Touch', Edgar Waters, *The Australian*, April 16 1966
'Dylan sings Dylan', Craig McGregor, *Sydney Morning Herald*, April 14 1966
'Folksong Pied Piper', Joe Cizzio, *[Sydney] Daily Telegraph,* April 14 1966
'Sydney's Wackiest Concert', Peter Michelmore, *[Sydney] Sun*, April 14 1966
'Advice to Dylan ... Stay Dylan', B.W., *Brisbane Telegraph*, April 16 1966 [sourced from the *Dylan Down Under* scrapbook]
'The Latter-day Dylan', Robert Westfield & Jim Monaghan, *Go-Set*, April 27 1966
'What's Happening, Mr Jones', Adrian Rawlins, *Farrago*, April 29 1966

'A Powerful Singer', *The Age*, April 20 1966
'It's Dylan The Devastating', Howard Palmer, *[Melbourne] Sun News-Pictorial*, April 20 1966
'The Concerts', Mick Counihan, *Lot's Wife*, May 17 1966
'Bob Dylan Destroys His Legend In Melbourne: Concert Strictly Dullsville', 'Stan' [probably Stan Rofe], *Variety*, April 27 1966
'Two Styles Of Dylan', A.M.M., *Adelaide Advertiser*, April 23 1966
'Dylan: The Fallen Idol', W.K. Parish, *On Dit*, May 4 1966
'Dylan: The Living Poet', Justine, *On Dit*, May 4 1966
'Cool Reception For Bob Dylan', Kim Lockwood, *West Australian*, April 25 1966
Letter from Rede Moulton, Crawley, *West Australian*, April 28 1966
Letter from M. Sydney-Smith, Scarborough, *West Australian*, May 3 1966
'Dylan—Man In A Mask', Rosemary Gerrette, *Canberra Times*, May 7 1966

Chapter 7
A transcript for the Stockholm press conference, Flamingo Hotel, Stockholm, April 28 1966, appears in *The Ghost Of Electricity*, along with the Klas Burling interview for Radio Three, Sweden, on the same afternoon, and the Copenhagen press conference, Hotel Marina, Vedbaek, April 30 1966. Other Dylan quotes are from interviews with John Cohen & Happy Traum (*Sing Out!*, October 1968); John Rockwell (*New York Times*, January 8 1974); and Ron Rosenbaum (*Playboy*, January 1978).

Another resource I have drawn upon in this chapter is the important interview with D.A. Pennebaker about the making of *Eat The Document* in *The Telegraph* #16.

The following contemporary reports provided further grist for the mill:

Pi Ann Tillman-Murray, *Idolnytt*, July 1966

'Man of Constant Sorrow', Pi Ann Murray, *Love*, August 1966

'Bob Dylan: An Ambiguous Picture Of Our Time', Annette Kullenberg, *Idun/VJ*, May 13 1966

'Bob Dylan—The Mystery', *?Pop*, August 1966

'Bob Dylan Better On Record Than On Stage', Ludvig Rasmusson, *Svenska Dagbladet*, April 30 1966

'A Notable, Difficult Artist', Peter Himmelstrand, *Expressen*, April 30 1966

'Dylan—A Sign Of Good Health', *Aftonbladet*, April 30 1966

'Dylan Doesn't Want To Sell Alibis', Ole John, *Politiken*, May 2 1966

Chapter 8

The transcript for the May 3 1966 London Press Conference, at the Mayfair Hotel, was compiled by myself from *Eat The Document*, *No Direction Home* (both on DVD); *Daily Sketch*, May 4 1966; *The Sun*, May 4 1966; and *Record Mirror*, *NME*, *Melody Maker* and *Disc & Music Echo*, all from May 14 1966.

Other resources I have drawn on in this chapter include 'Loves And Hates Of Bob Dylan' from *Jackie*, June 17 1965; 'Dylan Shocked By British Fans' by Norrie Drummond, *NME*, June 17 1966; and Bob Dawson's interview with Robbie Robertson in the May 28 1966 issue of *Melody Maker*.

The following contemporary reports provided further grist for the mill:

'Dylan Brings Own Group', *Melody Maker*, April 30 1966

'Bob Dylan At The Adelphi', George D. Hodnett, *Irish Times*, May 6 1966

'Applause At Dylan Show Was Dutiful', *Dublin Evening Press*, May 6 1966

'Oh What A Shock For Dylan Fans!', Norman Barry, *Sunday Independent*, May 8 1966

'The Night Of The Great Let-Down', J.K., *Dublin Evening Herald*, May 6 1966

'In Defence Of Bob Dylan', letter by Mary Morrissey, *Sunday Independent*, May 15 1966

Letters from Dermote Meleady and 'The Ghost', *Dublin Evening Herald*, May 19 1966

Letter from Disgusted of Foxrock, *Dublin Evening Herald*, May 21 1966

'Cat calls At Dylan Opening As Fans Cry Traitor', *Disc & Music Echo*, May 14 1966

'Dublin: Night Of The Big Let Down', Vincent Doyle, *Melody Maker*, May 14 1966

'I Can't Dig A Ditch', The Diary, *Belfast Telegraph*, April 29 1966

'We'll Be Nice To You', *Cityweek*, May 12 1966

'Talking To A Modern Myth', *Ulsterweek*, May 12 1966

'Commercial Dylan', Nicholas Williams, *NME*, May 13 1966

'Has Fame Spoilt Dylan?', Peter Gibbs, *Western Daily Press*, May 12 1966

'Dylan Down Beat', *Bristol Evening Post*, May 11 1966

Marilyn Johnson, Brislington, letter to *Bristol Evening Post*, May 14 1966

Jenny Leigh, Bristol, letter to *Melody Maker*, May 28 1966

Miss L. Cutler, Upper Gornal, letter to *Melody Maker*, May 28 1966

Erica Davies, Merthyr Tydfil, letter to *Melody Maker*, May 28 1966

'As I Was Saying', Jon Holliday, *South Wales Echo*, May 12 1966

Chapter 9

The Dylan quotes are from interviews with Neil Spencer (*NME*, August 15 1981) and Mikal Gilmore (*Rolling Stone*, September 27 2012).

Other resources I have drawn on in this chapter include the invaluable *Like The Night*, C.P. Lee's history of the Free Trade Hall '66 concert

(Helter-Skelter, 1998); *Bob Dylan: The Unreleased Recordings* by Paul Cable (Dark Star Books, 1978); as well as a communiqué from Graham Ashton to *The Telegraph*, quoted by John Bauldie in *Ghost Of Electricity*; a transcript of a radio interview with Willy Russell and provided by Spencer Leigh; and a letter to Tito Burns from the Free Trade Hall manager, reproduced in *Telegraph* #55, and derived from the Free Trade Hall archive, now housed at the Central Reference Library, Manchester.

Bob Dawson's interview with Robbie Robertson in the May 28 1966 issue of *Melody Maker* again proved useful, as did interviews with D.A. Pennebaker and Mickey Jones from *Telegraph*, issues 16 and 56 respectively. Two pieces in the *Independent*, one by Andy Gill from January 23 1999, the other from Andy Kershaw on September 22 2005, entitled (somewhat presumptuously) 'How I Found The Man Who Shouted Judas', staked their respective claims for 'the man who shouted Judas'. Both claimants are now sadly deceased, and so can't be interrogated further.

The following contemporary reports provided further grist for the mill:

'Bob Dylan', by D.D. [probably really B.D., see below], *Melody Maker*, May 21 1966
'Dylan The Legend Disappoints', *Birmingham Evening Mail*, May 13 1966
'Times Are A-Changin' And So Is Bob Dylan', *Redbrick*, May 18 1966.
T. Hardern, Nantwich, Cheshire, letter to *Disc & Music Echo*, May 28 1966
Barbara Ellis, Sheffield, letter to *Disc & Music Echo*, June 11 1966
'Pop Goes Bob Dylan—And Boo Go Fans', *Leicester Mercury*, May 16 1966
'Dylan Booed—But Stays Ahead On (Electric) Points', David Sandison, *The Illustrated Chronicle*, May 20 1966
Christine Kynaston, letter to *Leicester Mercury*, May 18 1966

Jane Szaraezyksji, letter to *Leicester Mercury*, May 18 1966
'Avec Dylan L'Intraitable', Jean-Marc Pascal, *Salut Les Copains*, July 1966
'A Plea For A Better Dylan', Jean-Marc Pascal, *Hullabaloo*, December 1966
R.A. McCann, letter to *Manchester Evening News*, May 21 1966
J.M. Whittaker, letter to *Manchester Evening News*, May 21 1966
'Dylan Fan', letter to *Oldham Evening Chronicle*, May 25 1966

Chapter 10

The transcript of the Paris press conference at the George V Hotel, Paris, May 24 1966, is sourced from *The Ghost Of Electricity* and a separate English translation of 'Thirty Questions to Bob Dylan', published in *Salut Les Copains*, September 1966. The Dylan quotes are from interviews with Hubert Saal (*Newsweek*, February 26 1968); John Cohen and Happy Traum, (*Sing Out!*, October 1968); Jann Wenner (*Rolling Stone*, November 29 1969); Ron Rosenbaum (*Playboy*, January 1978); Barbara Kerr (*Toronto Sun*, March 26–29 1978) and Jonathan Cott (*Rolling Stone*, November 16 1978).

Other resources I have drawn on in this chapter include Barry Feinstein's fabulous collection of 1966 photographs, *Real Moments: Photographs Of Bob Dylan* (Omnibus Press, 2008) and *Days In The Life: Voices From The English Underground* by Jonathon Green (Pimlico, 1998); as well as D.A. Pennebaker's interview and Barry MacSweeney's article in *The Telegraph*, issues 16 and 56, respectively.

The following contemporary reports provided further grist for the mill:

'Folk Fans Walk Out On Dylan', Andrew Young, *Scottish Daily Mail*, May 20 1966
'The Legend In Black', R.W., *Daily Record*, May 20 1966

'Dylan Faces Second Night Of Cat Calls', *Scottish Daily Mail*, May 21 1966

'A New-Look Bob Dylan Electrifies, Barry MacSweeney, *Newcastle Sunday Sun*, May 22 1966

'Almost a poet', Beat Hirt, *Pop*, July 1 1966

'Dylan Comes To Fourth Street', Bill Diehl, *St Paul Dispatch*, July 4 1966 (republished in part in 'Columnist Raps Bob Dylan's "Scorn" In Home State Performance', *Variety*, July 13 1966)

'Les Varietes—Bob Dylan A Paris', Claude Fleouter, *Le Monde*, May 26 1966

'Bob Dylan: Go Home!', Jacques Bourdette, *Paris Jour*, May 26 1966

'Bob Dylan ou l'evoque', Claude Kroes, *L'Humanité*, May 26 1966

'With A Mixture of Folk, Rock And Comedy, Dylan Shows He Can Take Every Insult …', Norman Jopling, *Record Mirror*, June 11 1966

'Bob Dylan at the Albert Hall', Peter Willis, *Peace News*, June 10 1966

'UPROAR at Bob Dylan Concert', Ray Coleman, *Disc & Music Echo*, June 4 1966

'Dylan Shocked By British Fans', Norrie Drummond, *NME*, June 17 1966

Outro

The Dylan quote is from an interview with Jann Wenner, *Rolling Stone*, June 1969.

Other resources I have drawn on in this section include *Baby You Can Drive My Car* by Alf Bicknell & Garry Mars (#9 Books, 1990); the author's own 1999 interview with Tom Keylock; 'Dylan Shocked By British Fans', Norrie Drummond, *NME*, June 17 1966; D.A. Pennebaker's interview in *Telegraph* #16 and outtake footage from *Eat The Document* of Dylan and Lennon in a London taxi, May 26 1966, as referenced in *Mojo* #1.

ACKNOWLEDGEMENTS

Inevitably, with a project like this, one hopes to invoke (in my case, for the nth time) the aid of the crème de la crème in that worldwide network of Dylan collectors, which happily remains largely intact thirty-five years after the formation of Wanted Man, the Dylan Information Office, gave it a focal point. Two of Wanted Man's founders have fallen by the way, John Bauldie and Dave Dingle. Both shared my fascination with the 1966 tour at a time when we were all working toward the same collective cause. John made the first attempt to reconstruct an accurate account of the world tour, 1991's *Ghost Of Electricity*. His executor, Margaret Garner, and literary custodian Bill Allison were kind enough to allow me to draw on John's photographic archive for my own version of the story. Thanks to you both, and to Bill for the attendant verbal banter, too.

Equally engaged—and somehow still alive'n'kickin', filling in innumerable chronological blanks through all the years—is the indefatigable Ian Woodward. Ian acceded to my many requests for texts and scans with almost indecent haste. Also looking over my shoulder at every turn has been New York's very own factotum of all things Dylan, Mitch Blank, ever willing to fire up the Xerox machine or pull up an image of yesteryear.

My one long-standing Australian correspondent, John Lattanzio, also put away his dusty astronomy books long enough, post-surgery, to summon Monash University resources to my aid. I thank him for this, and for introducing me to the effervescent Adrian Rawlins back in 1994. (A video exists somewhere of that verbal bout!) Zac Dadic also communicated with me, at length and at the death, correcting and embellishing my account of the Australian leg at every turn. Can't thank you enough.

Rod MacBeath, another long-standing correspondent, this time from the home of the folk-ballad, willingly shared scans from multiple decades of Dylan-collecting after (too many) years out of touch.

Others who shared their memories of 1966 shows for (and after) a lengthy article of mine on '1966 Line Recordings' in the *Telegraph*, back in 1986, were John Kappes and Graham Ashton. Hopefully, you're both still out there in the gloaming. Ditto Pete Howard, who many years ago gave me an invaluable hoard of photos from the Newport Folk Festival, and forgot to ask for them back. Our paths may not cross as often as they used to, but he deserves more than a nod of thanks for favours rendered through the simple years.

Among the fortunate few who saw the 1966 shows and kept notes, and then answered this researcher's pleas for help, are Simon Gee and Spencer Leigh, two of the most knowledgeable music men on the planet. C.P. Lee, whose 1998 study of the May 1966 Manchester show blazed a trail, shared his Judean thoughts over coffee in 'Central Ref.', taking a break from other historical quests for Manchester's elusive musical muse. Barney Hoskyns was ever at the end of an iPhone e-mail, if a name was needed to fact-check some fifty-year-old fallacy, even as he worked on his own history of Woodstock music, the excellent *Small Town Talk* (Faber & Faber, 2016).

Of Dylan's companions on the road in 1966, I was fortunate enough to interview Tom Keylock and Jules Siegel in 1999 and Richard Alderson in 2016. It was the first time any of them had been interviewed at length about the infamous world tour. I especially thank soundman Alderson for an afternoon of insights and humour in sunny Brooklyn.

Those who chased up elusive scraps of newsprint in the public libraries of the world—not always successfully, but hopefully sharing the thrill of the chase—include that great Kinks kronikler, Douglas Hinman, in Boston; Colin Harper in Belfast; Peter Cox and Jon Hulme Down Under; Richard Lyons in Oldham [!]; and Steve Shepherd in Liverpool. Elijah Wald also generously shared some of the more obscure Newport 1965 reviews thrown up by his recent study of that infamous festival and its historical background (*Dylan Goes Electric*, Harper Collins, 2015).

Andy and Pia Muir came to my aid with translations of weird and wonderful Scandinavian press reports that were all Greek to me. While for the copies of those reports, and countless others, I once again tip my hat to Scott Curran, whose private collection of music papers should be in the Library of Congress—and very soon will be. Thankfully, he gave me access without a trip to Washington. A trip to the New York Public Library, though, was necessary—and, as ever, a delight thanks to the helpfulness of the staff and the ease of access to many important US papers from the era of print.

Glenn Korman helped make sense of the trail of audiotapes and applied his vast archival experience to the thorny issue/s of Sony as curator of the most important artist in post-war popular music.

Ian and Isabel at Route Publishing proved a hardy crew, having signed on board as we were about to set sail. They made it back to land—just in time. Mike DeCapite gave the book the once over with his Time (of) Life eagle eye, at the usual rate for the scantest of rewards. The input of all three of you has made for a better book by far.

Last but hardly least, Jeff Rosen generously allowed me to reference many of the mono board tapes that had languished in storage boxes all these years, in between my increasingly belligerent demands for Sony to release every single goddamn note they have of this astonishing moment in time. Once again, the resources of the New York 'Dylan office'—as I continue to call it—were put at my disposable, even after I managed to destroy one of their music players which seemed to take particular offence to a CD-R of the legendary Paris '66 set and refused to spit it out. Especially helpful at every turn, even when they had real work to do, were Parker Fishel and Damien Rodriguez.

Hats off to you all.

Till the next time ... a dose of Fotheringport Confusion.

www.dylanjudas.wordpress.com
www.route-online.com